THE NOBLE SCIENCE OF THE GHAZAL

The Noble Science of the Ghazal

The Urdu Poetry of Mirza Ghalib

BRIAN QUAYLE SILVER

MANOHAR
2015

First published 2015

ISBN 978-81-7304-794-7

Published by
Ajay Kumar Jain *for*
Manohar Publishers & Distributors
4753/23 Ansari Road, Daryaganj
New Delhi 110002

Lasertypeset by
A J Software Publishing Co. Pvt. Ltd.
New Delhi 110005

Printed at
Salasar Imaging Systems
Delhi 110035

How is it, Ghalib, that your grief, resurrected in pieces
has found its way to this room from your dark house in Delhi ?

ADRIENNE RICH (1969: 68)

Contents

Foreword

All modern critics of Ghalib, including the author of this interesting volume, are the children of Altaf Husain Hali (1837-1914), whose seminal *Yādgār-e-Ghalib* (Memorial to Ghalib), first published in 1897, is still widely read and admired. Hali's work placed Ghalib in the perspective of Indo-Muslim poetry and poetics; more importantly, it also placed him in the vanguard of the coming century. Ghalib was shown as a poet who repaid reading even by a modern reader, notwithstanding the fact that 'Asiatic' or old style Persian poetry was no longer popular or highly regarded in India, and 'the taste for Asiatic poetry was day by day being absorbed by the European civilization'[1]—that is, the popularity of indigenous literatures was being swamped and overshadowed by the prestige commanded by English. Although there was 'nothing major or important in Ghalib's life except his poetry and literary activities, yet this one thing has made his life a grand event of the concluding era of the (royal) capital'.[2] Hali granted that his book wasn't likely to be of a type which would be considered of any use to the country at that time, or which would be seen as fulfilling a felt need,[3] yet he wrote his book out of a sense of personal attachment to Ghalib; and Ghalib's life and poetry did have material from which the nation could draw useful lessons.

Hali asserted Ghalib's modernity, but not in the form of direct statements. Rather, he attributed to Ghalib qualities of mind and art which signalled an open or implied break with the tradition. For example: 'It is clear that not only in poetry, but also in his manners, dress and address, food habits, life-style, and even in the art of living and dying, Ghalib disliked to follow the popular, conventional ways.'[4] A couple of pages on, we find Hali telling us that the older masters showed their excellence and virtuosity by improving upon the themes and modes of their forebearers, whereas Ghalib 'constructed the mansion of his ghazal on entirely different foundations. His ghazal mostly consists of themes which are unique, and which haven't at all been touched by the creative genius of other poets. Even plain themes were rendered by him in such a way as to make them entirely novel, and they are supplied with such subtleties as are not to be found in the works of other masters.'[5]

Hali's other major contribution in 'modernizing' Ghalib was to emancipate him from a trap which was to a certain extent of Ghalib's own making. Until about the end of the eighteenth century, Indians writing in Persian were quite confident of their right and position as Persian writers; they regarded Indian Persian as something not essentially different from Iranian Persian, and felt themselves to be entirely competent and capable readers, producers, critics, and evaluators of Persian literature. The term *sabk-i-hindī* (Indian style) may not have been known then, but a distinct and valid Indo-Persian identity was well established in the minds of readers and writers of Persian in India. Persian words and phrases were used in Urdu with a healthy unconcern for their 'original' and 'authentic' Persian connotation, or construction, or pronunciation. Just as in Indian Persian, authority lay with the Indians, so in Urdu, authority lay with actual users of Urdu, and not with some shadowy master figure in far away Iran.

All this seems to have changed with the advent of the nineteenth century. Indians developed in the field of Persian some sort of a self-hatred. Nothing that the greatest Indian Persian poet, lexicographer, or linguist did, could stand the scrutiny of the *ahl-i-zabān* (educated native speaker), and an Indian could never be described as *ahl-i-zabān* in Persian. Ghalib, third generation Indian himself, seems to have discovered the putative inadequacies, and the unreliability, of Indian Persian poets and grammarians in 1827-8 when, during his sojourn in Calcutta, some persons objected to some of his Persian usages on the authority of Qateel (1747/8-1818), a Hindu who converted to Islam, and went on to become a major Persian writer of the late eighteenth and early nineteenth centuries. Ghalib flatly refused to accept Qateel, or any other Indian for that matter, as an arbiter in matters of Persian poetry and usage. Even in his Persian apologia in verse, which he composed to appease Qateel's supporters, he wrote:

God forbid, I am not a bad mouther,
And whatever I say, I don't say on my own,
But those who are expert knowers of Persian,
Are all of this view and belief
That Qateel was by no means from the native speakers,
He certainly didn't come from Isphahan;
Doubtless, he is not worthy of reliance,
His utterances are not suitable as authority.

• • • •

How can I release myself from the hands of Talib, and Naziri, and Urfi?

• • • •

One who has travelled to such destinations,
Of what account would he hold such as Qateel and Vaqif.[6]

This couldn't by any stretch of interpretation be treated as acknowledgment of the authority of Indian Persian writers. In this poem, Ghalib spared the great Bedil (1644-1720), his childhood hero, but in later life, he denounced even Bedil. He wrote to Abdul Ghafoor Surur in March/April 1859, 'Nasir Ali, and Bedil, and Ghanimat, for what does their Persian count? Examine the poetry of each of these with the eye of justice; to see the bracelet on your arm needs no looking glass.'[7] Ghalib didn't much bother about the contradiction inherent in his position: as an Indian Persian writer, or a user of Persianate constructions and phrases in his Urdu poetry, he was open to the same ridicule that he heaped upon Qateel, and Bedil, and others. To the end of his life he continued to belittle Indian Persian writers (except Khusrau) and to claim exemption for himself, on grounds of 'natural affinity' with the language of the Iranians, and an equally putative discipleship of an 'Iranian master of the standard, pure language of Iran'.[8] No one was really fooled, but Ghalib's fulminations against Indian Persian writers affected his own reputation as a master of Persian poetry. Shibli Nu'mani's five volume history of Persian poetry, called *She'r ul 'Ajam* (Poetry of Iran) barely mentions Ghalib.[9]

Hali and those who came after him dealt with the problem of Ghalib's Persian in a typically modern manner. First of all, Hali declared that Ghalib's Persian was as good as that of the Iranians, especially the Iranians who wrote in the Indian Style. They, Hali declared, were the true masters of innovation and imagination.

Although the current Iranian fashion may be against them, all that this proves is that, 'if something was constructed in the past according to a particular mould, it cannot be fitted later in a mould of another design'.[10]

Now this is a peculiarly modern argument: if the current trend was in favour of the ancients, it didn't prove that the late arrivals were unworthy; it was just that each age had its own preferences, and one need not conform to the other's. Hali also made the interesting point that Ibn Khaldun held that practice and study could enable a person to write Arabic like a native. So, Hali's argument ran, if one could achieve a native's competence in Arabic, then why not in Persian, which, 'in comparison to Arabic, is a much narrower and smaller language'.[11] He quotes Macaulay to the effect that non-native speakers cannot compete with the native speakers in writing poetry of a high order. For once, Hali rejects that august authority, saying that this may be true of 'Europe, where in fact, poetry is the representation and interpretation of nature . . . and the demands of such poetry can be discharged properly only in the mother tongue'.[12] Ghalib therefore was in a win-win position: he wrote in a poetic tradition where one need not be a native speaker to achieve excellence; and he had, in fact, a native's command of Persian.

Hali also invested Ghalib with a romantic halo, a halo which was of particular appeal to the modern Indian, who was being assaulted day in and day out by stories and anecdotes and fiats proving British (or 'English') excellence, almost always at the expense of Indians; their morals, their mores, their intellectual and spiritual attainments, always being somehow found wanting by 'European' standards. In such a climate of feeling, it was extremely comforting and reassuring to know that there was one Indian who was generous to a fault, a gallant gentleman, a witty conversationalist and letter writer; a proud and self-respecting Indian who also had a sense of humour. Above all, he was a lonely figure, one who was much admired, but not in proportion to his talents, and was little understood, and was often accused of obscurity. In short, something like a Keats in the *avatār* of a Browning.

'Once he (Ghalib) went straight from the (Red) Fort to the house of Navab Mustafa Khan, and began to say' writes Hali, 'Today the Presence honoured me greatly, expressing appreciation. I took with me today a qasida in felicitation for Id. After I had recited it, he graciously commanded, "Mirza, you recite beautifully". Upon this, the Navab and Mirza Ghalib sat together for a long time, deploring the callous and unappreciating times.'[13] Ghalib was thus like a prophet in his own country, and essentially, out of synch with the times.

The question of whether the image of Ghalib the man and Ghalib the poet, as reflected by Hali, was authentic, is misplaced. Doubtless, it wasn't false in any substantive sense. But much more importantly, it was an image that evoked positive feelings in the mind of the twentieth century Indian, and fulfilled some of his deeply felt needs. Hali defined, for the next hundred years, the role model of a great poet. The English educated Indians loved every detail of Ghalib's image as purveyed by Hali. S. M. Ikram, historian and Ghalib scholar, and a distinguished member of the Indian Civil Service, wrote, 'The best book on Ghalib written from the modern critical point of view was composed by a person who was practically illiterate in English, that is, Hali'.[14]

Hali's view that it was possible for a non-native speaker to compose poetry in a foreign tongue as successfully as in his own, is of a piece with his views about the norms for judgement in literature. Without actually saying so, Hali had implied throughout his powerful theoretical pronouncement attached as preface to his book of poems (1893) that there are universal norms for literary excellence. Again, without stating this in so many words, Hali made clear that 'universal' meant 'English' or 'European'. Known as the *Muqaddama*, the preface became a work in its own right, and is still the most influential literary theoretical work in Urdu. In a section notorious for its dogmatism, quotability, and abiding influence, Hali prescribed for the poet a recipe for good poetry based on what he thought were the ideas of Milton and Macaulay.[15] He prefaced his remarks by saying that 'the treasury of nature is always open for the poet. And there is no dearth of its true food for the power of imagination. Thus, instead of sitting at home, devising flowers and petals of paper, he should observe the sights of the power of God in forest and hill, and in his own being'.[16] So much for qualities, attributes and conventions, specific to different literary cultures. There is, instead, a totalizing agenda aimed at flattening out all local differences.

(2)

Hali's agenda is but a coda to the Westocentric, anti-pluralistic regimen that was the order of the day in late nineteenth century European worldview. Where modern authors like Brian Silver (and there are not many like him), make a radical departure from Hali is in recognizing that foreign cultures should be approached on their own terms. It is somewhat ironical that Urdu had to wait for Western scholars like Bausani, and Silver, before it could know that its literature had the right to be read in its own idiom, and on its own terms. As Brian Silver says in his Introduction, 'Without an understanding of the urdu Ghazal, any inquiry into Indo-Musilm culture will necessarily be incomplete. . . . The literary explorations in the following pages are motivated by the desire to see the ghazal, as shaped by a master practitioner of the genre, within the traditional perspectives of Indo-Muslim culture.' One of the benefits that this study has derived from such an approach is an understanding, and demonstration, of the fact that the Urdu ghazal is not so limited in scope as both its friends and detractors have apparently persuaded themselves to be the case.

Of course, Brian Silver seeks the support of Western concepts of meaning and Western modes of rhetorical devices to prove the worth of his enterprise. It is another irony of history, that it will come as a surprise to most mainline Urdu critics that such support is possible, and valid. For it was Hali and his followers who taught Urdu poets and readers that rhetorical devices were to be eschewed by the poet so that he could write 'natural poetry'. All poetry 'tainted' by metaphor, or complexity, or ambiguity, or the use of wordplay and similar 'gimmicks' was by definition non-serious, unworthy of expressing lofty, personal or universal sentiment—which was the true office of poetry, as explained by Macaulay, and proved by the practice of Walter Scott and other 'European' masters. It is therefore good to see Brian Silver say that the poetic techniques he has discussed to demonstrate the Urdu ghazal's 'dynamic nuclear structure' are, 'ellipsis, inversion of word order, phonetic manipulation, repetition, parallelism, comparison and contrast, interrogative forms, allusion, personification, meter, rhyme, elision, and those techniques, such as hyperbole, ambiguity, paradox, and kinetics in imagery, which particularly distinguish Ghalib's poetry'.

One must note two things here before venturing further into Brian Silver's territory: Most, if not all, of the categories listed by him above would leave Ralph Russell, and his collaborator Khurshidul Islam, cold, and somewhat puzzled. The response of Nazm Tabataba'i (1852-1933), Ghalib's next great critic after Hali, wouldn't have been very different. Although classical Urdu literary theory recognized many of the categories listed above by Brian Silver, their stock had run so low by the end of the nineteenth century that even a confirmed classicist like Tabataba'i felt uncomfortable with most of them. Tabataba'i however did place high regard on the interrogative, and other forms of non-falsifiable statements. It may be worth recalling here that the distinction between falsifiable (*khabariya*) and non-falsifiable (*inshā'iya*) statements was made by Arab grammarians in the ninth century, and they were quick to recognise the semantitic potential of *inshā'iya* statements. It is only now that this point has been investigated by Western literary critics.[17] Brian Silver doesn't seem to have studied Tabataba'i on this point, and seems to have noted the uses of the interrogative mode on his own.

The other point to be remembered here is that mechanical application of the categories listed by Brian Silver can easily become a soulless exercise, if not a travesty of one's own self. Brian Silver avoids this fate, common to many academic undertakings by not labouring on any one thing; and by singling out some key concepts, or emotion/meaning bearing words, from the corpus of Ghalib's Urdu ghazal. Some of these words, like *shauq*, *'ishq*, *ulfat*, and *muḥabbat*, are known to all readers and listeners of ghazals. The value of Silver's exegeses is in the fact that he understands these and other words to exist as a part of a matrix, or mosaic. He says, 'The words, motifs, and images of the ghazal are important, not in isolation, but rather, in their relationships to each other, for it is the primary function of the ghazal to portray various types of relationships, and to examine, analyse, and suggest different tensions and connections between the individual elements of existence'

The above insight helps Brian Silver avoid many pitfalls into which many Westocentric critics of the ghazal fall with distressing regularity. However, the tradition which enables the ghazal to achieve meaningfulness is so different from that of the Western lyric, that misprisions (though not in the Bloomian sense) are bound to occur. One such misprision is to read, or hope to find, autobiography and/or social reality in the ghazal, unmediated by the conventions of meaning or poetry. Brian Silver comes out successful here too, though not without conceding that 'the impact of a glimpse of the beloved behind her veil, is, in purdah society, quite understandable—hence the emphasis in the ghazal on *seeing* the beloved' (Chapter II). This concession to Russell and Islam ignores the fatal contradiction in their position, for they are equally emphatic that 'pederastic' love (or boy-love, or whatever) plays a large part in the ghazal because of the segregation of the sexes.[18] Now man/boy lovers were not in purdah, so then what was the need to place so much stress on 'seeing'? Surely it is more persuasive to argue that the emphasis on 'seeing' refers to the idea of *liqā-e rabbānī* (coming face to face with God)?

Another part of this work which I would single out for special mention is Brian Silver's treatment of what he calls 'the personae of the ghazal'. Although the persons in the world of the ghazal are essentially stereotypes, or conventions, centuries of poetic practice, and individual invention, have invested them with the force of metaphor, and of living symbol, rather than mere icons. Brian Silver provides a long, analytical list of ghazal-characters, some of whom, as he points out, are drawn from real life. He does not explore their metaphorical potential, but emphasises their inter-connectibility. He follows the list up with a thorough analysis of *yār* (beloved, or one of the many words used for beloved), giving many of the associations and connotations that the word can give rise to in Ghalib. This is followed by a description of what Brian Silver calls the 'landscape of the ghazal'. In some ways, this chapter is even more satisfactory than the previous one, and melds well with the last chapter, entitled 'An Analysis of Three Selected Ghazals'. The previous chapter concluded on the following note, 'The limitations inherent in the traditional settings of the ghazal . . . should not pose an insurmountable challenge for the capable poet. . . . When Ghalib does desire novelty, for example, he may introduce fields of brilliant henna running to the horizon of the desert . . . or vast reefs of coral blazing in the ocean as a metaphor of the poet's lamp burning in the dust storm of the desert'. The basic idea, as Brian Silver recognizes, was to express one's own 'perspective through an established genre' rather than create new codes of meaning.

This leads us nicely into the concluding arguments in the book about how and why ghazal poetry can provide an occasion for greatness. There are good ghazals and bad ghazals, just as there are good poets and bad poets. It is perhaps easier to write a bad ghazal than a bad sonnet. But it is certainly much harder to write a good ghazal. The weight of the past is enormous, and ever present in the ghazal poet's psyche. The ghazal is essentially a palimpsest, a pre-existing site, to be worked over anew. Its topoi, in the words of Brian Silver, 'acquire, from generations of poets, through the process of connotative accretion' ever new meanings, providing us with ever new ways of looking at the world.

This book therefore is an attempt to reach the world of the ghazal, and of classical Urdu poetry generally, through the mediation of Ghalib. Brian Silver's approach is non-patronizing, non-romanticising: a serious scholar is studying a major poet of an alien tradition. And not so alien either. Brian Silver has access to the Indo-Muslim tradition from two fruitful routes. He is a substantial musicologist and professional level sitarist in the classical Hindustani musical style. He has also a sound knowledge of Urdu, and of Ghalib. The result is a happy creation, a rich book which should be a source of delight and profit to the expert, as well as the lay reader.

Allahabad SHAMSUR RAHMAN FARUQI
27 June 1996

NOTES

1. There are numerous extant editions of *Yādgār-e-Ghalib*; for facility of reference, I have cited from the first edition, Kanpur, 1897. For this quote, see p. 5, op. cit. All translations from Urdu and Persian are by me.
2. Ibid., p. 3.
3. Ibid., p. 420.
4. Ibid., p. 116.
5. *Yādgār*, p. 119.
6. Masnavi called 'Bād-e Mukhalif', in *Kulliyat-e Ghalib Farsi*, edited by Murtaza Husain Fazil, vol. I, Lahore, 1967, pp. 290-1. Talib (*d.* 1626), Urfi (*d.* 1590), and Naziri (*d.* 1612) are major poets of the Indian style. They're Iranians, and therefore acceptable to Ghalib. Nurul Ain Vaqif, flourished 1740s, was of Lahore.
7. Khaliq Anjum (ed.), *Ghalib ke Khutut*, vol. II, Delhi, 1985, p. 594.

8. For 'natural affinity', see Khaliq Anjum, op. cit., vol. IV, Delhi, 1993, pp. 1447, 1477. For the Iranian Master, see Khaliq Anjum, op. cit., vol. II, Delhi, 1985, p. 744, and vol. III, Delhi, 1987, p. 1202. For a detailed discussion, see Malik Ram: *Fasāna-e Ghalib,* Dehli, 1977, pp. 52-77.
9. Published in Urdu from 1909 to 1912, this five-volume work is still extremely influential. It has been translated into Persian, and is made use of by all Persian scholars worth the name.
10. *Yādgār*, p. 429.
11. Ibid., p. 434.
12. Ibid., p. 435.
13. Ibid., p. 90.
14. S. M. Ikram, *Āsār-e Ghalib,* Bombay, n.d., p. 188, originally published, 1939.
15. Altaf Husain Hali: *Muqaddam-e She'r o Shā'irī,* Allahabad, 1953, pp. 65-77.
16. Ibid., p. 65.
17. See for instance, John Hollander, *Melodious Guile: Fictive Patterns in Poetry,* Yale University Press, 1988. The second chapter, entitled 'Questions of Poetry', is devoted to the possibilities of semantic richness in the interrogative.
18. Russell and Islam: *Three Mughal Poets: Mir, Sauda, Mir Hasan*; Harvard, 1968, pp. 98-9, 103n, and passim. Recently, Ralph Russell has reemphasized his position on these points. See his 'Rejoinder' to Frances Pritchett and William Hanaway in Muhammad Umar Memon (ed.), *Annual of Urdu Studies,* no. 10, 1996.

Introduction

'The understanding of another culture or civilization', writes Milton Singer, 'requires that the foreign traveller rid himself of ethnocentrism and look at another culture in its own terms (1972: 3). Many civilizations have created in poetry their most eloquent expression of a cultural identity; such is the case with Indo-Muslim civilization. As C. M. Naim has observed, 'of all the gifts that the two great cultures, Hindu and Persian-Muslim, brought forth in India, perhaps the greatest is the Urdu language and [its] literature; and the most precious part of that literature is the Urdu *ghazal*' (1974: 186).

It thus becomes clear that, without an understanding of the Urdu ghazal, any inquiry into Indo-Muslim culture will necessarily be incomplete. Not only is the ghazal 'the most popular of all the classical forms of Urdu poetry' (Russell 1970a: 141), it is also the quintessential expression of Urdu cultural sensibilities. Descriptions of Indo-Muslim life, such as Ruswa's *Umrā'o Jān Adā* (1961, 1963), the first modern (1899) Urdu novel (Russell 1970b: 132), or Ahmed Ali's *Twilight in Delhi* (1966) illustrate amply the integral role that the ghazal plays in the Urdu-speaking world of the Indo-Pakistani subcontinent—though first-hand observation of any literate conversation in Urdu would demonstrate just as well the ghazal's central function in the full verbal expression of an idea. In the words of one prominent Urdu critic, Rashid Ahmed Siddiqi, 'our culture is molded in the ghazal, and the ghazal is cast in the mold of our culture; in both are combined direction and pace, color and harmony, and esteem and honor' (1969: 11).

Certainly no practitioner of the Urdu ghazal is more renowned than Mirza Asadullah Khan 'Ghalib' (1797-1869). The most outspoken declaration of Ghalib's pre-eminence has been made by Abdul Rahman Bijnauri, who wrote in 1921 that 'India has two divinely inspired books: the Holy Vedas and the *Dīvān* of Ghalib'

(1969: 123). Most appraisals of Ghalib's importance share the tone, if not the degree, of Bijnauri's encomium: Ram Babu Saksena considers Ghalib to be 'the brightest star in the firmament of Urdu poetry, and the most towering genius of his age' (1940: 158), and Sardar Jafri assigns Ghalib the position of 'the most beloved Urdu poet'([1958]: 3).[1] As 'the first "modern" Urdu writer' (Schimmel 1975a: 216), Ghalib's reputation has spread well beyond the Urdu-speaking world. No other modern writer of the subcontinent—with the exceptions of Rabindranath Tagore and Muhammad Iqbal—has inspired such an extensive range of critical and biographical literature in a variety of languages, and the celebration of Ghalib's death centenary in different countries in 1969 revealed him to be a literary figure of worldwide significance.

Yet in spite of—or perhaps, because of—their clear preeminence, both the Urdu ghazal as a poetic genre, and Ghalib as an Urdu poet, have been the centers of energetic controversy. Criticism of the ghazal as a form limited in its range of expression may be found in the first modern analytic treatise on Urdu poetry (written in 1893 by Altaf Husain 'Hali', 1837-1914), the *Muqaddama-e-she'r-o-shā'irī* (n.d.: 119-78). Muhammad Sadiq's *History of Urdu Literature* is even more outspoken in its assertion that 'the ghazal stands very low in the hierarchy of literary forms'(1964: 19). Negative appraisals of Ghalib, similarly, range from Sayyid Abdul Latif's early English book on Ghalib, in which he speaks of 'ghazal writers like Ghalib stalking, however gloriously or pompously, on the conventional ground'(1929: ii), to the characterization by Mirza Yas 'Yagana' Changezi (1883-1960) of Ghalib as 'an old-time thief [who], along with being a thief, is inarticulate' (1969: 10).

Such controversy provides both the background and the stimulus for this book. The literary explorations undertaken in the following pages are motivated by the desire to see the ghazal, as shaped by a master practitioner of the genre, within the traditional perspectives of Indo-Muslim culture. To make such an attempt is by no means contrary to the goals of criticism, for as I. A. Richards has written,

> That the one and only goal of all critical endeavors, of all interpretation, appreciation, exhortation, praise, or abuse, is improvement in

communication may seem an exaggeration. But in practice it is so. The whole apparatus of critical rules and principles is a means to the attainment of finer, more precise, more discriminating communication. There is, it is true, a valuation side to criticism. When we have solved, completely, the communication problem, when we have got, perfectly, the experience, *the mental condition* relevant to the poem, we have still to judge it, still to decide upon its worth. But the latter question nearly always settles itself; or rather, our own inmost nature and the nature of the world in which we live decide it for us. Our prime endeavour must be to get the relevant mental condition and then see what happens. [1929: 10]

Some excellent work has already been done in English in an attempt to analyze the ghazal objectively in traditional perspectives, in order to describe the 'mental condition' relevant to the poetry. Ralph Russell has documented very effectively the social contexts of Urdu poetry, as well as the Weltanschauung of the ghazal (1969, 1970a; also Russell and Islam 1968); the network of themes and imagery in both Urdu and Persian poetry has been illumined in the numerous writings of Annemarie Schimmel, most notably in this connection in *A Dance of Sparks,* her study of Ghalib (1979); C. M. Naim has made futher important contributions to both areas (1967, 1970, 1972, 1974). Following gratefully in their steps, I would like to offer as my contribution to the study of Urdu poetry, 1) an examination of the uniquely dynamic structure of the ghazal—as exemplified in the Urdu *Dīvān* of Ghalib—both in the ghazal itself, and in its presentation to, and reception by, its audience; and 2) an exploration of the full range of connotations surrounding certain basic topoi in Ghalib's ghazals, in order to explicate the role that diction and imagery play in the highly compressive structure of the individual couplet.[2] The organization of the chapters is as follows:

The concept of a dynamic nuclear structure is introduced in the first chapter, in a discussion of the essential formal elements of the ghazal; this nuclear structure greatly facilitates, through various techniques of compression, the completion of a full, effective poetic statement in the two lines of the individual ghazal couplet. Techniques discussed include ellipsis, inversion of word order, phonemic manipulation, repetition, parallelism, comparison and contrast, interrogative forms, allusion, personification, meter, rhyme, elision, and those techniques, such as hyperbole, ambiguity, paradox, and kineticism in imagery, which particularly distinguish Ghalib's poetry. The chapter concludes with an examination of certain social contexts of the ghazal, and the ways in which these affect the compressive and nuclear structure of the genre.

An analysis of the elemental relationships portrayed in Ghalib's ghazal poetry is begun in the second chapter, in answer to critical characterizations of the ghazal as a genre limited in scope. The central premise of this analysis is the proposition that the topoi—words, motifs, and images—of the ghazal are important, not in isolation, but rather, in their relationships to each other; for it is the primary function of the ghazal to portray a wide spectrum of relationships, and to examine, analyze, and suggest different tensions and connections between the individual elements of existence. The chapter continues with a close analysis of two complete ghazals in terms of the relationships they portray, and concludes with a summary of some of the thematic conventions of the genre.

A connotative analysis of every couplet in Ghalib's *Dīvān* which includes the major words for love (*'ishq, shauq, muḥabbat,* and *ulfat*) is contained in the third chapter, in order 1) to outline definitively the full range of connotations which love—the central topic of the ghazal—has for Ghalib; and 2) to begin to assemble a connotative concordance (of the basic words and images of the ghazal) of the sort that literate Urdu speakers may be said to have accumulated intuitively through extensive and sustained exposure to Urdu poetry. These couplets are presented in original English translation, and have been newly arranged according to topoi.

The connotative analysis continues in the fourth chapter, focusing on the central characters in the personae of the ghazal: the beloved (*yār*), the rival (*g͟hair* or *raqīb*), and the lover (*'āshiq*); and further in the fifth chapter, in an examination of the most important spatial centers in Ghalib's ghazals: the lane of the beloved (*kū-e-yār*), the lover's house (*ghar, k͟hāna,* or *makān*), and the desert (*dasht, saḥarā,* or *bayābān*).

An analysis in the sixth chapter of the nuclear structure and connotative networks of three of Ghalib's most famous ghazals concludes the book, in the context of a discussion of the ghazal's capacity for scope and variety in poetic expression.

NOTES

1. Even those writers who do not attempt such a sweeping characterization of his importance will usually consider Ghalib to be among the three or four greatest Urdu poets; further proof of his prominence may be found in the extent to which his work is included in anthologies of Urdu poetry. Yusuf Husain Khan's *Urdū Ghazal* (1957) includes, from a total of 337 pages, 22 by Mir Taqi 'Mir' (*c.* 1722-1810), 20 by Ghalib, 19 by 'Hasrat' Mohani (*c.* 1875-1951), and 13 by Navab Mirza Khan 'Dagh' Dehlvi (1831-1905). Zaki Kakorvi's *Ghazal Encyclopaedia* (1968), devoting 268 pages to a selection of at least a few verses by a much larger number of poets, contains 7 pages each of Mir, Ghalib, and 'Jigar' Muradabadi (1890-1960), with all other poets having fewer pages. David Matthews and Christopher Shackle's *Anthology of Classical Urdu Love Lyrics* (1972) assigns, of its 166 pages of text and English translation, 16 to Ghalib and 12 each to Mir, Insha'allah Khan 'Insha' (*c.* 1756-1818), and Momin Khan 'Momin' (1810-1851/2). Muhammad Abd-al-Rahman Barker's *Classical Urdu Poetry* (1977) alots, from 425 pages, 24 to Ghalib and to the *marṣiya* (elegy) poet Mir Babar Ali 'Anis' (1802-74), and 19 to Muhammad Iqbal (*c.* 1877-1938). Muhammad Sadiq's *History of Urdu Literature* (1964), finally, devotes 32 pages to Iqbal, 30 to Ghalib, and 12 to 'Akbar' Allahabadi (1846-1921).
2. Aside from the writings of Naim already cited (1970, 1972), the best efforts at textual analysis of individual couplets and their structure have been made by Shamsur Rahman Faruqi in his Urdu journal *Shabkhūn* (published from Allahabad), in various issues from 1969 through 1972, in an irregular feature which he has entitled *tafhīm-e-Ghālib*, or 'Understanding Ghalib' (Faruqi 1969-72); this feature, when it appears, devotes a full page to the analysis of a single *she'r*. Faruqi has also published a useful article (1971: 718-32) entitled *Ghālib kī ek ghazal kā tajzīya* ('An analysis of one of Ghalib's ghazals') in which he gives a close reading and discussion of the well-known ghazal, *jab tak dahān-e-zakhm na paidā kare ko'ī* [215: 1-12]. Otherwise, there are numerous commentaries (*sharḥ*, pl. *sharḥeṅ*) on Ghalib; these, particularly those by Mehr (n.d.) and Chishti (1959), are useful in the explication of difficult words and idioms, allusions, and certain ambiguities—though there is little here that is equivalent to close textual criticism, with its particular attention to structure and connotation.

   Similarly, only a few extended studies have been published of the occurrence of individual words, images, and image-clusters in Ghalib. The chapters in *A Dance of Sparks*, cited above, focus on Ghalib's dance, fire, and calligraphic imagery, and his treatment of the martyr

Hallaj (Schimmel 1979). Khurshidul Islam's *Ghalib* includes an appendix of 'those words which have been used repeatedly in Ghalib's early poetry, and their asociated words and couplets' (1960: 231), in which some fifty pages of Ghalib's verses are gathered and arranged according to their use of twenty-nine distinctively Ghalibian words; this list and anthology are useful, but only Ghalib's early poetry is treated, and there is no discussion at all of the implications of these words and their associations. Asloob Ahmed Ansari's short article, 'Some recurrent images in Ghalib's poetry' (1969-70: 84-96) is extremely useful so far as it goes, but in most cases no more than six couplets are selected to illustrate a particular word or image; Ansari's book, *Naqsh-e-Ghālib* (1970), an important and pioneering work in many respects, is not much more exhaustive in its discussion of any given topos.

A few topical anthologies, finally, are to be found, with such captivating titles as *Gul-pāre*—'Flower-fragments', by Kazim Ali Khan, Advocate (n.d.); *Gulhā'e Pareshāṅ*—'Scattered Blossoms', by Ilyas Ahmed, Retired District Judge [1957], and *Gulistān-e-Hazār Raṅg*—'The Garden of a Thousand Colors', by Sayyid Baha'uddin Ahmed, Former District Decision Judge (1970); this last includes a foreword by Maulana Abdul Kalam Azad. These are useful, after the fashion of a dictionary of quotations, in comparing different poet's treatments of certain words, though in some cases the poet is either unidentified or unknown, and there is no analysis or discussion.

I should emphasize that the works in the first two categories, whatever their limitations, are indispensable to a full consideration of Ghalib's opus, while the topical anthologies are helpful for general background. I feel much indebted to these writers, and hope to have expanded upon their unquestionably valuable contributions in the following pages.

Acknowledgments

The research for this book was conducted in London, Pakistan, and India from 1969 through 1971, under the generous auspices of a Ford Foreign Area Fellowship, administered by the Social Sciences Research Council and the American Council of Learned Societies; during these two years I received valuable guidance and support from the late Ralph Russell and the late S. Ehtisham Husain Rizvi. My work at this time was also enriched by meetings and informal interviews with Urdu poets and scholars too numerous to mention, but whose interest and encouragement I gratefully acknowledge.

I am particularly indebted to my two *ustāds* of Urdu, the late Professor Varis Husain Alavi and Professor C.M. Naim, for their generosity in time and knowledge in the course of my studies with them, and to the late Professor Annemarie Schimmel, who assisted and encouraged me, when I was teaching at Harvard, in the pursuit of my work in Urdu literature and Indo-Muslim culture.

Finally, I am grateful to my readers at the University of Chicago, the late Professor A.K. Ramanujan and Professor Norman Zide, for their helpful suggestions in the completion of this manuscript, and again, to Professor Naim as my manuscript advisor, for his criticism, inspiration, and advice during the course of our long association.

BRIAN QUAYLE SILVER

Note on Transliteration and Text

All Urdu words are transliterated according to the general scheme used by Platts in his *Dictionary of Urdu, Classical Hindi and English* (1930: vii); with the following important exceptions: 1) *ghain*, the twenty-fifth letter of the Urdu alphabet, is represented here by the widely accepted *gh* (instead of Platts' *g*); 2) *vāv*, the thirty-third letter, which Platts transliterates as both *v* and *w*, is here consistently rendered as *v*; and 3) *che*, which Platts transliterates as *ć* is here represented by a simple *c*. Personal and place names are given in their common English spellings, without diacritical marks.

All references to Ghalib's Urdu poetry are taken from the *Dīvān* edited by Sardar Jafri [1958] in parallel Urdu and Devanagari text. The ghazals are numbered from 1 to 235; I have supplied the number of the verse. A reference of [1: 1] indicates the first verse of the first ghazal. The same numbers also apply to various other editions of the *Dīvān*, such as that of the Taj Company, Lahore [1938], or the two editions by Malik Ram (n.d., 1969a). Because of the general availability of many such editions, I have given only occasional verses in transliteration, except for the complete ghazals discussed in Chapters 2 and 6.

The word ghazal has not been italicized, since the term may be said to have entered the lexicon of Western literature through the work of such poets as Adrienne Rich (1969, 1971), whose English ghazals have been anthologized in the widely distributed *Norton Introduction to Literature* (Hunter 1973: 497-501), and Jim Harrison (1972). It should be noted, however, that significant differences remain between these poems and the Urdu ghazals which inspired them (Silver n.d.).

CHAPTER 1

The Structure of Ghalib's Ghazals

> The great ghazal writers are like Hamlet; they bind themselves in a nutshell and still count themselves the kings of infinite space.
>
> MUHAMMAD SADIQ (1964: 19)

The single most distinguishing feature of the ghazal is its capacity for poetic compression. Formally, the ghazal consists of a series of couplets sharing a common rhyme scheme and meter but not necessarily related in content; the nutshell to which Sadiq refers is the separate, individual couplet. Each couplet (*she'r*) must contain a complete thought, and in the best ghazals, this thought is expressed in a manner that creates internal and external resonances, overtones, and echoes that enhance richly the elemental thought itself. In a single couplet, in short, the ghazal poet must achieve the complete statement of an idea to which poets in other cultures would usually devote a longer poem.

The evocative power of the individual ghazal couplet is such that it may be quoted in a personal context (in conversation or in a letter), or in a public speech or a poetic recitation (called a *mushā'ira*) and may provoke a wide variety of responses. Such responses range along a continuum from a gentle smile of comprehension and recognition on an individual face to ten or twenty seconds of pandemonium, punctuated by a chorus of cries demanding the verse's repetition, in an audience of thousands. When the same verse is translated into English, there is every likelihood that it will seem, on the printed page, obvious and uninspiring. At this point the Western observer may be inclined to ask: What is there in this poetry, contained within a single couplet, that can so move an audience?

In beginning to answer this question, it is illuminating to turn to a passage by Donald Keene on the Japanese *haiku*, a genre comparable in its conciseness to the ghazal:

> The *haiku*, for all its extreme brevity, must contain two elements, usually divided by a break. . . . One of the elements may be the general condition—the end of autumn, the stillness of the temple grounds, the darkening sea—and the other the momentary perception. The nature of the elements varies, but there should be the two electric poles between which the spark will leap for the *haiku* to be effective; otherwise, it is no more than a brief statement. [1955: 40-1]

To be effective, the ghazal couplet, like the *haiku*, must contain at least two different elements existing in a certain relationship based on tension. Examples of such relationships may be found in two of Ghalib's own couplets, both of which make some sense in English translation, and thus may serve as a fitting introduction to his poetry:

1.1 Just see the pleasure of discourse—that what *he* said
I knew, as though exactly that were in *my* heart [158: 2]
1.2 There are in this world many other masters of eloquence
People say that Ghalib's style is something different
[63: 11]

In the first verse Ghalib alludes to the power of speech (of which poetry is perhaps the most persuasive genre) to evoke a recognition of the familiar that makes the poet one with his audience: the poet observes from his own life something within the audience's range of experience, and the audience recognizes in the poet's experience their own. In the second couplet Ghalib begins by praising the eloquence of his contemporaries; he then craftily concludes with the observation that everyone finds his style of poetry unique. In the first couplet, a relationship of familiarity unites the poet with his audience; in the second, the poet is distinguished from his contemporaries by a relationship of novelty. In both verses, there is a spark which jumps between the elements of the first and second line, and it is this spark which makes each verse 'more than a brief statement' (Keene 1955: 41). The analogy of the spark—far-fetched as it first may seem—expresses very well the sort of internal dynamic structure, based upon tension, that distinguishes the ghazal from what I will cautiously call more linear forms of poetry.

By linear poetry, I mean poetry which is read or recited in an uninterrupted forward progression, and which has an essential continuity of thought from beginning to end through a sequence of lines. In many respects, the ghazal seems at first glance to be linear, particularly when it is described in some variation on the general theme of 'orient pearls at random strung' which one encounters in writings on oriental poetry. The sequentiality of the ghazal, and the impression of a linear structure, is suggested further by the description I have heard, but cannot trace, of the ghazal as a sequence of chocolates handed out in genteel fashion by the poet, who says, 'Try this one—it has a cherry core'—(the listener tastes slowly, savoringly)—'and now try *this* one—it has an almond nougat'—(the listener chews thoughtfully, with relish)—'and this one has a rum center'—(the listener is transported).[1]

But a closer examination of the pearl or chocolate analogies, along with a backward glance at Sadiq's description of the ghazal poet confined within a nutshell, provides a future key to an understanding of the ghazal: in each image there is an aspect not only of sequentiality, but of concentration as well. Pearls, as we know, are formed over time by a process of accretion around a central nucleus; in the historical sense, as discussed below, there is an accretion of meaning around the individual elements of a ghazal over a period of time, with repeated and sometimes varied usage of an idea by a chronological sequence of poets. In the likeness of the chocolate, there is the effect of refinement and distillation; in that of the nut (at least, the walnut), there is a clear sense of convolution that evokes the internal logic of the ghazal couplet. It is through these aspects of accretion, concentration, and convolution—all perceived in an essentially circular form—that it is possible to begin to see the couplet in a nuclear form.

The Nuclear Structure of the Ghazal Couplet

I have chosen the word nuclear to describe the structure of the individual ghazal couplet for several reasons. The *Oxford English Dictionary* defines nuclear as 'pertaining to, having the form or position of, a nucleus', and nucleus (originally from the Latin for kernel or inner part, and related to the word for nut) as 'that which forms the center or kernel of some aggregate or mass' (1971: 1952-3). In this sense the ghazal is distinctly nuclear: there is in each couplet a central idea or image around which words and often other images 'are grouped, collected, or compacted' (1971: 1953). The analogies given above—pearl, chocolate, and nut—are all nuclear; yet they are also essentially static, and while useful, they capture only part of the full effect of the ghazal couplet.

The term nuclear is even more appropriate when applied to the dynamic structure of the ghazal, where the individual elements of the couplet exist in a complex relationship around the basic idea, and where a central network of tension holds the various elements together in some sort of equilibrium. To borrow a phrase from Lévi-Strauss, the ghazal consists of a complex of tensions arranged in 'bundles of relationships' (1967: 207), and thus satisfies particularly well the definition given by Rene Wellek and Austin Warren that 'a literary work of art is not a simple object but rather a highly complex organization of a stratified character with multiple meanings and relationships' (1956: 27).

Since so many of the connotations of the word nuclear involve some aspect of the biological or physical sciences, it is particularly satisfying to find such imagery in one of Ghalib's most evocative couplets, a verse which may be translated into English without elaborate explanation:

1.3 haiṅ zavāl-āmāda ajzā āfrīnash ke tamām
mihr-e-gardūṅ hai cirāgh-e-rahguẕār-e-bād yāṅ [106: 2]

A word-by-word translation would be

are decay-inclined things/elements creation-'s-all
sun-in-heavens is lamp-of-road-of-wind here

and in a translation better suited to English syntax:

all the elements of creation are inclined toward decay
the sun in the heavens is [but] an oil lamp in the wind's path

In the first line, there is a general statement describing an irreversible action—decay—which is presented in a context of indefinite urgency; *āmāda* means both 'inclined' and 'bent upon', hence the ambiguity of the degree of urgency. The words in the first line, moreover, are abstract—*elements, creation, inclined, decay*—and there is an emphasis provided by an inversion of the normal spoken prose order on both process (the first word is *are*, the first phrase is *are decay-inclined*) and totality (the last word is *all*.) The first line, therefore, creates a certain tension of expectation.

In the second line, a cluster of concrete and real images—*sun, heavens/sky, lamp, path, wind,* and *here*—is catapulted into the consciousness of the reader or listener by the abstract statement in the first line. The effect of the second line by itself (that the sun is a lamp in the wind's path) is ambiguous: the lamp may blow out but will not necessarily do so. But the first line establishes that the lamp *will* blow out eventually, and will do so *here* (emphasized as the last word in the second line).

What is distinctly nuclear in this couplet is the fact that the first line, after its initial reading, will be perceived differently in all subsequent readings once the second line has been read. In this sense, the structure of the couplet involves a circularity of logic: the reader's perception is drawn to return to the first line, in order to re-examine the statement that 'the elements of creation are all inclined toward decay', and to interpret it anew as meaning 'the very elements of this creation are *all* subject to, even bent upon, destruction'. The blowing out of the sun, moreover, is no gradual process of decay; it is an apocalyptic event. The magnitude of the event may be perceived in a variety of perspectives. The religious person, inclined to take his earthly existence as of no significance in comparison to God's reality, could easily see the sun as having the insubstantiality of a mere oil lamp; the same person might well perceive decay or destruction as a path to union with the Divine, for Sura 55: 16 of the Qur'an observes that 'all that is on earth will perish'. On the other hand, someone with no existential certainty of a divine presence could react with horror at the unimaginable prospect of the sun's extinction.

The primary impact of this verse exists in the metaphor of the sun as a lamp. This telescoping visual comparison is effective not only because the lamp and the sun are both burning, but they are both round, and flame-colored. Such a comparison is typical of Ghalib because it is kinetic—in motion—with a sense of potential or unleashed energy, while a similarly appropriate comparison of the rose to the beloved's cheek is merely static. Yet beyond this sense of energy, which is quite apprehensible in translation, there are additional devices of compression which endow the verse with a greater sense of density and force than the English paraphrase reveals.

The inversion from normal prose order as a device of emphasis has already been noted above. One of the distinctive features of Urdu syntax is a broad flexibility in the possible word sequence of a sentence. There is in English some latitude for alternation of word order: 'Here the sun of heaven is. . . .'; 'The sun of heaven here is. . . .'; 'The sun of heaven is here . . . '; 'A lamp in the wind's path is here the sun of heaven'; and so forth—and an occasional English poet, such as Gerard Manley Hopkins, may exploit these possibilities to the fullest. Yet an Urdu poet has the option of beginning the above thought with *lamp, wind, path, is, here, sun, of,* or *heaven,* or of ending with any of the same words, without any effect of contrivance. Thus Ghalib is able to enclose his statement with the emphatic 'Are . . . all' and 'Sun . . . here' in order to clarify the meaning and heighten the impact of each line. (Conversely, certain words may be de-emphasized by their placement in the first line, in order to provide for the element of surprise in the second.)

Other compressive techniques which contribute to the effectiveness of the above verse include elision and the use of the *eẓāfa.* The word *yahāṅ* (here) is contracted for metrical reasons to the monosyllabic *yāṅ,* and *gardūn* (heavens) is shortened to the nasalized *gardūṅ;* other common examples include *agar* (if) to *gar, merā* (my) to *mirā,* or *jahān* (world) to *jahāṅ,* all contributing to a greater compactness of the line. The *eẓāfa,* the Persian particle usually transliterated as *i* or *e,* functions in the addition of an adjective to a noun, or more commonly (particularly in Urdu poetry), as the genitive, as in

mihr-e-gardūṅ hai cirāg͟h-e-rahguẕār-e-bād yāṅ
or
sun-of-heaven is lamp-of-wind here.

While the use of three *ofs* seems ponderous in English translation, as would the use of the common Urdu genitive *kā* three times in the original, the proliferation of the *eẓāfa* in Persian or Urdu sounds perfectly fluent and natural, and at the same time allows for the construction of highly compressed phrases. By the same token, the use of the genitive *ke* in the previous line, as the only occurrence of the *kā-ke-kī* form in the entire couplet, gives an added impact to the word which ends the first line, *tamām* (all).

Probably the greatest compression in this couplet is that created by the use of contrast and comparison, between the *heavens* and *here*, between the air-element of *wind* and the fire of *sun* and *lamp*, between the totality of *all* and minute particularity of *elements*, and finally, in the vertiginous manipulation of perspective in comparing the (eternal) *sun* to the (momentary) *lamp*, and by extension to the previous line, to *ajzā*, which has a connotation in the modern context of 'elements' as essential particles, or atoms. In such a comparison, the perspective ranges instantaneously from the microscopic to the astronomical, so that in effect, the ghazal does indeed come to 'a binding of infinite space'.

Tension and the Nuclear Structure

The presence of tension in the structure of the ghazal couplet should be evident from the verse just examined. While I have not found any discussion of 'tension' as such in Urdu criticism on the ghazal, the concept is a useful device, as I hope to demonstrate, for explaining the indigenous understanding and appreciation of the ghazal. Since the element of tension is central to this discussion of structure, I would like to review in this chapter some of the connotations that the word has in Western literary analysis, then apply these connotations in an analysis of the ghazal. As Cleanth Brooks has written in an excellent article entitled 'I. A. Richards and the Concept of Tension',

> The element of tension in literature is, of course, not new. The father of criticism discerned it in Greek tragedy and commented on it. Even that solid neo-classicist, Samuel Johnson, clearly acknowledges it—in his treatment of metaphor, at least. Tension has always been a factor in determining literary and artistic unity, regardless of the historical period. But in our own day it has emerged as an important, if sometimes problematic, aspect of literary structure, and because it upsets older ideas of decorum, it has demanded new insights into its positive functions and a fresh discussion of its proper limits. [1973: 135]

Brooks proceeds to paraphrase Richards (because he sees Richards' treatment of tension as more implicit than explicit) in a discussion of the tension between 'inclusion' and 'exclusion'; in this parlance, 'inclusion' refers to elements included in a poem, and 'exclusion' to those elements not included.

> Most actual poems fall somewhere between the extremes, but poems that

lie near to either extreme undergo accordant risks, reveal characteristic virtues, and sometimes characteristic defects. Thus too much dependence on exclusion will result in a trivial and anemic poem. Such poems do not provide the reader with new insights, i.e., new ways of putting into a pattern what we had usually taken to be unrelated and perhaps even irreconcilable elements. They do not sufficiently exhibit the power of the plastic imagination. . . .

Yet poems founded on inclusion, it must be conceded, have their characteristic failures too. If the poet tries to include too much of the heterogeneous, if he lacks the power of imagination to reconcile the disparities, if he increases tension beyond his power to control it, then the poem simply explodes into incoherence. What happens to his over-ambitious metaphors will illustrate: the 'heterogeneous ideas yoked by violence together' have been forced by sheer will power to touch momentarily, but because merely yoked by violence and not truly reconciled, they fly apart. [1973: 138-9]

The above passage, with its discussion of inclusion and exclusion, is particularly applicable to the ghazal, which by virtue of its form forces the poet to exclude all but a very few words and images for use in each 'poem' (couplet), and challenges him to include as much meaning as possible within the confines of two lines. The discussion of tension is also very much to the point *vis-a-vis* the ghazal couplet, where there is always some basic tension, usually between the first and second lines (sometimes called hemistiches).

Some connection, implicit or explicit, will exist between these two lines. The second line may be comparative (in the sense of establishing a similitude) to the first, or contrasting (establishing a difference), or corroborative (giving a specific example to illustrate a general statement in the first line, or *vice-versa*). The first and second lines may exist as question and answer, or an expression of cause and effect. Since the two lines will in some sense be different, their very difference produces a tension which combines with the metric arrangement of the ghazal to bind the two lines into a unified couplet. Following Brooks' statement above, and modifying it to suit the ghazal: If the two lines are too similar (or limited in their combined perspective) and 'do not provide the reader with new insights', the results will be 'a trivial and anemic poem'. If the two lines are too different (or too disparate in their individual perspectives), if the poet 'lacks the power of imagination to reconcile the disparities, if he increases the tension beyond his power to control it, then the poem simply explodes into incoherence'.

The 'leaping spark' suggested by Keene as an analogy for the effect of the *haiku* provides an illuminating example of tension. As just observed, the two halves of the *she'r* (couplet) provide two points between which a poetic spark may leap. The brilliance of the spark depends upon two factors: the distance between the poles, and the strength of the charges held by the individual lines. If the distance is too small, the spark is weak; if the distance is great, there will be no spark at all unless the poet can charge each line with a sufficient energy of meaning. If the poet is successful, his couplet has the effect of providing a spark which does not simply leap from one pole to another, like a man jumping across a stream, but rather extends over the full distance between the two poles for the duration of its existence, illuminating the surrounding area brightly, and the more remote areas dimly and ambiguously.

It is important to note that beyond the basic, elemental tension existing between the lines of most couplets, there may be other tensive poles between which sparks of recognition and understanding may leap. In the following verse by Ghalib, as in many couplets composed in the longer meters, there are four distinct conceptual units (two in each line) which contain, in effect, a total of seven tensive poles, as represented by seven grammatically complete clauses:

1.4 na thā kuch/to k͟hudā tha | kuch na hotā/to k͟hudā hotā
ḍabūyā mujh ko hone ne | na hotā maiṅ/to kyā hotā
[33: 1]

A literal translation would be:

not was something then God was
something not had been then god would-have-been
sank/drowned me—1) being/existence—2)
not had-been I then what would-have-been

1) is an object indicator, 2) is a past tense transitive indicator, particles which have no equivalent in English. In a comprehensible translation, the verse would be:

1.4 when there was nothing, there was God

had nothing been, God would have been
my being has been my ruin
had I not been what would have been [33: 1]

The basic tension here exists in the implicit comparison between the poet and God, a comparison obvious from the symmetrical and parallel syntax of the couplet; within each line, a secondary tension exists between the concepts of being and non-being, so that, as already noted, there are seven distinct 'poles' of tension within the couplet, with cognitive 'sparks' leaping among them in an illumination of the relationships between being and non-being, and between self and God. The different interpretations possible from this single couplet are evident in the following English translations (of varying quality) by different writers:

When there was nothing there was God
Had nothing been, God would have been
My being has brought about my fall
Had I not been, what would have been?

Ahmed Ali (1969: 31)

Before all being, God was there
Without all being God would be
My being has been all my ruin
O, but for being, God I'd be

H. D. Saraswat (n.d.: 3)

When there was nothing, God was; and if there were nothing still God would be
My being has been my undoing; if 'I' were not, what would there have been?

Malik Ram (1968: 64)

When I was not born I was God and had I not been born I would have remained God. My being here has been the cause of my ruin. What would have happened if I were not born?

K. N. Sud (1969: 73)

Thou wert, O lord, when there was nought
Thou wouldst be still, if there were nought

It is my separate existence
that made me forget
my true identity with God!
What would I be, if I were not!

Had I not clung to mine ego
and this phenomenal existence,
I should have realized
my true Diving Being.

J. L. Kaul (1957: 81-2)

When there was naught, existed God,
If all turned Void, He'd still be there,
Doomed am I, for I *am*,
Whatever could be if I were not?

Qurratulain Hyder (1970: 80)

The Urdu original of this couplet illustrates a number of compressive and tensive devices not seen in the earlier verse (1.3). Here is an example, as shown in the divergent translations, of a *she'r* which may be read with different intonations. Since traditional Urdu writing has no punctuation, it is up to the reader to supply pauses and intonation from the context of the poetry, and from his own experience. The second half of the second hemistich of this verse may be read either with extreme seriousness ('If I had not been, *what would have been*?' with the intonation—indicated in English by underlining—expressing fear, doubt, or uncertainty) or with a shrugging, casual carelessness suggesting that nothing would have been lost in not being.

The asking of a question, 'what would have been?', illustrates another rhetorical device of the ghazal. By asking a question without answering it explicitly, the poet leaves open a range of possible answers. For the reader with no clearly defined ontology, the concept of non-existence, whether of one's self or of the entire universe, is difficult to comprehend. For the person with a strong religious sense, however, the answer to the question is clear: If I had never come into existence, I would have remained in the presence of God and would never have had to be separated from Him.

Ellipsis is another compressive device found in this couplet, not just once, but three times. In each phrase using the Urdu conjunction *to* (then), there is an implicit *agar* (if) at the beginning of the phrase. Such an ellipsis is not uncommon in Urdu. In addition to the *if . . . then* construction (with the *if* left unstated but clearly implied), double clauses using *jab* (when) . . . *tab* (then) may leave the earlier element implicit and unstated. The grammatical relationship between pronoun and verb in Urdu, moreover, permits the omission of the pronoun, so that in some phrases (particularly those in poetry) the verb will indicate the number, gender, and sometimes the person of the subject. In other cases, particularly those using some form of the verb *honā* (to be), the verb itself may be eliminated, with the verbal function evident from the context. Such ellipsis may only achieve a shortening of the poetic line or (as will be shown in the next chapter) may increase the breadth of possible interpretations of the verse, and hence increase the density and conceptual charge of the central statement.

Moving from purely grammatical compressive devices to logical techniques, we find in the above couplet a rather compelling use of paradox in the distinction between man and God, and the states of being and non-being. The paradox is enriched and further explained by a knowledge of traditional Sufi thought. Ghalib says that being has made him sink or drown; on one idiomatic level this may mean that being has been his ruin, in the sense of the ruin of his reputation. But on a deeper level, the statement also suggests that existence has made him, paradoxically, non-existent. In the Sufi distinction between reality (*ḥaqīqat*) and the unreal (*majāz*), the former is the reality of God, into whose divine presence all other things are absorbed, while the latter is the deceptive, seeming 'reality' of earthly life, in which man, through an illusion of selfhood, is separated and distinct from the divine reality, and hence unreal. There is even a further paradox in this couplet in the assertion that God's reality is transcendent, so that He would exist even if nothing at all in the entire universe existed.

This delving into mystical metaphysics, while not constituting a formal allusion, will evoke for the person knowledgeable in the history of Sufism an implicit echo of the famous pronouncement by Mansur al-Hallaj, the Sufi martyr who was executed in AD 922 for his earlier proclamation of *anā'l-ḥaqq,* 'I am God/Truth/Reality'. The very syntax of the verse, as is shown in English translations, provides the scope for an implicit comparison of the poet himself with God. At the same time, this allusion in no way prevents the alternate interpretations, in which the poet may be expressing a desire for union with—and terror at separation from—God, or may simply be evoking the horror of contemplating the prospect of death in earthly life.

It should be clear by now that the internal structure of this verse is extremely dense and compact, through such devices as 1) ellipsis, in the implied *jab* (when) or *agar* (if) signalled by the later *to* (then); 2) inversion, with the normal prose order of *kuch na thā* changed to *na thā kuch* for emphasis on the negative, and for the same reason, the use of *na hotā maiṅ*; 3) phonemic manipulation in the use of a single retroflex sound, *ḍ* in *ḍabūyā* to highlight the ruin of the poet through existence; 4) repetition of the words *hotā* (would-have-been) four times; *na* (not) and *to* (then) three times; and *thā* (was), *kuch* (something—but here used with *na* to mean 'nothing'), and *k͟hudā* (God) twice each, to emphasize the central ontological concerns of the verse; 5) parallelism between the first and second halves of the first line, and between the second halves of the first and second lines, with the resulting 6) comparison and contrast between God, and existence and non-existence, and between the poet and God, being and non-being; 7) the asking of an unanswered question ('had I not been, what would have been?'); 8) paradox, as noted above, along with 9) allusion to Hallaj and the Sufi concept of reality; and finally, 10) ambiguity not only in the absence of punctuation, but in the subtle use of implication in most of the other techniques just described. The effortless compression and combination of all these different techniques in a single verse provides a superb example of *sahl-e-mumtana'*, the deceptive simplicity so highly prized in Urdu poetry: the subtle fusion and even concealment of diverse elements, held in equilibrium by primary and secondary nuclear tensions which extend into the mind of the reader or listener to invoke his own experience and perceptions. Like the earlier example (1.3), this verse illustrates brilliantly the circular logic in the nuclear structure of the ghazal couplet, for the second line demands, if not a re-reading of the first, at least a recollection of it, by virtue of the various parallelisms and contrasts among the two lines, the four half-lines, and the seven clauses. While this process of recollection and re-perception occurs to some extent in all good poems, it is dominant in the ghazal because of the compactness of its structure, as well as the conventions surrounding its recitation (see below). In the verse just examined, then, one's mind travels back in a circular pattern from the end of the couplet to the beginning, while the paradoxes of being and not being, and of God's existence and non-existence, pull the mind deep into the complex questions of the couplet with an extraordinary centripetal nuclear force.

The effect of this couplet and the one before it is, in short, one of awe. In a chapter entitled 'Tensive Language' in his book, *Metaphor and Reality*, Philip Wheelwright has written:

> [The] language that strives toward adequacy . . . is characteristically tensive to some degree and in some manner or other. This is true whether the language consists of gestures, drawings, musical compositions, or . . . verbal language consisting of words, idioms, and syntax. A gesture in the worship of a tutelary daemon, or a phrase of the Lord's Prayer, is originally and properly alive and tensive. It may become commonplace and perfunctory through careless usage, which would mean that its original linguistic vitality had been lost so that its survival is merely a result of social habit; but when the gesture or the phrase reflects the religious aura that first surrounded it and gave it significance for an authentic worshipper, it has the power to elicit awe. [1968: 46-7]

In most respects, this passage might well have been written about the ghazal. Like liturgy, the ghazal is subject to much formalization and prescription, and so may be—depending upon the predilections of the individual participant as either poet or listener—performed and experienced with a sense of awe, or merely executed and appreciated as a matter of convention and habit. What follows is a discussion of formalization and prescription in the form and context of the ghazal.

The Structural Conventions of the Ghazal

The celebrated Arab philosopher Ibn Khaldun (1332-1406) defined poetry as 'an effective discourse, based on metaphor and descriptions, divided into parts [i.e. verses] agreeing with one another in meter and rhyme, each one of such parts being independent in scope and aim of what follows it' (Browne 1964: vol. 2, 87). Following this traditional pattern, the Urdu ghazal (like the later classical Persian ghazal, and the Turkish ghazal) consists of a sequence of discrete, internally complete couplets sharing a common scheme of meter and rhyme. There is frequently no apparent compelling thematic unity among the couplets, so that each verse—*she'r*, from the Arabic infinitive noun meaning ' "to know"; "to speak in verse" ' (Platts 1930: 728)—as previously noted, is essentially a complete poem in itself. There is, however, a type of ghazal called *musalsal* (continuous) in which all the couplets are sequentially linked by a linear progression of thought (see the first ghazal in chapter VI); other ghazals may contain a section, called *qiṯ'a-band* (literally, 'fragment-binding') in which two or more couplets are intended to be read together as a unified sequence (see 3: 81).

Most Urdu ghazals have at least five couplets, and a few have as many as fifteen or more. The first line (*miṣra'*, from the Arabic infinitive meaning 'to throw down' [Platts 1930: 1041]) of the ghazal establishes the metric structure for each succeeding *miṣra'*; the initial *miṣra'* also introduces the rhyme scheme to be followed in the second *miṣra'*, and in the second *miṣra'* of each succeeding couplet. For this reason, the first *miṣra'* is called the *miṣra'-e-ṯarḥ* (literally', line of procedure'), as the verse line which sets the example in meter and rhyme for all the following verses.

The rhyme pattern of the Urdu ghazal usually consists of a double rhyme, which has as its component parts a true rhyme (*qāfiya*, from the Arabic verb 'to follow' [Platts 1930: 786]) and a repeated rhyme (*radīf*, from the Arabic 'to ride behind' [Platts 1930: 590]). This pattern may be represented as ax, a^1x; b, a^2x; c, a^3x; and so forth, with *a* and it derivatives representing the *qāfiya* (true rhyme), *x* the *radīf* (repeated rhyme), and *b*, *c*, etc. the non-rhyming first lines of each succeeding couplet. The first couplet, called the *maṯla'* (from the Arabic 'to rise' [Platts 1930: 1044]), has this double rhyme in both its first and second lines, while the rhyme in succeeding couplets occurs only in the second line. The second couplet, called the *ḥusn-e-maṯla'* (literally, 'beauty of the first couplet'), is conventionally expected to be even more beautiful or ingenious than the first; by the same token, the verse before the last couplet, the *maqṯa'* (from the Arabic 'to cut' [Platts 1930: 1056]), is called the *ḥusn-e-maqṯa'*, and is expected to be of a particular excellence (Gibb 1958: vol. I, 81). In the last couplet (*maqṯa'*), the poet usually includes his nom de plume (*takhallus*, from the Arabic 'to become safe and secure' [Platts 1930: 313], presumably in the sense that the poet is protecting himself and his beloved from the public discovery of his love; see below).

The following verses are the first (*maṭla‘*), thirteenth, and fourteenth and last (*maqṭa‘*) from one of Ghalib's most famous ghazals, and illustrate the form just outlined:

1.5 bazīca-e-aṭfāl hai dun*yā mire āge*
hotā hai shab-o-roz tamā*shā mire āge* [209: 1]

1.6 go hāth ko jumbish nahīṅ āṅkhoṅ meṅ to dam hai
rahne do abhī sāghar-o-mī*nā mire āge* [209: 13]

1.7 ham-pīsha-o-ham-mashrab-o-ham-rāz hai merā
Ghālib ko burā kyoṅ kaho *acchā mire āge* [209: 14]

A rough English translation of these couplets, creating the general effect of the ghazal-like rhyme (but using, I emphasize, ***different*** *qāfiya* words in English from those in Urdu), would be:

1.5 The world is but a bauble for children's ***play*** *before me*
It is a constant spectacle, night and ***day*** *before me*

1.6 Though the hand cannot move, there's life left in the eyes
Let the goblet and the flask of wine now ***stay*** *before me*

1.7 He works with me, drinks with me, shares my confidence
The evil you would speak of Ghalib, do not ***say*** *before me*
[209: 1, 13, 14]

The rhyme pattern, in summary, is:

(dun)***yā*** *mire age*	=	ax	= ***play***^{1} *before me*
(tamā)***shā*** *mire age*	=	a^1x	= ***day***^{1} *before me*
meṅ to dam hai	=	b	= in the eyes
(mī)***nā*** *mire age*	=	a^2x	= ***stay***^{1} *before me*
ham-rāz hai merā	=	c	= confidence
(ac)***chā*** *mire āge*	=	a^3x	= ***say***^{1} *before me*

The *radīf* (repeated rhyme) in the Urdu verses consists of two words with a total of four syllables, while the *qāfiya* (true rhyme) consists of one syllable which is usually the last syllable of a multisyllabic word, and which has as the consistent rhyming element the final and long vowel *ā*. In general, Ghalib's *radīfs* range from one to four syllables, and rarely consist of more than two words, though theoretically, a *radīf* may be nearly a complete line, with only one additional word—the *qāfiya* word—occurring at the beginning of the line.

As should be evident from the above example, the *radīf* itself may impose a certain vague unity of mood throughout the whole of the ghazal. In some ghazals the unified tone may be obvious, as in Ghalib's ghazal using the *radīf hā'e hā'e* (alas! alas!) or that with the *radīf kahāṅ* (where?); the first is clearly a lament throughout all the couplets, and the second an Urdu equivalent of the Latin *ubi sunt.* In ghazals using the more characteristic verbal or adverbial form as a *radīf,* there will be a more superficial sense of unity (if at all) created by the *radīf.* (It is perhaps relevant to note here that the apparent disunity of the Persian ghazal has been reexamined by such writers a Wickens [1952] and Hillman [1974]. While an examination of the unity or disunity in the Urdu ghazal of Ghalib is not the central concern here, the question will be raised in the next chapter, and discussed again in the last.)

Beyond this formalization and prescription (in Wheelwright's word) of rhyme and stanzaic structure in the ghazal, there is the entire area of metrics (along with rhyme, the other major component of traditional Urdu prosody), as well as the traditional Indo-Persian rhetoric, all of which constitute a network of conventional restrictions within which the ghazal must be composed. I have summarized the nature of rhyme at some length because it is especially pertinent to the discussion which follows of the ghazal's social context. A sustained examination of Urdu metrics and rhetoric, such as that already done in English by Captain G. D. Pybus (1924), is unnecessary here. For our purposes, it will be adequate to summarize briefly the dominant traditional rhetorical figures which provide tension, and contribute to compression, in the individual ghazal couplet. Some of these figures, in fact, have already been pointed out, though they have not been identified by their technical names.

Allusion, or *talmīḥ* (plural *talmīḥat*): Urdu poetry is filled with references to people and places, most of which are drawn from Persian and Arabic sources. We have already seen the implicit reference in 1.3 to a verse from the Qur'an and in 1.4 to Hallaj, the historical martyr. In Ghalib's poetry one may encounter specific Qur'anic figures such as Adam, Moses, Joseph and

Zuleikha, and Christ, as well as figures from Arab and Persian history and legend, such as Laila and Majnun, Sohrab and Rustam, Shirin and Farhad, and mythical creatures such as the Simurgh or the Phoenix. In some cases, epithets may be used in place of names, with Moon of Canaan (*māh-e-kan'ān*) referring to Joseph, or Mountain-Digger (*koh-kan*) referring to Farhad. Such allusions, like the Lord's Prayer (mentioned by Wheelwright), may evoke a response ranging from mechanical acknowledgement to awe, with the degree of intensity determined by 'the sensitivity and disposition of the individual participant' (Wheelwright 1968: 47). In this case, the reader or listener, not the poet, is responsible for providing the electric charge of meaning and familiarity, though an excellent poet will use the allusion in some novel and striking way that will bring the reader's own spark of recognition to a particular brilliance.

Comparison: Comparison in the ghazal occurs primarily in the visual realm, with the same general devices one finds enumerated in Western rhetoric. Both metaphor (*iste'ārā*) and simile (*tashbīḥ*) occur frequently, the latter involving a link of the tenor and the vehicle (in I. A. Richards' terminology [1936]) through such words as *mānind* (like), *jaisā* (as, like), and *yūṅ* (thus). More technical types of figures also occur in Urdu, such as the synecdoche (*majāz-e-mursal*) and metonymy (*kināya*), in which an object is indicated by one of its parts, or by some related thing; a frequent example of this in Ghalib is *dar-o-dīvār* (door-and-wall, for 'house'), a phrase Ghalib uses in one ghazal (59) as the *radīf.* Another important type of figure that occurs in Urdu poetry is the poetical aetiology (*ḥusn-e-ta'līl*), or fanciful assignment of cause; the blushing of the rose is an example commonly given in rhetorical treatises, and in Ghalib's poetry, an example typically more kinetic would be the 'restless' movement of the waves in the ocean, or of the dust motes in sunlight, as an indication of the desire of all things to be united with the ultimate divine reality. Such images are based on the more general sort of personification indicated in the category *tashkhīṣ*.

To a great extent, as Bausani has noted, the visual imagery of Persian and Urdu poetry is seen as 'bi-dimensional decorative visual play', by which he presumably means the two-dimensional effect of arabesques, carpets, and perspective-less miniature paintings (1956: 52). Explaining such imagery, Bausani cites the traditional 'formal harmony of comparison', in which things are likened purely on the basics of their visual appearance, as when a lock of hair is compared with a polo-stick (1958: 148). He points out the degree to which such congruence is usually observed, by referring to Shelley's ode, 'The Cloud', in which the moon is likened to a maiden walking across the sky, with her feet 'breaking the woof' of the sky here and there for the stars to peer through; such a conceit, says Bausani, would be intolerable in Urdu poetry, for obviously the moon has no feet; only a face can be like the moon (1956: 52-4). Typically Ghalibian examples of such purely visual comparisons would be the eyebrow as a bow to launch the arrows (eyelashes) of the beloved's eye or glance; or more uniquely (and tri-dimensionally), the wave as a severed tongue.

Contrast (*tazādd*) in the ghazal is indicated in a variety of ways both visual and circumstantial. Ghalib will frequently juxtapose the past (when one's fortunes were usually better and there may have been an occasional rendezvous with the beloved) with the present (when the poet is suffering terribly); or the beloved's house (with its assembly—*bazm, maḥfil, majlis*—of admirers and its gaiety of conversation, flowers, and affection) with the poet's wretched cell of woe (where he sighs icy sighs, weeps tears of blood, tears his collar, and swoons from weakness); or again, the poet's cell with the desert (where the poet, leaving behind his wretchedness, wanders in sublime and energized madness). Such contrasts may be indicated by explicitly antithetical word such as then-now (*pahle-ab*), here-there (*yahāṅ-vahāṅ*), and I-thou (*maiṅ-tū*), or by an implicit description of circumstances. Ghalib's verses also include the frequent juxtaposition of descriptive opposites, either in the form of the oxymoron (*ṣifat-e-mutaẓādd*), such as 'the delight of pain', or in outright antithesis (*taẓādd*), such as night and day, life and death, ocean and desert, and union and separation.

Such comparison and contrasts obviously involve a degree of tension; images are pushed apart by contrast (yet held together within the couplet) or yoked together 'by the power of the plastic imagination', though they be dissimilar; Ghalib's early poetry is characterized by imagery which so often seems 'yoked by violence together' (Brooks 1973: 139), in that it is difficult for the mind to assimilate the comparison—not because of the distance between the objects compared, but because of the sheer complexity generated in the comparison, or the excessive attention to minute detail. In writing such poetry, Ghalib was merely following the conventions of the declining *sabk-e-hindī*, the Indian style of Persian poetry (the final master of which was Bedil [Ghani: 1960], whom Ghalib admired greatly), with its convoluted imagery of exaggeration which, though grotesque to modern tastes, was much appreciated in its time.

The *hyperbole* (*mubālagha*) of Urdu and Persian poetry, it is safe to say, knows no limits. The beloved's waist, for example, is so slender as to be thin as a pin, or even, on occasion, to disappear altogether. Ghalib's use of hyperbole is usually less decadent, or at least more dynamic—as when he exaggerates the rushing of his tears to become a flood which will obliterate entire cities, or in inverse exaggeration, he compresses the vast expanses of the desert into a fistful of sand, or the sun into an oil lamp. The startling manipulation of the audience's perspective through the use of antithesis, exaggeration, and telescoping compression is a common technique which Ghalib uses to challenge the assumptions and ordinary perceptions of his audience.

Ambiguity and paradox: By the same token, Ghalib has demonstrated a skillful command of ambiguity (*īhām*) and paradox (*mu'ammā* or *ta'miya*). A single word may be ambiguous, for example, in one of three ways: it may be used with its common meaning intended and its secondary meaning only suggested, or *vice-versa*, or it may be used with both meanings intended to be of equal importance in the verse. At a more complex level, an entire phrase, line, or even a couplet may be ambiguous or paradoxical. A very common sort of ambiguity exists in the identity of the beloved, who by convention is represented entirely by masculine verbs and adjectives (there is no gender in Urdu pronouns), even though a female beloved is clearly intended; aside from the question of the actual gender of the beloved, there is also a choice to be made as to whether the beloved should be interpreted as being human or divine, or as existing on both levels. Other uses of ambiguity and paradox may be even more subtle and complex, and it is certainly in such finely wrought verses as the two (1.3 and 1.4) discussed above that Ghalib has created some of his most eloquent poetry.[3]

Yet this poetry, no matter how effective it may seem on the

printed page, cannot be appreciated fully without some understanding of the traditional contexts of its appreciation, and the way in which its distinctively dynamic structure is related to those contexts.

The Structure of the Ghazal in its Social Contexts

An understanding of the socio-cultural context in which the Urdu ghazal is composed and read is enormously important to a comprehension of the ghazal itself. Most critical literature on the ghazal has assumed in the reader a knowledge of these contexts; Sadiq's *History of Urdu Literature* (1964), for example, makes no more than an occasional passing reference to the circumstances under which the ghazal was traditionally composed, recited and circulated. Regarding the importance of the ghazal in its cultural context, the statement by Rashid Ahmed Siddiqi (quoted in the Introduction) that 'our culture is molded in the ghazal, and the ghazal is cast in the mold of our culture'(1969: 11), though seemingly correct to the specialist, is typical in its vagueness, and essentially meaningless to someone outside the Urdu cultural milieu.

Yet the social importance of poetry in general, and the ghazal in particular, should be apparent to anyone having a moderate familiarity with the culture of the Urdu-speaking world. The ghazal, with its structure based in individual couplets, has maintained a particular vitality that enables it to be quoted or recited in a wide variety of circumstances both informal and formal. At the former extreme is the phenomenon through which well-known ghazal couplets become part of Urdu colloquial expression, and are quoted—often without a knowledge of the poet's name—as proverbial, epigrammatic statements in the course of a conversation. At a somewhat more formal level, a particular couplet is frequently used to illustrate a point in writing or in public speaking. In the most formal of circumstances, ghazal poetry is recited at a *mushā'ira*, a popular form of poetic symposium at which the ghazal is by far dominant genre (Naim 1974: 187).

In informal conversation with Urdu speakers, one sometimes encounters situations in which a known couplet is suddenly perceived in a new and different light, so as to be applicable to a particular set of circumstances that has just arisen. To give a topical example: after the resignation of Richard Nixon as President of the United States in 1974, an Urdu-speaking friend remembered two couplets by Ghalib:

1.8 Uncommitted sins—those only longed for—should have their reward as well
If, O God these sins committed must have their punishment [231: 10]

Or in a similar vein:

1.9 We have heard of Adam's leaving Paradise, but
We left your lane having been *truly* disgraced [220: 3]

These couplets both have the basic tone of complaint carried by much ghazal poetry. The first complaint is made unambiguously to God, while the second could be made either to an earthly beloved (whose doorstep and lane are two of the traditional haunts of the poet), or again, to God—the divine beloved. In ordinary circumstances one would be inclined to sympathize with the poet's complaint; supporters of Nixon, claiming the insignificance of his 'misjudgements', could quote the couplets in this sense. For critics of Nixon, however, there could be a savory reversal of the traditional sympathy, in seeing the American public as the beloved, haughty and tyrannical, and Nixon the cringingly proud (whatever his circumstances) and wretchedly supplicating lover.

The quotation of the ghazal couplet, or a complete ghazal, as a literary device is evident in many Urdu novels, or even in novels written in English about India. The first-person narrator in *Umrā'o Jān Adā* (written in 1899) frequently quotes one or more ghazal couplets, often of her own composition, and the "author", Mirza 'Ruswa', to whom Umrao Jan is "telling" her story, often retorts with more couplets, often of her own (Ruswa 1961, 1963). Ahmed Ali's *Twilight in Delhi* (written in English and published in 1940) includes occasional Persian and Urdu couplets in the streams of its characters' consciousness (Ali 1966), and even Forster's *A Passage to India* (1924) includes a reference to a couplet quoted from Ghalib in the course of a conversation: '[Aziz] recited a poem by Ghalib. It had no connection with anything that had gone before, but it came from his heart and it spoke to theirs. . . .

The poem had done no "good" to anyone, but it was a passing reminder, a breath from the divine lips of beauty, a nightingale between two worlds of dust' (1952: 105-6).

The quotation of his own or another poet's ghazals in letters was commonly practised by Ghalib; on a few occasions, in fact, he would introduce new verses in a letter written to a friend (see Ghalib 1968a; 89-90; the *maṯla*' and *maqṯa*' appear in the *Dīvān* as 217: 1, 3). In addition to those ghazals included in letters, Ghalib arranged during his lifetime the compilation of hand-written manuscripts of his verses (Latif 1929: 20-5). The vernacular press was introduced in India in the early nineteenth century, but it was not widely used in printing until the middle part of that century, so that the first published edition of Ghalib's Urdu poetry did not appear until 1841 (Schimmel 1975a: 216). In addition to manuscripts (and later, printed books) of the works of a single poet, the anthology (*tazkira*) of verses from various poets along with brief biographical notes was then another source of ghazal poetry for those who could afford to purchase such manuscripts.

At a more formal level, the ghazal couplet may be used as an illustrative device in public lectures and speeches. C. M. Naim recalls an occasion in 1956 when Jawaharlal Nehru, as Prime Minister of India, quoted a couplet by 'Akbar' Allahabadi (1846-1921) in response to a fierce attack on the Congress party by a rebellious party member:

A mere sigh, and we get a bad name
He commits murder, and no one comments.

As Naim observes:

> This very well-known and quite typical ghazal couplet expressed the late prime minister's feelings more poignantly than any other remark could have, as was evident from the thunderous applause that followed. In quoting a couplet from an Urdu *ghazal*, Nehru expressed not merely his personal inclinations but displayed a habit common among the millions of admirers of Urdu poetry who come from all parts of the subcontinent and from all strata of society. [Naim 1975: 186]

The most formal context for the recitation of the ghazal is the *mushā'ira*, which probably developed, according to Annemarie Schimmel (1975a: 171) in connection with the poets of Delhi during the lifetime of Khwaja Mir 'Dard' (1721-85). The *mushā'ira* in its present form seems to be unique to Urdu speakers, though it unquestionably had its origins in Persian and Arabic culture: the word itself is Arabic (in correct form, *mushā'ara*), meaning a poetic contest (Steingass 1892: 1242). According to a personal communication from C. M. Naim, the *mushā'ira* in Iran consists of a one-to-one competition, with the first contestant reciting a couplet, the second reciting another couplet beginning with the ending letter of the first couplet, and the first contestant following suit, until one of the two is unable to recite. Naim observes that such competitions, called *bait-bāzī* (couplet-play) in India, are still popular in Iran, with alphabetically arranged anthologies published to assist the competition.

According to M. Mujeeb, the *mushā'ira* became popular in India during the nineteenth century:

> It had originated in the practice of poets reciting their odes in the courts of rulers or in the houses of patrons; now it became much more democratic, because a literary medium had been discovered which stimulated a few larger number of people to exercise their mind in the composition and appreciation of poetry. The style of the *qaṣīdah* [ode] fell into the background, the *ghazal*, with its opportunities for terse, epigrammatic expression, came to the fore. Hardly any educated person would have been willing to admit that he did not have the intelligence or taste to appreciate poetry, and most aspired to the ability at least to string meaningful words together for attracting notice and winning applause and esteem, and it also happened that people who had no aptitude for versification persuaded or paid others to write *ghazals* for them. *Mushā'irahs* were held in the courts of Oudh and Delhi, but anyone well-known enough to play the host could hold a *mushā'irah.* The general procedure was to send an invitation and announce at the same time a *miṣra'-i-ṭaraḥ,* a half-verse to show the meter and rhyme in which the *ghazal* was to be composed. When the poets had assembled, and generally they took their time, a candle was passed around, being placed before the poet who was to recite his poem. Much importance was attached to the order in which poets were requested to recite, the beginners and the less well-known coming first, those with established reputations coming later, and often—perhaps too often—unpleasantness was caused by a poet being asked to recite too soon or before another poet whom he considered his inferior. Poets had their own circle of admirers, who were anxious to see that the eminence of their literary hero was recognized and that he got his due share of applause, and *mushā'irahs* sometimes led to bitterness and conflict. . . .
>
> The *mushā'irah,* for all its obvious drawbacks, was a means of public appraisal of cultivated expression. There was much quarreling over the

meanings and uses of words and idioms, but there was also an elaboration of concepts, particularly of personality, love, beauty and freedom. This century was the century of Mīr and Ghalib, in which the poet attempted to build out of the ruins of institutions the ideal of a new man and a new faith.

Many poets who attained literary fame can also be regarded as typical representatives of the culture of this period, Mirzā Assadullāh Khān Ghālib being among the last. [Mujeeb 1967: 515-16]

Ghalib's own letters, in fact, contain periodic references to *mushā'iras* in which he participated (Russell and Islam 1969).

All the features enumerated in the above passage would be apparent to any reasonably observant person with a good knowledge of Urdu who attends a contemporary *mushā'ira.* (In the present era, the candle, in its rotation among the participating poets, has in effect been replaced by the ubiquitous microphone—to which the poets must go themselves—a concession from the previously intimate *mushā'iras* to the larger audiences today; otherwise, the customs of the *mushā'ira* have remained essentially unchanged.) Yet some further description is necessary, particularly concerning the relationship of the ghazal's structure to its recitation, in order to explain the full appeal the ghazal still holds for speakers of Urdu.

In the *mushā'ira* the poet begins the recitation of a ghazal by saying that he will 'submit' a couplet (the verb is '*arẓ karnā*). He then recites the first line of the *maṭla* to establish the meter and rhyme scheme of the poem for the sake of the audience. After a pause, which builds up a certain suspense as to what the second line (following the meter and rhyme of the first) will be, the poet often recites the first line a second time to emphasize the formal patterns as well as the thought of the first line, and perhaps to heighten the suspense; (at least some of the knowledgeable members of the audience will be searching for possible words to rhyme with the *qāfiya* in order to anticipate, following the thought of the first line, what the second line will be.) Then the poet delivers the second line, and the most attentive members of the audience, excitedly following each word of the second line, may shout the new *qāfiya,* which they may have already anticipated, and the *radīf,* which is the same as that in the previous line.

For example, returning to the couplet translated earlier in the chapter (1.5): after hearing bāzīca-e-aṭfāl hai dun*yā mire āge*

recited once or twice, followed by a pause, the alert listener would be in a position, after hearing

hotā hai shab-o-roz tamā—

to shout, along with the poet

—*shā mire āge*!

The audience would be assisted in its anticipation of the second line and the *qāfiya* not only by the formal metric and rhyme structure of the first line, but also by a knowledge of the traditional figures of speech, words, images, and motifs (which will be introduced in the next chapter) which predominate in the ghazal. But returning for a moment to the discussion of tension: the recitation of the first line creates, through the audience's expectations of the second line, a state of heightened suspense which is relieved by the conclusion of the second line. Such tension is external—between the couplet and the audience, and as mentioned above, the degree of tension will be determined by the knowledge and responsiveness of the audience.

Often to give the audience an opportunity to persue an outstanding couplet, a fellow poet or some prominent person among the assembly guests may repeat the couplet, or request a repetition by cries of '*mukarrar*! *mukarrar*!' ('repeat! repeat!'). Sometimes an alternate interpretation may be suggested by emphasizing different words or giving different phrasing or intonation to a line, as was possible in 1.4, given the lack of punctuation and the ambiguity of the verse; or the couplet may have been particularly pleasing, and some listeners may request a repetition in order to memorize it on the spot for some future quotation. Occasionally, it has been observed, a polite request for repetition may signal that the listener has perceived some defect in the couplet, and the alert poet would attempt to correct the fault in the subsequent recitation (Russell and Islam 1968: 121).

If an audience is not pleased by a recitation—and style is sometimes of as much importance as substance—the indications of disapproval in a contemporary *mushā'ira* can range from noisy inattention to outright ridicule, and sometimes an unfortunate poet is hooted and shouted into defeated silence. An occasional poet, however, refuses to compromise his standards, and may deliberately provoke audiences he feels to be of inferior sensibility. Such a poet in his early years was Ghalib, who was often chided for the abstruse quality of many of his verses, influenced (as noted above) by the *sabk-e-hindī*. The story is told of a *mushā'ira* at which Ghalib was present, and where a respected member of the audience, in order to apprise Ghalib that many of his listeners felt his verse to be too outré, quoted a couplet of utter nonsense swearing that he had read it somewhere in Ghalib's *Dīvān* (Russell and Islam 1969: 40).

Another poet may play directly to his listeners, and recite a couplet 'designed mainly to enable them, given their prior knowledge of the rhyme scheme, to complete for themselves the second line of his couplet without his needing to recite it at all; and those who have seen this happen know how much the audience enjoys the experience' (Russell 1969: 121).

When a couplet has been enjoyed through various recitations to everyone's satisfaction, the poet proceeds to the next verse, and the audience, hearing the first line of each new couplet, tries to anticipate the sense, and perhaps the *qāfiya*, of the second line. Sometimes a new couplet may be given greater force by preceding it with a summary recitation of the previous couplet, or of the first couplet in the ghazal. The process of repetition (and it is to make the following point that I have discussed at such length the formal recitation of the couplet in a *mushā'ira*) provides each member of the audience a chance for careful scrutiny of each verse, in light of the fact that one's mind travels back and forth, even circularly, among the various elements in the nuclear structure of the couplet as it is recited.

It is also relevant to mention here that the ghazal is often sung, and that Ghalib had enough awareness of the musical potential of the genre to specify that one of his ghazals should be sung in the *rāga Jhinjhotī* (Russell and Islam 1969: 319). In current practice, the musical rendering of a ghazal allows fully as well as a spoken or chanted recitation (see Qureshi 1969) for a careful examination of the nuclear features of its structure; if anything, there is an even greater degree of repetition, and an additional opportunity for highlighting and underscoring particular words and phrases in the ghazal, and for creating suspense, in the musical rendition of the ghazal (Silver 1978).

In another paper (Silver 1972), I have discussed the *mushā'ira* as one variety of *maḥfil* (cultural gathering with performance), and have compared the structure of the ghazal to that of other Indo-Muslim temporal arts (particularly Hindustani classical music and Kathak dance). In that discussion I mention the importance of the element of serious play (as defined by Huizinga and others) in all these genres, and I think it would be appropriate here to conclude this chapter with an extended passage from Huizinga's *Homo Ludens* which refers directly to poetry in the context of play. The rather striking applicability to the ghazal of Huizinga's remarks should be immediately apparent, though I have italicized statements which seem particularly descriptive of the ghazal and the *mushā'ira.*

Let us enumerate once more the characteristics we deemed proper to play. It is an activity which proceeds within certain *limits of time and space,* in a visible order, *according to rules freely accepted,* and outside the sphere of necessity or material utility. The play-mood is one of *rapture and enthusiasm,* and is sacred or festive in accordance with the occasion. *A feeling of exaltation and tension accompanies the action, mirth and relaxation follow. . . .*

The definition we have just given of play might serve as a definition of poetry. The rhythmical or symmetrical arrangement of language, *the hitting of the mark by rhyme or assonance,* the deliberate disguising of the sense, the artificial and artful construction of phrases—all might be so many utterances of the play spirit. To call poetry, as Paul Valéry has done, a playing with words and language is no metaphor: it is the precise and literal truth. . . .

Whether in myth or lyric, drama or epic, the legends of a remote past or a modern novel, *the writer's aim, conscious or unconscious, is to create a tension that will 'enchant' the reader and hold him spellbound. Underlying all creative writing is some human or emotional situation potent enough to convey this tension to others. But there are none too many of these situations—that is the point. Broadly speaking, such situations arise either from conflict, or love, or both together.*

Now both conflict and love imply rivalry or competition, and competition involves play. In the great majority of cases the central theme of poetry and literature is strife—i.e., the task that the hero is to perform, the trials he has to undergo, the obstacles he has to surmount. The very word 'hero' for the chief protagonists is telling enough. *The task will be extraordinarily difficult, seemingly impossible.* More often than not it will be tackled as the result of a challenge, or a vow, *a promise or whim of the beloved.* All the motifs carry us straight back to agonistic play. [1955: 132-3]

Again, the Greek word for assembly or contest, represents 'the conflict of characters in a drama' (Webster 1957: 28). An entry into the world of the ghazal, like that into Greek drama, demands the suspension of many conventional Western expectations of poetry. In both genres, reality is presented in a highly formalized structure and style of expression that at first experience seem stark, even transparent. Yet both are concerned fundamentally with conflict, and when the conventions and codifications of the genre are learned, that conflict is portrayed, even recreated, with an effect of deep absorption, whether the tone be comic or tragic.

NOTES

1. Perhaps this is an attempt to respond to Hali's critical observation that ghazal couplets are similar to English bonbons, 'different in precise shape but all having the same taste' (n.d.: 136).
2. The English rhyming words here are different from the Urdu, and have been chosen to provide a rhyme in the translation.
3. All of the processes discussed up to this point can be translated to some extent into English. But a whole realm of word-play exists in Urdu, both on the semantic and orthographic levels, which is utterly untranslatable. While simple alliteration can at least be pointed out in English, along with such devices as synonyms and homonyms (*tajnīṣ*), other types of devices such as the chronogram, or various plays on the shapes of letters or the use of dots, cannot be duplicated or even adequately described in English without great difficulty; no attempt to do so, except in rare instances, will be made in the following pages.

CHAPTER 2

The Elemental Relationships of Ghalib's Ghazals

> The narrowness of the ghazal's straits is not equal to love
> I need more latitude to tell my story
>
> GHALIB [235: 8]

There can be no doubt that the structural limitations of the ghazal, outlined in the previous chapter, pose a formidable challenge to the poet seeking to be truly original; at the same time, these limitations themselves enable the inferior poet to indulge in facile versification, and the question of where versification ends and true poetic creation begins has been at the heart of the controversies surrounding the ghazal for the past hundred years.

The basic source of the ghazal's controversiality lies not in the restrictions of its form, but in the limitations of its thematic content and imagery. Hali spoke of the entire corpus of Urdu ghazal *dīvāns* (collections of the verse of a single poet) being condensable into a hundred or hundred and twenty-five pages of basic subject (n.d.: 138). Sayyid Abdul Latif referred to the 'few conventional ideas' of the ghazal, and the 'definite number of stereotyped phrases and words which are repeated from one ghazal to another and by one poet after another' (1924: 25), and Muhammad Sadiq similarly decries the ghazal's conventionality (1964: 14).

In comparison with modern Western poetry (with its relatively unlimited range of topics and motifs and its freedom from formal restrictions), the ghazal must certainly seem at first view to be rigid, excessively stylized, and even archaic and decadent; it would seem to limit the possibilities for individual poetic expression so that the poet, confined to the repertoire of conventional images (see below), can only rearrange these images to produce, at best, a minor effect of novelty. It might also seem that the use of the same vocabulary of words and images over a period of centuries would result in semantic depletion, and that the basic Persian imagery would cease to have valid meaning in the Indian context; of the Urdu ghazal, Latif writes: 'Persian in conception, Persian in feeling, Persian in tone, Persian in imagery, and Persian even in local coloring, and Persian in its esoteric connotations, the erotic poetry in Urdu lives on in a few conventional ideas' (1924: 25).

Such objections, however, miss a very basic point, which is the central proposition of this chapter, and to a considerable extent, of the analytic approach used thereafter: that the words, motifs, and images of the ghazal are important not in isolation, but rather in their relationships to each other, for it is the primary function of the ghazal to portray various types of relationships, and to examine, analyze and suggest different tensions and connections between the individual elements of existence. The appeal of the ghazal lies in its challenge to the poet: to make the most resourceful use of a limited number of familiar thematic elements in expressing, most often symbolically, new perspectives on existing relationships, and most commonly, those relationships involving some form of strife.

Just as Huizinga, quoted above, commented on the importance of strife to poetry, Wheelwright has written in his chapter on tensive language that

> In all organic life there is a ceaseless but varying struggle between opposite forces, and without such struggle the organism would go dead. . . . In man the basic organic strife shows itself in various tensions, of which he may be unconscious or at most partly conscious—the tension between self and other persons, between self and physical environment, between love and antagonism, between one's impulses and the decisions of rational thought, between the life-urge and the dark fascination of death. As man gropes to express his complex nature and his sense of the complex world, he seeks or creates representational and expressive forms . . . which shall give some hint, always finally insufficient, of the turbulent moods within and the turbulent world of qualities and forces, promises and threats, outside him. His life oscillates between contrary pulls, and out of his Dionysian condition he seeks, and sometimes for lingering moments attains, an Apollonian vision. But if the vision is not to be escapist and a merely stubborn refusal to face things a they are, it will bear traces of the tensions and problematic character of the experience that gave it birth. [1968: 45-6]

It should be clear from its dominance and popularity—as well as from a brief perusal of a score of couplets—that the ghazal has no dearth of verses hinting at strife, or at tension between love and hate, self and others, or life and death. The question may then be asked: how accurate are these representations of strife and tension, couched as they are in such traditional terms, and if accurate, how eloquent? To answer this, let us turn to Ghalib's most famous ghazals, and consider them, verse by verse, as they might be presented in the leisure of a *mushā'ira.*

Ghazal: ko'ī ummīd bar nahīṅ ātī

The first ghazal is relatively simple; it has few allusions, and—atypically—only a moderate amount of dependence upon the particular thematic conventions of Urdu poetry, so that an uninitiated person may make at least partial sense of it without prior explanation. The sequence of couplets runs:

2.1 ko'ī ummīd bar nahīṅ ātī
ko'ī ṣūrat naz̤ar nahīṅ ātī

2.2 maut kā ek din mu'ayyan hai
nīṅd kyoṅ rāt bhar nahīṅ ātī

2.3 āge ātī thī hāl-e-dil peh haṅsī
ab kisī bāt par nahīṅ ātī

2.4 jāntā hūṅ s̤avāb-e-ṭā'at-o-zuhd
par tabī'at idhar nahīṅ ātī

2.5 hai kuch aisī hī bāt jo cup hūṅ
varnā kyā bāt kar nahīṅ ātī

2.6 kyoṅ na cīkhūṅ keh yād karte haiṅ
merī āvāz gar nahīṅ ātī

2.7 dāgh-e-dil gar naz̤ar nahīṅ ātā
bū bhī ae cāra-gar nahīṅ ātī

2.8 ham vahāṅ haiṅ jahāṅ se ham ko bhī
kuch hamārī khabar nahīṅ ātī

2.9 marte haiṅ ārzū meṅ marne kī
maut ātī hai par nahīṅ ātī

2.10 ka'be kis muṅh se jā'oge G͟hālib
sharm magar tum ko nahīṅ ātī [162: 1-10]

2.1 No hope is fulfilled
No prospect appears

2.2 A day is appointed for death
Why does not sleep come at night

2.3 Laughter used to come at the state of the heart
Now nothing is laughable

2.4 I know the reward for obedience and abstinence
But my nature is not inclined that way

2.5 There is something that makes me remain silent
Otherwise what wouldn't I say

2.6 Why shouldn't I shriek—would she[1] remember me
If she didn't hear my voice

2.7 Even if you can't see the scars on my heart
You mean to say, Doctor, there's no smell of burnt flesh

2.8 We are in that place from which, even to us
Comes no news at all of ourselves

2.9 We die in the desire for death
Death comes, and doesn't come

2.10 How can you approach the Ka'ba, Ghalib
[Have you no shame at all
But of course, you have no shame] [162: 1-10]

Ghalib begins the ghazal in a voice of pathos, pure and simple: 'No hope is fulfilled' is the first hemistich of the initial couplet, the *miṣra'-e-ṭarḥ* of the ghazal. The *radīf, nahīṅ ātī* (does not come), requires a feminine singular subject for its verb—so that the poet's choice of options is already somewhat limited. The *radīf* suggests a pathetic tone here, or at least an anxious mood: something does not come—or since *ānā* is a compound verb—something is not fulfilled, or does not appear, even though it is expected, or its absence noted and perhaps questioned. There is thus a certain vague unity of mood that will be imposed throughout the ghazal by the *radīf* and its implicit tensions: the poet observes that something does not come, which means that he is aware that something should come, or used to come, or might have come, but in fact does *not* come.

The poet repeats the first line: 'No hope is fulfilled.' By the very nature of the ghazal, the audience will expect either a contrasting statement, or perhaps a corroboration and elaboration in the second hemistich; the knowledgeable listener may also be mulling over possible rhyming words. The poet recites the second half of the *she'r*: 'No prospect appears.' The audience has a corroboration of the first statement, with the additional pleasure of encountering the ambiguity of *ṣūrat*, which in its primary sense here means 'possibility' or 'prospect', though it also has the richly associative meaning of 'face', 'form', or 'shape' as faint echoes to the meaning clearly intended. Thus, at the same time one is reflecting on the implication of 'no prospect appears', one may also sense peripherally that neither does a face (or perhaps the form of the beloved) appear in the poet's (and one's own) perception. In the traditional love poetry of the ghazal, of course, any hope, any question of 'prospect', would be solely for union with the beloved, or lacking that, at least a glimpse of her radiant face. For though the basic sense of this couplet can and will be applied to a multitude of meanings, the beloved here is almost certainly hidden behind the veil of simplicity.

The audience knows, before the first hemistich of the next couplet is recited, that it will prepare for some statement in the second hemistich that something (grammatically feminine) *does not come.* The poet proceeds: 'A day is appointed for death.' The two central words, *maut* (death) and *mu'ayyan* (appointed, fixed, ordained) resound in recitation, linked by their alliteration, their common derivation from Arabic, and a semantic bond joining them with an implicit sense of the inescapable edict of *qismat* (fate); between them stands *din* (day), Sanskrit in ancestry, but at the same time having a definite prosaic sense given by the qualifying *ek* (one), which makes it not *the* day of death, but merely *a* day of death. Once again, there is a tension in the air of the *mushā'ira,* for the audience knows that the second hemistich will carry either a comparison or contrast to, or variation upon, the phrase 'does not come', as well as some rhyming word ending in *-ar.*

The poet continues with a statement that is both contrasting and corroborative: 'Then why does sleep not come all night'? In a split second the inner tensions of the couplet's nuclear thought are revealed: day contrasts with night, and death has an implied consonance with sleep. But is 'day' used in the sense of a full terrestrial day, or merely in the sense of daylight? If the former is true, then death may come at any time, and it is no wonder that worry troubles our sleep; if the latter is true—and daytime is associated with death—then the nighttime should be free of anxiety, and so may be associated with life. The asking of an explicit question, 'why?', adds another tension, for a question demands an answer, and the answer must be supplied by the listener, if not by the poet, who presumably has an answer of his own—and who, in any case, does continue to worry. It is probable that the poet, exhausted with life or love, ardently desires death; sleep is an imitation of death, though an inferior alternative. Yet in his intense love, or his longing for death, the poet is too restless to sleep.

Ghalib begins the third couplet by saying that one (presumably he) used to laugh at the state of the heart—literally, 'before came, at the heart's state, laughter'—a direct contrast in the past tense to the three examples (in 2.1 and 2.2) already given of something not coming or not appearing in the present. In so short a line there is much ambiguity: neither is the laugher identified, nor the possessor of the heart, nor the actual state of the heart itself. Even the word *āge* means both 'in the future' and 'in the past', though by context the meaning here is clearly 'past'. By convention, the *ḥāl-e-dil* refers to the *ḥāl-e-dil-e-'āshiq* (the state of the lover's heart), and since the poet is traditionally identified with the lover, he is probably speaking of his own heart—though possibly, before he fell in love, the poet laughed at the lamentation and misery of some other lover. The poet continues his recitation: 'Now [the first word of the second line, in parallel contrast to *before*, the first word of the first line] it [laughter] doesn't come at anything.' Again, the one who does not laugh in the second hemistich is not specifically identified, though most probably it is the poet, who is so miserably in love in the present that he is incapable of laughter.

This *she'r* is a statement of the extreme dejection and misery which the lover feels at times—though as we shall see later, Ghalib is also capable of feeling rapturous ecstasy in his love (the state of love being a sort of delirium oscillating between wretched suffering and joyous intoxication). It is a statement made in an extreme simplicity filled with pathos; as Tabatabai has observed, it is a couplet which Mir, the poet of pathos and simplicity, might envy (1954: 185). The diction is soft, and pure Hindi; the dominance of *ī*, which occurs three times in each line, enhances the softness of the diction, and probably suggests a sense of vulnerability through emphasis of the feminine gender. It is difficult to recreate in English the probable effect this couplet has in Urdu; 'Now nothing makes me laugh' is just as simple, but somehow too sullen, and too unrefined.

In the fourth verse, Ghalib admits that he knows the rewards for obedience and devotion or abstinence. For the second hemistich, 'But my nature is not inclined that way', Chishti suggest two interpretations. In the first, Ghalib eschews righteous behaviour which has the gathering of rewards as motive; the true lover finds obedience and devotion (an alternate meaning for *zuhd*) their own reward. In the second interpretation, the poet is stating his independence: it is simply not within the capacity of his nature to be obedient and abstinent, and there is nothing he can do to alter this, since his nature is decreed by fate. The first reading is deeply ethical; the second is a smooth piece of logical sleight-of-hand used by the poet to excuse his vices (1959: 691-2). Mehr suggests a slightly different interpretation—that knowledge alone (of the rewards of virtue) is not enough; the grace of God must give the emotion which insures the realization of that knowledge through action (n.d.: 531).

In the fifth couplet, Ghalib has created a superb example of potentially explosive energy through the contrast between the first and second lines. He begins his recitation with the deceptively delicate 'There is something that makes me remain silent'; apparently the poet has something to tell (and traditionally he has a great deal to say, as we shall see)—so why does he remain silent? He explains in the second hemistich that if he begins to speak, nothing will remain unsaid (the line has a striking similarity to the evocative line of blues poetry, 'Don't start me talkin'—I'll tell everything I know'). Mehr suggests a variety of possible reasons for the poet's silence: 1) he has something he wants to hide; 2) he is afraid of speaking, least he reveal the name of the beloved and disgrace her; 3) he is bursting with complaints, which would anger the beloved if she should hear them; 4) even if the poet complains, his words will have no effect on the beloved, so that it is more seemly to remain silent; and 5) the poet's complaints may prove a source of joy and amusement to his rivals for the affections of the beloved (n.d.: 531-2). There is also a possible allusion to Mansur al-Hallaj, the Sufi executed for his utterances, which were considered by the orthodox to be blasphemous. Ghalib, with some thought of his own life, prefers prudent silence. This couplet, in short, demonstrates the fine and delicate balance between the poet's wisdom and his emotion: he knows that if he opens his mouth to utter even a word, the consequences could be enormous—and so he persists in his uneasy silence.

The next *she'r* is in direct contrast to the one preceding. Ghalib has lost control, and instead of maintaining his cautious silence, he has begun to cry out: 'Why shouldn't I shriek—would [you/she] remember me if my voice didn't come?' The verse has a subtle element of paradox: he feels that he cannot succeed, no matter what he does, in gaining the beloved's attention. One possible reading would be that the poet feels he must shriek continuously in order to remind the beloved of his existence, and he is asking with some sarcasm whether, in her indifference, she would remember him at all were he not to shriek. Chishti suggests that the poet raises such a commotion because the sounds of his suffering please the beloved (1959: 692), and Mehr interprets the couplet as a genuine question by the poet: were he to stop screaming, would the beloved notice the sudden and unusual silence, and inquire what had happened to the poet—thus being tricked into bestowing upon him some of the attention he so desperately desires (n.d.: 532)?

The seventh couplet continues the vein of irony. Ghalib begins with the hemistich, 'If the scars of the heart do not appear'—referring to the scars branded on the heart by the heat and pain of love, and introducing a pleasing contrast of *naẕar nahīṅ ātā* (masculine) to the *naẕar nahīṅ ātī* (feminine) of the first couplet. The stage is now set for a fusion of image and sound, which emerges in the startling and explicit 'even the smell, O Doctor, doesn't come?' There is also the metaphor of branded scars being exaggerated to a literal brand with the smell of burnt flesh, and the added touch of irony in giving the obviously ignorant advisor/

friend (who ideally should console the lover) the title of 'Doctor' or 'curer', when he is oblivious in every sense to the symptoms of the lover's plight. (An alternate interpretation of 'curer' would be the beloved, who as the cause of the lover's pain and suffering, also has the power to cure it.)

The eighth couplet involves, as do some of Ghalib's finest verses, an irresolvable logical paradox that catches the reader's intellect and pulls it into the nuclear forces of a riddle: 'We are in that place from which, even to us, comes no news of ourselves.' The couplet was probably intended to describe the vertigo and intoxication of the lover's state of *be-khudī* (loss of self), but it can describe a variety of situations of ecstasy, distraction, astonishment, and alienation (see 1.4 for a similar paradox).

The ninth *she'r* continues the element of paradox, though here the level is less elevated and more playful: 'We die [figuratively] in the desire for [literal] death; thus death comes [figuratively], and doesn't [literally] come.' To make complete sense in English, the verse must be put more colloquially: 'We're dying to die; we die, and don't die.' The desire for death is due to the wish for an end to suffering, probably the suffering of love. But no matter how ardently we desire to die, that last relief is denied us. If one takes the longing for death as a wish for union with the divine beloved, then the words take on an additional sense of depth and frustration.

The final couplet includes, as is conventional in the ghazal, the poet's *takhalluṣ* (pen name): 'How can you approach the Ka'ba, Ghalib—aren't you ashamed?' Ghalib is speaking to himself, to one of the many guises that his personality may assume in the *maqṭa'* of a ghazal. He ends here on a note of humorous self-reproach—how can Ghalib, who is such a notorious sinner (see 2.4), have the presumption to make the pilgrimage to Mecca? In another reading, however, the reproach may be heard in ironic tones, with Ghalib himself turning the tables on the unwary pious drudge who dares to judge him on the basis of ordinary sins, in ignorance of his extraordinary love.

This introductory ghazal illustrates several techniques used within individual couplets to express a single idea, as well as the relationships which may exist among the couplets in a ghazal. Admittedly, as most writers on the genre observe, the ghazal tends to be characterized by the discreteness of its couplets. and there is no doubt that any one of these verses could be taken out of context and quoted with complete integrity and appropriateness in a variety of unrelated situations. Yet it should also be evident in this ghazal that there is a sort of internal organization to the poem as a whole which may be seen metaphorically in terms of architecture, orchestration, or choreography: there is a broad spectrum of tones, moods, voices, images, and thoughts, but there is also some degree of linkage and recurrence in these aspects. The unity imposed by the *radīf* ('does not come', in this case) has already been mentioned; within this unity, the poet adopts a number of stances, so as to engage his audience in different ways. The first couplet is a simple statement, with the pathos enhanced by a powerful but subtle word-play. The second, again with no specific human subject, poses a question of profound gravity. The third continues both the strict grammatical impersonality and the implication of the poet's personality. These first three verses are essentially consonant in their seriousness and pathos.

The fourth *she'r* introduces the grammatical person of the poet, and with it, an expression of pride and self-assertion. The fifth and sixth couplets continue the grammatical personality of the poet, with the fifth imbued with a gentle humor, and the sixth pervaded by the slightly hysterical irony implicit in the question—or exclamation—'why not?!' The irony continues, drier and under tighter control, in the seventh verse, where the poet addresses directly and questions, even taunts, some meddling, bumbling friend. The tone becomes more serious in the eighth *she'r*, though the poet here reaches the highest level of vertigo and mental energy (*junūn*—madness) in the ghazal. In the ninth couplet the poetic voice again becomes playful, and culminates in the *maqṭa'*, with its ironic question in each hemistich. All of this combines to form a coherent progression from seriousness and pathos to serious playfulness, with the questions in the second, sixth, and tenth verses functioning as devices to engage the audience directly. That the second and penultimate couplets both deal with death gives the ghazal a certain symmetry. This is not to say that an altering of the order of the couplets would be impossible; in fact, poets often rearrange the sequence of their verse at the time of recitation, or even omit or add certain verses. What I do suggest, rather, is that the experience of this particular ghazal (and to some extent of other of Ghalib's ghazals) is more than the sum of its parts.

As for the portrayal of the tensions and strife of real existence, these ten couplets offer an admirable variety of tensive subjects, tones and circumstances—even dilemmas: 1) hopelessness and deprivation; 2) fear of death in spite of its calm certainty; 3) laughter and melancholia; 4) independence from conventional ethics or religion, and probable punishment as a result; 5) self-control versus abandon; 6) hysterical complaint about the beloved, and again, the question of self-control—with auditory imagery; 7) complaint again, with visual, olfactory, and kinaesthetic imagery; 8) disorientation and utter self alienation; 9) the paradox of dying to die; and 10) confrontation with co-religionists, or with God. Admittedly, the two rather strident verses, 2.6 and 2.7, do not reach a stage of humane universality, but remain essentially petty, if snipishly clever. Yet the best of these couplets are like a mirror, in which individuals in a wide variety of contexts may find some reflection of their own circumstances and moods.[2]

Ghazal: yeh na thī hamārī qismat . . .

A second well-known ghazal by Ghalib illustrates a greater degree of complexity; whereas the previous ghazal was in a short enough meter to permit only one cogent statement in each hemistich (with exceptions, such as 'death comes, but doesn't come'), the following ghazal includes two distinct clauses in almost every hemistich:

2.11 yeh na thī hamārī qismat keh viṣāl-e-yār hotā
agar aur jītā rehtā yehī intiẕār hotā

2.12 tere va'de par jīye ham to yeh jān jhūṭ jānā
keh k͟hushī se mar na jāte agar e'tibār hotā

2.13 tirī nāzukī se jānā keh bandhā thā 'ahd bodā
kabhī tū na toṛ saktā agar ustuvār hotā

2.14 ko'ī mere dil se pūche tire tīr-e-nīm kash ko
yeh k͟halish kahāṅ se hotī jo jigar ke pār hotā

2.15 yeh kahāṅ kī dostī hai keh bane hai dost naṣeḥ
ko'ī cāra sāz hotā ko'ī gham gusār hotā

2.16 rag-e-saṅg se ṭapaktā voh lahū keh phir na thamtā
jise gham samajh rahe ho yeh agar sharār hotā

2.17 gham agarce jān-gusil hai peh kahāṅ bace keh dil hai
gham-e-'ishq gar na hotā gham-e-rozgār hotā

2.18 kahūṅ kis se maiṅ keh kyā hai shab-e-gham burī balā hai
mujhe kyā burā thā marnā agar ek bār hotā

2.19 hū'e mar ke ham jo rusvā hū'e kyoṅ na gharq-e-daryā
na kabhī janāza uṭhtā na kahīṅ mazār hotā

2.20 use kaun dekh saktā keh yagāna hai voh yaktā
jo dū'ī kī bū bhī hotī to kahīṅ do-cār hotā

2.21 yeh masā'il-e-taṣavvuf yeh tirā bayān Ghālib
tujhe ham valī samajhte jo na bāda-khwār hotā [21: 1-11]

2.11 This was not our fate—that there be union with the beloved
If we had lived longer, there would have been this same waiting

2.12 If we lived on your promise, know this: that it was false, we knew
For we would have died of happiness if we had trusted it

2.13 We knew from your own delicacy, that your promise too was weak
You could never have broken it, if it had been strong

2.14 Let someone ask my heart of these half-pulled arrows
From where would this pricking come, if the heart had been pierced clean through

2.15 What kind of friendship is this, that a friend becomes an advisor
There should be someone to console, someone to share grief

2.16 From the vein of the stone would drip that blood which could not be stemmed

If that which you know to be grief were to become a spark

2.17 Grief destroys the soul; how can one be saved as long as there is a heart
Were there not the pain of love, there would be the pain of life

2.18 To whom could I speak, and what say?—that the night of separation is calamity
What would have been the harm in dying, if it had been but once

2.19 Disgraced as I was in dying, why hadn't I drowned in some river
There would never have been a bier to be carried, and nowhere would there have been a grave

2.20 Who can see Him, for He is unique—that incomparable one
If there were even a trace of duplication, we would have encountered it somewhere

2.21 These questions of mysticism, this discourse of yours, Ghalib
We would have thought you a saint, had you not been a drunkard [21: 1-11]

The first couplet begins with the statement, axiomatic in ghazal poetry, that is to be no union with the beloved (*viṣāl-e-yār*). In pre-twentieth century Urdu poetry, the beloved is almost always inaccessible for one reason or another: her haughtiness, social restrictions, or the lowliness of the poet's position (outside society as he is). Ghalib speaks in the past: 'It *was* not our fate', which would signal to the alert listener what Ghalib makes explicit in the second line: 'If we had lived longer, there would have been this same waiting.' The poet assumes a voice from beyond the grave, having died, perhaps from the exigencies of love. There is curious usage of 'this' in 'this same waiting'—is the poet, though dead, still waiting to be united with his beloved? The two most important elements in the couplet, *viṣāl-e-yār* (union with the beloved) and *intizar* (waiting), are set in effective contrast, and at the same time linked through their rhyme and their placement in the second half of each line as the *qāfiya* (true rhyme).

The poet, continuing the past tense in the second verse, describes indirectly the circumstances leading to his demise by saying what did *not* cause his death: happiness. After the general declarative voice of the first couplet, he now addresses the beloved directly, saying that she should know that *he* knew her promise (to meet him) to be false—he would have died of joy had he believed it. The clear but unstated conclusion to be drawn is that he died, instead, from grief and suffering. The beauty of this couplet is that it introduces the unexpected—that the poet could not bear the joy of the beloved's true promise—and thus corroborates the statement of the first couplet: that one way or another, the poet cannot be united with his beloved, for he will die either from the traditional excess of suffering, or from the more startling excess of joy at believing her promise.

One minor but pleasing aspect of this couplet is the ambiguity of *jān* in the first line; to *yeh jān jhūṭ jānā* may be read both as 'know this, [that we] knew [your promise to be] false'; and '[we] knew this beloved to be false'; *jān* may be either the imperative 'know', or the noun, 'beloved' or 'sweetheart'. In the latter case, *jān* (which also means 'life' and 'soul') would echo the verb *jīnā* (to live) in the first line.

The third couplet continues the tense, though here with no clear implication of speaking after death. The mood suggests that the beloved has asked, in response to the previous verse, how the poet knew her promise to be false. Ghalib invokes the traditional delicacy of the beloved (whose waist, in the exaggerated descriptions of other poets, may become so thin as to be invisible), and makes comparison between her physical and temperamental delicacy and the delicacy, or weakness, of her promise: he knew (echoing the 'knew' of the previous couplet) that her promise was weakly bound. This comparison is an example of the correspondence of ideas in the two halves of single hemistich; but Ghalib extends the comparison into the second hemistich: he again praises the beloved for her delicacy (while implicitly chiding her for her fickleness of mind) by saying that she would not have had the strength to break a strong promise, as inevitably she would try.

In the fourth couplet Ghalib compliments the beloved once more on her delicacy, in referring to her 'half-pulled arrows'—her glances (metaphorically speaking) with their power to strike the poet's heart. There is here an implicit allusion to the more elaborate metaphor of the eyelashes launched by the bow of the eyebrow, and a probable suggestion of the captivating power of the beloved's half-closed eyes. Eager to tell the story of his suffering, the poet says, 'Let someone ask my heart about the effect of your arrows launched with a half-pulled bow', since he knows that those arrows, not being launched so forcefully, would seem to others to be less painful. He assumes the beloved is too disinterested to ask, though since he is addressing her directly he hopes that she may take the hint and inquire herself. But his eagerness to speak is such that he does not wait for anyone to ask, and gives the answer directly: 'From where would this [delicious] prickling come, if the arrows had passed all the way through my heart?' Since suffering is a source of pleasure to the lover, he is acknowledging the beloved's generosity in so wounding his heart as to leave a continuous rankling.

In the fifth couplet, as in the fourth, Ghalib speaks in the present, inquiring of anyone who may be listening: 'In what kind of friendship does the friend assume the role of an advisor'? The advisor (*naṣeḥ*) is actually one of the villains in the poet's life. The true friend, understanding that the poet knows what he is doing, and that he in fact desires to suffer, will unselfishly offer consolation and try to alleviate the poet's suffering through sympathy. But the true friend is all too rarely found, and most alleged friends turn out to be meddlesome.

The sixth couplet includes one of Ghalib's most innovative and striking images. He begins with the somewhat puzzling statement that 'From the stone's vein would drip such blood that could not be stopped'. This presents the listener with an entirely unfamiliar conceit, the bleeding stone (though the image is almost certainly an extension of the 'heart of stone' associated with the beloved). Even the second line—'If that which you know to be grief were to become a spark'—is initially obscure; (this is an example of the sort of couplet which would have to be repeated in its recitation for the full impact of its imagery and thought to be felt). Grief may be perceived in terms of heat (the lover's sighs are hot from grief—as well as paradoxically cold from despair), and if through exaggeration this heat generates a spark (sighs can be 'spark-shedding'—see 6.4), the power of that spark would be such that it could so wound or melt a stone as to make it bleed; this image also recognizes, most probably, the fact that two stones struck together produce a spark, and that the veins that may be seen in many rocks are visually similar to the veins in flesh. The unstated implication here is that, if the poet's grief can cause stones to bleed, think what the consequences will be for the poet's heart—which, unlike the beloved's, is of mere flesh. There is a further pleasing contrast between the intermittent spark (fire), and the unstemmable flow of blood (in the same elemental category as water), though both spark and blood are yoked metaphorically together by their common color (fire is treated in Urdu poetry as being red).

In the seventh couplet—one of Ghalib's most famous—he steps out of the realm of love, only to return to it by implication. The source of all our troubles, he says, is the fact that we possess a heart which will inevitably be destroyed by grief (and here there is an echo of the previous verse); as long as one has a heart, grief—whether from love, or from a multitude of everyday troubles (the result is the same)—will come to destroy us. Though the poet most probably would prefer to suffer from the grief of love, he recognizes that everyone is besieged with grief—so that this is the sort of couplet, capable of a wide range of individual applications, that may be quoted aphoristically to suit almost any occasion of tribulation and grief.

After the previous couplets describing the pain of separation from the beloved, Ghalib alludes directly in the eighth couplet to the *shab-e-gham*, the night of grief, of separation from the beloved, which is the direct opposite of the *viṣāl-e-yār* of the first *she'r* in the ghazal. He realizes that no one will listen to him, and that no one will understand what he is saying—and that, moreover, he is incapable of finding words to describe his pain. To say that it is a calamity is a gross understatement; it is nothing less than death, a recurrent dying. 'What would have been the harm in my dying only once?' he asks. Instead, he must suffer these nightly deaths, the million momentary deaths every minute of each night.

Ghalib refers to the ignominy of his death in the ninth couplet, lamenting that he wasn't simply drowned in some far river, so that there would be no need to take out his body in a funeral procession, nor to bury him in his grave. By one conventional expectation, the poet dies friendless and unmourned; Ghalib here suggests indirectly that at his death there would be no friends to mourn him, carry his bier, bury him and tend his grave, so that he is being evasive in saying that his drowning would have saved everyone the trouble of carrying and burying his corpse. On the other hand, even if he *were* to be mourned, the procession and grave would be a source of disgrace to him, as well as to the beloved, through the gossip that would inevitably result. The ultimate message of this verse is serious, though there is an element of rich irony in his explorations of the nature of his 'disgrace'.

The tenth couplet represents an abrupt change in mood from the rest of the ghazal, as Ghalib speaks unequivocally in the tones of *ḥamd*—praise for God—at the same time that he demonstrates his own wit and ingenuity. The sense of the verse translates easily enough into English, but the verbal subtleties remain locked in the Urdu. 'Who can see Him', Ghalib begins, 'for He is unique, the singular one.' The double emphasis on unity and singularity through the words *yagāna* and *yaktā* (derived from the Persian *yak*, for the number one) is the central feature of this hemistich. The question, like most questions in the Urdu ghazal, is rhetorical: the answer is clearly implied to be that no one can see God. In the second hemistich Ghalib ostensibly supports his first statement by saying, 'If there were even a hint of duality, we would somewhere have encountered it'; yet at the some time he is giving very strongly the sense of duality and encounter, not only in the visual sense—through the use of the idiom *do-chār honā*, which means literally 'for two [eyes] to become four' (i.e. to meet two more eyes)—but in the olfactory sense as well, through the use of *bū*, which means both 'scent' and 'trace'. If one were facing the beloved, one would see his eyes, as well as sense his scent. The effect of proliferation, moreover, is achieved by the double mention of oneness in the first line, and the sequential mention of two and two-four in the second. Ghalib is thus able to affirm both the uniqueness and omnipresence of God, at the same time as expressing the intense desire to encounter Him, to experience His presence personally.

After the stunning pervious couplet, Ghalib begins the *maqṭa*' in apparent continuation of mystical revery, addressing himself (as convention requires) by his *takhalluṣ*, in a reference to his discourse (possibly in the preceding verse) on some of the problems of Sufism. Then he reverses himself: 'We would have thought you to be a saint, if you had not been a wine-bibber'. The irony here is double, depending upon one's interpretation of wine-drinking as mere debauchery, or as the pursuit of the wine of mystical love.

This ghazal, like the one preceding, demonstrates a certain unity to the extent that its *radīf—hotā* (the conditional from of the verb *to be*) recurs at the end of each verse. The word *hotā* occurs in the senses of 'if there had been', 'there would have been', 'if there were', and 'would that there were'; in almost all cases, expectations and hopes are contrasted with realities through this grammatical structure. All the couplets but two (the fifth and ninth) have an explicit word—*agar* or *jo*—meaning 'if', which imposes a further unity (beyond that of the *radīf*, to which the 'if' is functionally related) on the ghazal as a whole.

There are also subordinate unities. The first four verses are in some sense continuous in their effect: the first speaks of the desire for union, and uses the verb *to live*; the second refers to the beloved's promise of union, and the fact that the poet *lived* on that promise, though *knowing* it to be false; the third couplet states that the poet *knew* from the beloved's *delicacy* that her promise was *weak*; and the fourth verse, referring implicitly to the beloved's delicacy, speaks of that weakness as manifest in the *half-pulled* arrows from her eyes. Similarly, couplets four and five, and seven through ten, include some questioning phrase, usually in the rhetorical mode, since no answer is really expected or even possible. There are four references to death in the ghazal, in the first and second, and eighth and ninth verses. Finally, there is a greater unity here than in many ghazals in terms of the person(s) addressed by the poet; only couplets two and three are addressed directly to the beloved, the sixth is to some indefinite companion, and the remaining couplets are all addressed to some unspecified listener, or perhaps to the poet himself, as in the *maqṭa'*, though without the appearance of *takhallus*.

There is also a certain uniformity in the poetic voices heard in this ghazal. Couplets one through nine are basically complaints, though two and three involve some assertion of the poet's superior wisdom (he had know all along that . . .), and the fourth is typical of Ghalib in its reference to the pleasure of pain. Then in the tenth *she'r* the mood changes abruptly to praise of God—yet there still remains a hint of complaint in Ghalib's expression of his longing for a glimpse of the divine beloved, though as he says himself, such an experience would be impossible. The *maqṭa*', while witty, concludes however faintly the plaintive effect of the poem as a whole: his fellows will never recognize his mysticism, but will always consider him to be a drunkard.

Within the general unities of this ghazal there are varieties a well. Four verb tenses are used: the past, past conditional, present, and present conditional (which functions as a subjunctive); only the future is not used explicitly, though it is implied in the present conditional. Three verbal moods are expressed; the declarative, interrogative, and exclamatory, both negative and positive, with only the imperative mood not evoked (unless the *jān* of the second verse is taken as a command). The poet speaks of himself (in two couplets as 'I', and in two couplets as the more universal 'we'), of the beloved, the sympathetic friend and confidant, the meddling advisor, God, and of course, Ghalib—addressed in the *maqṭa*' as a different figure from the person speaking in the poetic voice; of the major characters of the ghazal's personae (see chapter IV), the rival alone is unrepresented. It is worthy of note, moreover, that on two occasions Ghalib uses the personal pronoun in one verse and uses no pronoun in the next, thus rendering the second statement more indefinite and inclusive without any loss of meaning: 'we knew' in couplet two, and '[I, we, he, etc.] knew' in three; 'my dying' in couplet eight, and '[I, we, he, etc.] drowned' in nine. The person intended is obviously the poet himself, but the absence of the pronoun enhances the inclusive ambiguity of the poetic statement.

There is a final characteristic, found in both the above ghazals, that I have not mentioned: their generally abstract quality. Both ghazals are devoted primarily to an exploration of the relationships between people, or between people and states of being or non-being. There is very little visual imagery, a point worthy of remark given the fact that Ghalib is frequently considered to be among the most visual of poets (Ansari 1969-70: 91). In the first ghazal, there are no visual references at all (though there are engaging, even paradoxical conceits), and in the second, only 2.16 contains a concrete visual image—the spark in the vein of the stone (though the eyelash-arrow comparison in 2.14, and the idiom *for two* [eyes] *to become four* in 2.20, are derived from visual perceptions). In images involving other senses, the first ghazal includes an auditory reference (the poet's shrieking) in 2.6, and an olfactory image (the smell of burnt flesh from the scars on the poet's heart) in 2.7. In the second ghazal, there are references to pain which to some extent arouse a sensory response: the pricking of the beloved's glances in the poet's heart (2.14), and grief transmuted into a spark of both heat and brightness (2.16); the pain and grief of love in 2.17 are essentially abstract.

Yet in spite of the abstract effect of these two ghazals, it would be difficult to describe them as monotonous. It should be clear that processes are operating in these ghazals which involve both unification and diversification. It should also be evident that there is only an occasional recourse to what might be called the stock-in-trade of the ghazal (those images in particular danger of being seen as clichés), as in the poet's heart with its scars in the first ghazal, or the beloved's eyelashes in the second. Instead, Ghalib has succeeded in portraying a considerable variety of the sort of relationships and tensions which may be found in actual life.

The Thematic Content of the Ghazal

If any dominant type of relationship may be perceived in the verses of the ghazals just examined, it is love. By its very definition, the word *ghazal*, an Arabic verbal noun, means 'speaking in the language of love or in verse; making love to women' (Steingass 1892: 887). By most of the conventions of Urdu poetry, as demonstrated in the majority of the verses discussed above, the love of the ghazal is rife with conflict and frustration, and hence a fertile topic for literary exploration (see Huizinga 1955: 132-3, quoted above).

The poet-lover, as he may be called, occupies a place at some distance from his beloved, and the tone he adopts in describing or attempting to alter his position may vary widely, according to his personal disposition. Many ghazal couplets deal rather passively in one way or another with a description exclusively of the beloved: her beauty, playfulness, cruelty, and so forth. In such descriptions, the opportunities for the poet to reveal his personality, or to express a new perception of a relationship, are somewhat limited; at best, he may display his ingenuity and wit in a choice of comparisons, or in some feat of extraordinary description.

Admittedly, a truly accomplished description may be as stunning in its effect in Urdu as is Romeo's of Juliet (I: v):

O, she doth teach the torches to burn bright!
It seems she hangs upon the cheek of night
As a rich jewel in an Ethiop's ear—
Beauty too rich for use, for earth too dear!

But by the very limitations of images in the ghazal, most descriptions of the beloved are merely conventional, and the number of comparisons that can be made are rather limited. In most ghazals, a routine simile likening the beloved's face to the sun or moon, or her stature to the cypress (with the compared object inevitably emerging as inferior to the beloved) does not lead very far. It is this unimaginative use of traditional images which many critics attack, and justly so.

The poet, on the other hand, may describe the effect the beloved has upon him. Here vastly greater possibilities exist for individualized expression, for the very manner in which the poet responds to the beloved, or to the emotions of love, will reveal a great deal about him. Often, in ghazals of lesser quality, there is no more sense of the poet as distinct individual than there is in Romeo's fume of sighs, when he is in love with love before meeting Juliet—and so portrays love in airy, insubstantial conventions. But for the skilled poet, there is enormous scope for personal and original statement in the subtlety with which he describes his relationship with the beloved, given the fact (as we shall see presently) that the beloved may represent a variety of desired objects or goals.

The lover, for example, may describe the way in which he follows the protocol of love, and the manner of his description will disclose much about his attitude toward love, or toward the beloved. In treating the conventional act of prostration before the beloved (as a gesture of respect and submission), Mirza Muhammad Rafi 'Sauda' (1713-80) composed the following couplet (1973: 78):

adab dīyā hai hāth se apne kabhū bhalā maikhāne kā
kaise hī ham mast cale par sajdā har ik gām kīyā

When did I ever let slip away the etiquette of the tavern
However much drunken I was in coming, I prostrated myself at every step

Here the gesture of prostration (*sajda*) is ostensibly a sign of respect, though implicitly—and obviously—the act is for him not prostration at all, but rather, gloriously drunken stumbling. Through this treatment of *sajda*, Sauda reveal his predilection for satire. Compare the uses of *sajda* in a couplet by Mir Taqi 'Mir' (1722-1810), composed in the same meter and rhyme scheme (1968: 107)

> sarzad ham se be-adabī to vaḥshat meṅ bhī kam hī hū'ī
> kosoṅ us kī aur ga'e par *sajda* har har gām kīyā

> Whatever impoliteness may have come from me, even in my wild state, was very slight
> I followed her for miles, but prostrated myself at every step

Here Mir portrays his immense devotion by evoking the great distances he has walked in search of the beloved, and while there is none of Sauda's sense of irony, there is a subtle double meaning suggesting that the act of prostration is at the same time a symptom of extreme fatigue, since he is in reality falling in exhaustion from the zeal of his love.

In each of these couplets, there is a distinct sense of the poet's particular nature: Sauda is witty, satirical, and bibulous (the wine, of course, may be earthly or spiritual, but we suspect that in Sauda's case it is of the more lowly vintage), while Mir is dedicated and sincere in his fulfilment of the arduous tasks of love. Each poet uses a stock image, but does so in such a way as to reveal some facet of his personality. The second-rate poet, in contrast, who portrays himself in ordinary prostration, is in no way memorable.

In speaking of the individuality or personal nature of a poetic statement, I do not mean to suggest that the tenor of a ghazal couplet should be taken as literally autobiographical. Most ghazal poets, including Ghalib, do not have an explicit beloved in mind when they compose the majority of their couplets (though one famous sequence by Ghalib is said to have resulted from his desolation at the death of a woman he loved; some of the couplets from this ghazal will be discussed in the following chapters). But the poet's characteristic attitudes toward the relationships and conflicts of life will often manifest themselves through his treatment of conventional themes, and the general frame of mind in a given era of a poet's life will often affect the ghazals composed during that period. Ghalib's pride, for example, is evident in many of his verses, as is his restless and inventive imagination; in terms of actual events, Ghalib's persistent but fruitless pursuit of a patron is probably reflected in his ghazals in recurrent images of powerlessness. One should not go the extreme, however, of assuming that in image of imprisonment, for example, refers in any way to some actual prison experience, as when Ghalib was jailed for gambling in 1847; the nightingale in a cage is just a nightingale, or at most a poet—and not Ghalib composing his verses in a Delhi jail.

The frustrations and strife of love may be presented in a variety of traditional configurations, usually involving a triad of participants, for as G. C. Narang has observed, 'the basis of love in the ghazal is the same eternal triangle' (1966: 52; also below). Narang's schematization of love is as follows, with the agents of love given in the first column, the objects of love in the second, and the hindering agents in the third:

Lover	Beloved	Rival
Lover	Love	Ascetic
Heart	Beauty	Doubt
Nest (heart)	Garden	Lightning
Nightingale	Rose	Flower-picker
Nightingale	Spring	Gardener, Autumn
Moth	Candle	Morning
Farhad	Shirin	Khusrau
Eye	Face	Veil

In a continuation of the above pattern, Narang outlines the conventional triads of mystical poetry:

Divine Love	Union/Revelation	Separation
Traveller	Destination	Thorn
Traveller	Path	Strong wind, Guide, Robber
Libertine, Drunkard	Divine wine, Cupbearer	Censor
Sublime madness	Truth	Intellect
Mystic	Spiritual knowledge	Theologian
Devotee	Extinction Submission	Ego

C. M. Naim has moved from the mystical level to discuss the adaptation of ghazal imagery to the twentieth-century context, with the poet as nationalist, the beloved as motherland, and the rival as England; or again, the poet as communist, the beloved as the masses, and the rival as the forces of capitalism. As Naim notes, the beloved in such poetry becomes oppressed by the rival, and ceases to be the traditionally cruel beauty of the past (1967: 106).

In general, however, the relationship of love, and the attendant conflicts, may be interpreted as involving almost any goal that may be attained only with difficulty. As Ralph Russell has observed, the beloved of the Urdu ghazal may be 'any person, or any ideal to whom or to which the poet, whether in real life or fantasy, is prepared to dedicate himself, sacrificing himself for its (her, his) sake and willingly accepting the hostility of his fellow men as an inevitable consequence of his love' (1969: 119-20).

Russell traces the nature of the poet's struggle to the medieval origins of the ghazal, and he sees the type of love portrayed in the ghazal—with its inevitable frustration—as essentially medieval in character. In traditional Indo-Muslim society, with its pattern of female seclusion and arranged marriages, love of the romantic sort exists most often outside marriage, so that, for example, the infrequency of union with the beloved in Urdu poetry reflects social realities; the impact of a glimpse of the beloved behind her veil is, in purdah society, quite understandable—hence the emphasis in the ghazal on *seeing* the beloved. On the generally anti-social tone of the ghazal's Weltanschauunng, Russell has observed:

> At first sight it seems an extraordinary fact that the most popular, the most esteemed literary form of medieval society—and the ghazal undoubtedly *is* that—is precisely that form in which all the conventions of that society, all its accepted institutions, and all its leading figures—kings, nobles, and learned divines—all are held up to the most unrestrained, vituperative ridicule and condemnation, and in which God himself is the target of sarcastic attack for His injustice to His creation. Upon reflection, however, one comes to the conclusion that the ghazal won its preeminent prestige not in spite of, but because of its content. . . . The cultivated, sensitive sections of such a society would have burst had there been no safety valve to reduce the pressure which their environment built up in them, and the rulers of society felt no great

difficulty in giving the seal of their approval to the ghazal as a, so to speak, licensed, institutionalized form of passionate protest against the world in which the poet and his audience were alike confined. [1969: 120]

This is not to say (nor does Russell imply) that the ghazal is a genre exclusively of cavil and complaint. When the ghazal is used as a vehicle for humanistic or metaphysical statement by a great poet, the perspective of vision rises beyond the chronological, geographical, and social limitations of the convention, to reach a universal sphere which is no less accessible to later generations than to the poet's contemporaries; in the case of an innovative poet such as Ghalib, this perspective, while meaningful to succeeding generations, was beyond the comprehension of many of his contemporaries. Ghalib's particular complex of visions is often cited, in fact, as being peculiarly ahead of his time. Many critics speak of Ghalib's modernity, in his ability to capture the particular feelings of *angst* and perplexity that so frequently trouble the citizen of our era, and the sense that life—or love—is not what it used to be (see Chapter VI).

I will return to this question of Ghalib's modernity from time to time, for it is central to a discussion of his popularity in the current era. Suffice it to say for the moment that Ghalib's poetic portrayal of relationships—those of love, those of people, places, and things, even those among the basic elements of the universe—is the essence of his ghazal poetry, and since his poetic vocabulary is confined primarily to traditional themes and images, the greatness that he does demonstrate must be found in his capacity to express relationships among these elements in cogent and meaningful ways.

The final chapter below will examine three more of Ghalib's complete ghazals, which like the two presented earlier in this chapter, are well-known and frequently quoted. But it is time now to turn to a specific analysis of some of the dominant and characteristic words and images which Ghalib uses to express the relationships of life, in order to determine with some objectivity the breadth of his vision, and the capacity of his imagination. Since love is said to be the central concern of the ghazal, Ghalib's concept of love will be the next subject of this inquiry.

NOTES

1. The beloved in Urdu poetry is grammatically masculine by convention, even when a female beloved is clearly intended; to make these translations more consonant with English poetic practice, I have used the feminine, except where God is clearly indicated as the beloved.
2. One of my first experiences in understanding a couplet quoted on a given occasion took place when an Indian friend, in an advanced stage of jet-lag, arrived in America for the first time; he recognized me in the unfamiliar surrounding of O'Hare airport, and smiling with bewilderment, quoted the eighth couplet of the above ghazal (2.8).

CHAPTER 3

The Phenomena of Love in Ghalib

If I don't have love, at least I have madness
My madness, at least, will bring you fame

GHALIB [149: 11]

'Whether the experience be that of Othello or of Khusrau Parwīz', Annemarie Schimmel has observed of both Western and Eastern poetry, 'the essence is the same: love, jealousy, and death'. The difference, she goes on to say, is that 'Persian poetry is learned poetry—much more than even the verses of John Donne and the other Metaphysical poets' (1979: 12).

Like its historical predecessor and stylistic and thematic wellspring, Urdu poetry must also be learned to be appreciated fully. The previous two chapters have attempted to demonstrate the degree to which a knowledge of the ghazal's distinctive form, structure, and context is essential to an understanding of the poetry itself. This chapter, and the two following, will explore some of the central topoi (which also must be learned to be understood) of Ghalib's Urdu *Dīvān*, in order to substantiate further the proposition made in chapter II: that *the words, motifs, and images of the ghazal are important, not in isolation, but rather, in their relationships to each other, for it is the primary function of the ghazal to portray various types of relationships, and to examine, analyze, and suggest different tensions and connections between the individual elements of existence.* Because of the extreme brevity of the ghazal couplet, each word, each image assumes a particular importance in the attainment of the greatest possible compression and, at the same time, clarity. As a result, most literate Urdu speakers may be said to carry in their own minds a personal concordance of these topoi based upon their own experiences.

These experiences may be of two types. The first, at least in origin, is objective and historical: the tradition of diction and allusion that comes to Urdu from Persian poetry. In Urdu, individual words and names, through a process of accretion, have taken on meanings and connotations from the entire poetic tradition. In the West, the name Absalom evokes a network of associations for the person versed in Biblical lore, and thus gives some clue to the substance of the novel by William Faulkner, just as the reading of that novel further enriches an earlier experience of the original story. By the same token, the name of Hallaj, to the lover of Urdu poetry, summons to mind not just the static image of an historical figure, but a whole network of states of mind and events culminating, ultimately, in accusation, trial, sentence, gallows, hanging, death, and martyrdom.

The second type of experience of these topoi comes from personal associations drawn from one's own circumstances. No doubt more than a few of the followers of the late Prime Minister of Pakistan, Zulfiqar Ali Bhutto, found ample occasion to apply the story of Hallaj to the execution of their leader, so that any subsequent reference to Hallaj which they might encounter in a couplet of Urdu (or Sindhi) poetry would assume a new range of significance.

The same is the case with imagery. For the initiated person, any reference to a single element from the triads of love (enumerated in the previous chapter) would call to mind not only the other two elements of the triads, but quite probably, elements from parallel triads as well. To mention the moth—that ultimate cliché of Persian and Urdu poetry—is also to evoke the candle and morning (or the moth's annihilation in the flames); but in an alternate configuration, the candle is a symbol for the poet (see 6.24 below), and there is no moth, but rather, the beloved's *maḥfil*. Yet still there is the threat, of dawn, the snuffing of the candle, the end of the sublime gathering, the smoke from the candle (see 3.47) rising, dark, as a sign of mourning. . . .

To answer Abdul Latif's allegation of the ghazal's monotony and repetitiveness, it seems reasonable to suggest that the use of traditional topoi in Urdu poetry (at least in the best poetry) is not a matter of mere repetition, for any word repeated a hundred consecutive times in the same context becomes, effectively, meaningless to the person repeating it. In the ghazal, on the contrary, a word or image attracts and gains meaning through a variety of associations, after having been perceived in different relationships and contexts over a long period of time. As a result, that word or image assumes a tensive quality, a certain semantic charge or potential which, in proximity to other similarly charged words or images, creates the distinctive spark of illumination that makes the ghazal 'more than a brief statement' (Keene 1955: 41).

To be sure, there is a danger of semantic depletion in the mere repetition of these topoi; as Wheeelwright noted, a phrase 'properly alive and tensive . . . may become commonplace and perfunctory through careless usage, . . . so that its survival is merely a result of social habit' (1968: 47). Were it not for the elements of conflict and competition in the ghazal, this danger would be particularly great, given the limitation of themes and form, even for the best of poets; certainly much low-grade ghazal poetry is little more than social habit. Yet these very limitations, and the challenges they offer and the competition they provoke, are not unlike the limitations of chess, another agonistic form of play which may be pursued into endless absorption.

Huizinga, cited above, speaks of the poet as the hero of a struggle. The ghazal poet portrays himself in endless strife with the beloved, and with his rivals. But the poet is also struggling with the formal and thematic restrictions of the ghazal, and he is in competition with fellow poets past and present (on whose poetic statements he tries to improve), and with the knowledge of his audience. Writing further on the relationship between poetry and competition, Huizinga suggests that:

> As a form of competition proper, archaic poetry is barely distinguishable from the ancient riddle-contest. The one produces wisdom, the other words of beauty. *Both are dominated by a system of play rules* [the italics are mine] *which fix the range of ideas and symbols to be used . . . ; both presuppose a circle of initiates who understand the language spoken. . . .* Only he who can speak the art-language wins the title of poet. This art-language differs from ordinary speech in that it employs special terms, images, figures, etc., which not everybody will understand. The eternal gulf between being and idea can only be bridged by the rainbow [or Keene's spark?] of imagination. The word-bound concept is always inadequate to the torrent of life. Hence it is only the image-making or figurative word that can invest things with expression and at the same time bathe them in the luminosity of ideas. . . . But whereas the language of ordinary life . . . is continually wearing down the image-content of words . . . , poetry

continues to cultivate the figurative, i.e. image-bearing, qualities of language, with deliberate intent.

What poetic language does with images is to play with them. It disposes them in style, it instills mystery into them so that every image contains the answer to the enigma. [1955: 133-4]

The pursuit of an opponent's king, of the solution to a riddle, of the affection of the beloved—all these quests have archaic roots. Yet their language, their idiom, continues to be used in the modern age with no loss of fascination. To understand the historical idiom of love in the ghazal, it is necessary to be aware of the early usages of certain central words—*'ishq, muḥabbat, ulfat,* and *shauq*—before examining the ways in which Ghalib has used them to denote love, and in which he has linked them with other words and images in his exploration of love's quest.

Of the four words, *muḥabbat* and *'ishq* have the oldest and most extensive range of associations, though only the former occurs (in a related form) in the Qur'an, describing the mutual love between man and God (Sura 5: 59). While there have been numerous debates over the centuries about the relative meanings of the two words (see Arkoun 1973: 118-19 and Giffen 1971: 63, 95-6), a basic distinction may be made. Lane's copious *Arabic-English Lexicon* indicates that the form *ḥubb* means 'inclination of the nature, or natural disposition, towards a thing that pleases or delights' (1865: 62), while *'ishq* is defined as 'excessive love; or attachment to women . . . or a disease of the nature of melancholia' (1874: 2054), though as Lane points out, both words may be used in connection with either chaste or immoral love. *'Ishq* probably had its first use in a mystical, dynamic sense by Hallaj (Schimmel 1975b: 72, 137) and thereafter became the central word in Sufi poetry for love. *Shauq,* according to Lane, means 'desire, or yearning or longing of the soul for a thing, or the emotion of love' (1872: 1620), and continued to be used as an aspect of mystical love (Schimmel 1975b: 132), though it is less important a word than *'ishq. Ulfat,* finally, does not seem to figure at all in the mystical lexicon.

To examine Ghalib's treatment of love, I have, as an initial effort, collected all of the couplets in the *Dīvān* which use any of these four words, and proceeding through *'ishq, shauq, muḥabbat,* and *ulfat,* have examined the range of associations and relationships which Ghalib connects with love. The remainder of this chapter, then, is the first step toward the desideratum, stated in the Introduction, of having a thorough and systematic analysis of certain important words in the *Dīvān*.

It would be misleading to imply that only those couplets which use one of the words that I have translated as 'love' deal with the subject of love; needless to say, numerous other couplets touch on one or another of love's aspects. Any couplet which refers to the beloved, for example, or to the beloved's attributes or behavior, will be exploring some of the ramifications of love. But I am concerned here with the specific denotation (which Allen Tate, in an article entitled 'Tension in Poetry', has called *extension*) in order to begin to analyze the connotations (Tate's *intention* [1965: 356]) of love in Ghalib's Urdu ghazals.

Generally speaking, Ghalib sees the state of love as occurring in two basic modes: the active and the passive. Neither mode is exclusive of the other, and at times Ghalib combines the two with great subtlety and ingenuity. But assuming for a moment the separation of the two categories, we may say that love in its passive complexion is seen as something of an affliction, even though the passivity of affliction may be transformed into an assertive act: the paradoxical choice to savor, in a manner at times almost ecstatic, the pain of suffering. Love in its active complexion, on the other hand, is an act of assertion against all odds: a flying in the face of traditional public values and norms, in pursuit of a goal which in the poet's mind transcends all others.

Within this couplet-bound microcosm of love, myriad relationships are created and examined. All are based upon some form of attraction, and most express a response to that attraction. Some relationships are static and formal, while others are dynamic, either in equilibrium or in flux. What seems most interesting to Ghalib is love as a manifestation of energy—or even an absence of energy—in the play of force which on the earthly level draws a man to his beloved, and which in the very cosmos holds the tiniest particles together in a manifestation of the Divine.

'Ishq

In Urdu poetry, *'ishq* is the word most commonly used for love. Platts defines *'ishq* as 'love, excessive love, passion for' (1930:

761), and the poets before Ghalib's time used *'ishq* to describe love in its various conditions. But in Ghalib's verses, *'ishq* is most commonly associated with love as suffering (witness the recurrence of the phrase *gham-e-'ishq*—'the grief/pain of love'), as well as the various states of dejection, derangement, desolation, and debilitation that accompany passive love. It is significant that the Persian meaning of *'ishq*, according to Steingass, is 'love; intensity of the passion and a blindness to the failings of the object loved; being sick or dying for love' (1892: 850), for Ghalib most certainly sees love in this sense in a majority of his *'ishq* couplets. This is not to say that he does not celebrate *'ishq*—he does, often with wit and ingenuity, and even passion. But as will be evident in the next major section of this chapter, he sees the most ennobling form of love as better expressed by the word *shauq*.

In discussing Ghalib's portrayal of love, it is worth noting at the outset that the great majority of his *'ishq* couplets (which total 52) do not refer directly to the beloved, but rather to some aspect of the lover's condition. In such couplets, the predominant effect created is of the destructive or disabling consequences of love, and of the poet's struggles to prevail. On the other hand, in those *'ishq* couplets which do include the beloved directly within their purview (only 8 out of 52), the tones range toward the ironic and assertive, as though the poet is simply using the beloved, however elegantly, as a foil to draw attention to himself.

'Ishq and the Beloved

It is important to emphasize here that the verses which follow in this chapter—as well as all verses in Chapters 4 and 5—are drawn from different ghazals throughout Ghalib's *Dīvān* and *do not occur there in the present sequence.* They are arranged here, in an artificially topical progression, in the attempt to reconstruct the sort of connotative concordance that someone thoroughly familiar with Ghalib's Urdu poetry would have developed, albeit unconsciously, over a long period of exposure to the *Dīvān.* (The decimal number to the left of each verse indicates the occurrence in these chapters, with past occurrences shown in parentheses. The numbers given in brackets at the right of each verse refer to the sequence of Jafri's Urdu-Devanagari edition of the *Dīvān*

[1958], in which the ghazals, but not individual couplets, are numbered. Thus, 154: 6 means the sixth verse of ghazal number 154.)

In only one verse containing the word *'ishq* is Ghalib even partially overwhelmed by his beloved:

3.1 Although, feigning indifference, we try to hide the secret of love
We become so lost in pretending, that she finds us out
[154: 6]

In ellipsis is the fact that the sight of the beloved so dazes the poet that he must concentrate with obvious difficulty on his pretence, thus betraying the secret of his love; what gives this couplet its freshness is the slightly paradoxical tension among the processes of hiding, losing, and finding.

Much more typical of Ghalib's attitude toward the beloved is his assertion (from elsewhere in the *Dīvān*) that:

3.2 If I don't have love, at least I have madness
My madness will, if nothing else, at least bring you fame
[149: 1]

The connection between love and resulting madness is proverbial in Urdu poetry. Ghalib's wit adds the causal link between his madness—as expressed in his poetic ravings—and the ensuing notoriety of his beloved which will result not only from the revelation of her identity, but from the skill of Ghalib's poetic description as well. Such self-acclaim, moreover, is one of the common voices in which the ghazal is traditionally composed; in this case, the power of Ghalib's boast is in its being symmetrical and succinct.

The poet-lover also commonly speaks in complaint. His madness may result from a variety of causes, not the least of which is the impossibility of union with the beloved. As evoked in the previous couplet, separation from the beloved may be the source of poetic rapture. But madness may also result from the cruelty of the beloved, or her indifference. Even the most determined of lovers may at times feel that there is no hope for his love, and that he is unable to bear the beloved's cruelty and indifference. In one couplet, Ghalib cries out in a voice of despair and reproach which nevertheless, in a tenuous way, maintains his distinctive pride:

3.3 What sort of faith can there be, how can there be love,
when all that's left is to dash out one's brains
So then—O stone-hearted one—why should it be on your
doorstep [127: 4]

The beloved's door is one of the traditional haunts of the distracted lover; but Ghalib has had enough of the beloved's stone heart and the stone of her doorstep, and he asks her why he should give her the satisfaction of being the publicly visible cause of his death, and of seeing him die. Any stone in the desert would be a more appropriate place to kill himself.

In the previous two couplets Ghalib addresses the beloved directly. But sometimes he must resort to a messenger, a stock character in the ghazal who transmits the poet's messages, thus maintaining the secrecy of a love which otherwise would disgrace the beloved.

3.4 She is bad-tempered, and my epic of love is long
To be brief even the messenger is uneasy with me
[206: 3]

The messenger is fidgeting at the prolixity of the poet's narrative. Ghalib laments the impossibility of conveying his myriad complaints and desires to his beloved. In a fine blend of self-assertion and self-ridicule (a combination we have seen previously in 2.10 and 2.21), he praises his poetry for its epic scope, and satirizes it for the elaborateness and detail of its expression. He begins by condensing his thoughts with three verbless phrases in a gallant attempt to be concise—'she [is] bad-tempered, and my epic of love [is] long; to be brief . . . '—then he loses patience, and bursts out with a full sentence, complete with verb, in spoken style: 'even the messenger has become uneasy with me!'

'Ishq and the Rival

All four of the remaining couplets which include the word *'ishq* and refer directly to the beloved also involve some consideration of rival lovers. In the first, no rivals are mentioned explicitly, but their existence is clearly implied:

3.5 Where is the honor of love, when cruelty becomes commonplace

I stop, seeing you cruel without reason [61: 3]

Ghalib is here rebuking the beloved for a failure to distinguish between the true lover and the pack of common profligates. By convention, only the true lover deserves real cruelty from the beloved as a test of strength and determination, and Ghalib proudly forswears his love in order to seek another more worthy and discriminating object for his devotion.

His search is not easy:

3.6 The rival's sweet-talk has had its effect
She doesn't even suspect us mute ones of love [104: 1]

When he has found a discriminating and worthy beloved, there is no question about the identity of the true lover:

3.7 Just see the irony in the efficacy of faithful love
The rival sighed, but she was angry with me [29: 2]

Her anger, of course, is a sign of her approval, but the burden of anger and cruelty, though the duty of the lover to bear, is no substitute for receiving the beloved's love. Ghalib laments that:

3.8 In love, it was the injustice of envy for the rival that struck me down
I am finally the victim of my enemy, though I was stricken for my friend [54: 4]

The logical play here between enemy and friend, and sickness and death, is typical of Ghalib in its unexpectedness.

The *'ishq* couplets just presented associated love with rapture, eloquent madness, threatened suicide, verbosity, righteous indignation, muteness, self-confidence, and sickness and death on the part of the lover; cruelty and only an occasional capacity for discernment on the part of the beloved; general ineffectuality and pettiness on the part of the rivals; and cowardice and impatience on the part of the messenger. In only two of these couplets does Ghalib have anything favorable to say about anyone other than himself: in couplet 3.1 he praises the beloved's enchanting beauty, and in 3.7, her powers of discrimination. Otherwise, the poet's laudatory efforts are reserved exclusively for himself. It is illuminating, moreover, to trace the frequency of pronouns and personal nouns in these eight couplets which focus ostensibly upon the beloved: 3.1 we / we, she; 3.2 me / my, thy; 3.3 [one] / thy; 3.4 she, my | messenger, me; 3.5 — / [I], thee; 3.6 rival | her, us; 3.7 — / rival, she, me; 3.8 rival, me / [I], enemy, [I], friend. While speaking of the beloved, Ghalib remains prominently in the picture, demonstrating a characteristic self-assertiveness—even at the expense of the traditionally dominant beloved—which we shall see throughout his verse.

'Ishq and the Poet

Such self-reference is further demonstrated when Ghalib leaves the beloved altogether, and in an allusion to the story of Shirin and Farhad, speaks of the conflict between lover and rival. Shirin was to be the queen of the famous Persian emperor Khusrau Parvez (known in the West as Cyrus the Great). According to legend, Farhad was in love with Shirin, and he was promised by Khusrau that Shirin would be his if he were able to accomplish the seemingly impossible task of digging a canal through the mountains to bring milk to the gardens and palace that Khusrau was building for Shirin. In his devotion to Shirin, Farhad agreed to the task, and to Khusrau's astonishment, completed the canal. Still determined not to yield Shirin, Khusrau sent false word to Farhad that Shirin had died, and Farhad, by various accounts, either killed himself or died of grief. Farhad (who traditionally had the poetic epithet *koh-kan*, or 'mountain-digger') is revered by poets as a perfect lover. But Ghalib's stance is typically skeptical:

3.9 Love, and labor for Khusrau's pleasure palace—how strange
We do not recognize Farhad's reputation as a lover
[102: 2]

What Ghalib is implying here is that even Farhad does not appear to him to be a worthy rival!

When he is standing alone, without direct reference to either beloved or rival, Ghalib—like most poets—becomes less defensive, and allows himself to explore the various ramifications of the traditional poetic concept of love. In a couplet from one of his most famous ghazals, Ghalib states with admirable simplicity what might be the basic tenet of the true lover:

3.10 How can we abandon our faithfulness
If there isn't love, at least let there be difficulty [149: 7]

The lover is not expected to be united with the beloved; hence, if there is no love (in the sense of union, or reciprocated love), the lover must prove his devotion through the endurance of extreme hardships. In another couplet, Ghalib gives an equally eloquent portrayal of the dedication necessary in true love:

3.11 Love does not yield to despair
Dedication and sacrifice are not fruitless like the willow
[96: 1]

Here there is ambiguity in the result of love: will the lover be victorious in achieving union with his beloved, or merely in having prevailed throughout all the struggles of love? What is important is that love will ultimately be its own reward for the true lover. (The effect created in English by 'willow'—a word associated with sadness—is reflected in the Urdu; Ghalib's conceit is brilliant, for it assigns hopelessness to the weeping willow because of its being fruitless.) The reference to the willow-tree, rare in the ghazal, creates a striking effect.

In a number of verses, Ghalib does portray a sensibility overwhelmed by hopelessness and grief. (As was evident in the previous chapter, the poet sometimes assumes a voice of utter despair to express his debilitation in the trials of love.) He begins one ghazal with the following *maṭla*':

3.12 Of the expression of love's dedication, I am no longer capable
The heart of which I was proud—that heart did not remain
[42: 1]

and concludes the same ghazal with:

3.13 I don't fear the injustice of love, but Ghalib
The heart of which I was proud—that heart did not remain
[42: 8]

Love rewards dedication with injustice. Ghalib's tone in the willow couplet (3.11) is filled with firm resignation. In these last two couplets his strength has deteriorated, with the *īhām* (ambiguity) of *nāz*—which can be both the poet's pride and secondarily the beloved's coquetry; the phrase *nāz-o-niyāz* is here broken down to have the secondary equivalent meanings.

In another couplet, Ghalib portrays his fate at the hands of love with complete simplicity:

3.14 Love, Ghalib, wrought its destruction
Otherwise I too was a useful man [181: 7]

The beauty of this verse lies in its movement from general to specific. Reflecting elsewhere on lovers in general, Ghalib portrays their condition without invoking himself:

3.15 You have asked for news of the arduousness of love's suffering
Those people gradually became anguish from head to foot [168: 4]

Both the above couplets refer to the past, with the clear implication that love results in death. The suffering of love is once portrayed as a sickness (recalling 3.8, in which the poet is 'sick from his friend') though here Ghalib tries to assume the role of doctor:

3.16 Listen: we are those who look after the patients of love
All right, if this is not so—could Christ himself have a cure [56: 1]

If love is incurable, so is its pain:

3.17 From love, my nature found the pleasure of existence
I found it the cure for pain, found its pain incurable [4: 2]

The paradoxical relationship of love and pain—evoked often, not only in Ghalib, but throughout the tradition of Islamic mysticism—is expressed in one couplet which links pain explicitly with pleasure:

3.18 Life cannot be spent without love, and here
There's not even the vitality to savor affliction [113: 4]

In a similar verse, Ghalib introduces a contrast between the grief of the age and the joy of love in the first line, then returns unexpectedly to an acknowledgement that love's pleasure is inseparable from pain:

3.19 The age's grief swept away the intoxication of love's joy
Otherwise even we used to enjoy the pleasure of anguish in those days [177: 3]

The anguish here is of course the anguish of love, and the pleasure, that delicious pain, described in 2.14, that results from the prickling of love's arrows. This couplet illustrates the figure of speech known as *ṣifat-e-taẓādd,* or oxymoron.

In another *she'r,* Ghalib refers to the bondage imposed upon him by love; the poet's heart, debilitated in 3.12 and 3.13, is here in a state of vitality:

3.20 A hundred times from the bond of love we were free
But what can one do, since the heart itself is the enemy of freedom [34: 5]

Love, in all its exquisite maliciousness, is personified in two further couplets which also refer to the heart:

3.21 Again, love has gone to inquire after the heart's wound
Taking as luggage a hundred thousand salt-cellars [234: 5]

3.22 To my heart, bloodthirsty love
Has written: beneficent master, long life! [52: 2]

Blood, similarly, is a motif which Ghalib uses with some frequency, usually as a transformation of grief (as in 'tears of blood' or 'a heart reduced to blood'), or as a by-product of slaughter by the beloved; in most cases, the importance of blood is secondary, as in the following verse, in which it is evoked as s symptom of lamentation:

3.23 From the root of every hair, at the moment of remembering, no blood dripped
It was the story of Hamza, not a recitation of love [23: 7]

Amir Hamza, the uncle of the Prophet Muhammad, was the hero of a popular romance (*dāstān*) which was read or recited purely for entertainment of a diversionary sort. That point Ghalib is making is that a story of true love evokes genuine grief; but the odd negative logic in the first line ('if blood doesn't drip, then . . . '), combined with the use of the word *carca* (which means both 'recitation' and 'gossip'), suggests that he has been listening to the account of some rival's love—an account which is merely long and boring.

Just as in the previous couplet blood is seen dripping from the root of every hair in the suffering of true love, Ghalib again uses numerical exaggeration (as in 3.20 and 3.21) to complete his thought:

3.24 The passion of love's madness gave me hearts by the thousands
Turning black, every drop of blood in my body became itself the core of a heart [114: 8]

In the medical thinking of Ghalib's day, the humor *saudā*, or black bile, was considered to be the cause of frenzy and melancholia; the diminutive form *suvaidā* represents the core of the heart (Platts 1930: 695, 704). In this couplet Ghalib exalts the extent and intensity of his love in a characteristic posture which, as will be evident in the second main section of this chapter, is more typical for *shauq* than for *'ishq*; otherwise, *'ishq* is more frequently associated with grief.

The Grief of 'Ishq

Gham (grief) is a word closely associated with love in traditional Urdu poetry: grief at the hopelessness of love, and at the impossibility of union with the beloved, or of obtaining any but the most casual or malicious attention. In several couplets translated above, Ghalib describes situations in which the poet is generally grief-stricken; but in each case that he uses the word *gham* in explicit connection with the word *'ishq*, he qualifies or expands the traditional viewpoint.

3.25 We too used to know little about the grief of love, but now
We have seen that, even when it was lessened, there was still the grief of everyday life [17: 5]

This couplet is a less famous, but no less effective, statement of the theme of the famous *she'r* (2.17) quoted in the previous chapter:

3.26 Grief destroys the soul; the heart destroys us all
Were there not the grief of loving, there would be the grief of living [21: 7]

Both couplets contrast *gham-e-'ishq* with *gham-e-rozgār*. The first couplet describes the poet's progression in wisdom from the stage before he was in love through a state of wisdom beyond love; the second reinforces the theme that the mere existence of the human heart is enough to insure a lifetime of grief. Both verses are eloquent examples of the capacity for individual ghazal couplets to reach a broad and universal idiom; the greater popularity of the second is probably due to the fact that it is from one of the better known ghazals, and that its internal double rhyme (the *zu-ulqāfiyetain* of traditional prosody) lends to its proverbiality a mellifluous musical effect.

In traditional imagery, the grief of love produces a scar (*dāgh*) upon the heart. Ghalib has written a startling couplet based on this theme:

3.27 Don't think me to be idle, for like the morning and the sun
The scars of love are the decoration of the collar of my shroud, still [68: 1]

Since the burning of love produces scars on the heart (see the reference in 2.7 to the smell of branded flesh), Ghalib is here likening himself to the rising sun, and his white shroud (with its collar-like rent) to the pale dawn; both his heart is burnt and his shroud scorched by the sun-like heat of his still-fervent love. Such logical incongruity is less disturbing in Urdu poetry than it is in English, since as stated in chapter I, one of the most important aspects of the simile is the law of formal harmony, which involves the visual congruence of images; here the round, burning sun invokes the small circular scars burnt on the poet's heart, and the white, spreading dawn invokes the white cloth of his shroud.

In another striking conceit, Ghalib says

3.28 Don't ask the spring of the joy from the scars of love's grief
Blossoming itself submits to the autumnal flow of the candle [76: 6]

As the fire melts the wax of the candle into a withered blossom, so the heat of love melts the heart. The phrase *mat pūch*—'don't ask!'—is frequently used by Ghalib as a rhetorical device suggesting either that any question would require an answer much longer than anyone would want to hear, or that the answer is painfully obvious. Both this couplet and the last are rich in a visual imagery that is at once ambiguous and evocative, particularly in the use of color; dawn and shroud are white, and here heart, rose, and flame are red.

The Struggle of 'Ishq

In three of the previous couplets, the phrase *gham-e-'ishq* occurs, thus establishing grief as one of the qualities Ghalib tends to associate most frequently with love (although if unimaginative repetition were as rampant in Ghalib as some critics would suggest, more occurrences of the phrase *gham-e-'ishq* would be expected.) It is significant that a word much less common in Urdu poetry—*nabard* (battle or contest)—also occurs three times in the *Dīvān* in *eẓāfa* compound (twice as 'war-of-love' and once as 'warlike love'). For Ghalib, love is clearly an engagement in the combative sense, though in keeping with his tendency to view *'ishq* as debilitating, the 'war or love' is such that few lovers, true or false, can prevail.

3.29 The foot was wounded in the beginning of the war of love
It neither serves me in flight, nor lets me stand to fight
[206: 7]

The wound here need not be entirely painful, given the poet's pleasure at his heart's wounds from the beloved's glance, though in this verse his attitude toward the wound is ambiguous.

The fate of the false lover in the war of love is clear:

3.30 He died at the threat, who was not equal to war
Love, warlike, was seeking a man [7: 1]

The mere threat of war was enough to slaughter the pretender to love. By what is not said here, it is clear that Ghalib considers himself fully equal to love's battle; his ridicule of the faint-of-heart lovers, the people of mere lust (*ahl-e-havas,* as opposed to *ahl-e-'ishq*), is even more pronounced in the following:

3.31 For the people of lust, victory is the desertion of love's war
The foot that has been raised is itself their standard
[168: 8]

By *mubālagha* (exaggeration), he depicts a cowardly lover so terrified of the war of love that he lifts his foot in flight as high as an upright flag, and at the same time pretends that it is his standard being borne victoriously away.

In a similar vein, Ghalib admits the inability of the heart to prevail in the struggle (*kashmakash*) of love:

3.32 Does anyone leave the struggle of love's anxiety
If the heart leaves as well, that itself is the heart's pain
[7: 5]

The Game of 'Ishq

The conceit of love as a game of chance occurs in a *musalsal* (continuous) ghazal which has a central theme of *ubi sunt,* as shown in the *radīf, kahāṅ* (where?):

3.33 The gaming house of love is free from us
Were we to go there, what of value is in our purse [86: 6]

In the entire ghazal Ghalib is mourning the loss of the days when he had the leisure for love, or the fortitude. Mehr suggests a formal comparison between the scars on the heart and coins, and between sallow complexion and gold, along with a plenitude of patience and devotion (n.d.: 281)—though these comparisons would hardly come to the mind of any but the most alert *Urdū-dān.* Taken by itself, this couplet is difficult to understand, though it is a novel and evocative verse in the context of the entire ghazal. (The punning connection which exists in English between 'free' and 'empty purse' is fortuitous, and does not occur in the Urdu.)

The Journey of 'Ishq

We have just discussed Ghalib's conception of love as a battle, struggle, or game. In another portrayal of love in dynamic (as opposed to static) terms, Ghalib used the phrase *safar-e-'ishq* (journey of love), which, though more conventional than 'battle of love', is given a typical Ghalibian conceit:

3.34 In the journey of love, weakness made me seek rest
At every step, I thought my shadow to be a bedchamber
[35: 6]

The phrase 'at every step' heightens the effect of an individual moment of fatigue; and if one remembers that the journey of love traditionally takes place in the desert where there is only sun, sand, and shadow, the paradox of this couplet is all the more clear. As Russell and Islam have noted, 'the cool shade is a pleasant concept in English, but it is even more so in a country where the intensity of the heat becomes almost unbearable in some seasons of the year, and in Urdu a wide range of metaphorical use reflects this fact' (1968: 152).

In another couplet, Ghalib explores a similar theme:

3.35 Why bear the pain of the road—there is love for fatigue
The foot cannot be lifted that's in the caravanserai, or at the goal [158: 5]

There is a clear *īhām* (ambiguity) here between the meanings of *manzil* as a resting place on a journey, and a final goal. In either case, Ghalib asserts that love is its own object, and that the essence of love is in loving.

Ghalib fuses several images in a verse combining visual with kinaesthetic sense:

3.36 In the road of love, the pace of the starry sky is
Slow, like that of one with blistered feet [178: 4]

The star-filled immensity of the sky over the desert-wandering lover is the central image, and the slowness of the celestial sphere's revolution is compared to the painfully slow gait of the lover, whose feet are blistered from his endless journey. There is also an implicit comparison between stars and blisters, and a very remote suggestion that the desert is covered with prints from the lover's blisters, just as the sky is filled with stars. Into these two lines are thus condensed an immensity of space and an enormity of time.

The Madness of 'Ishq

The wandering of the desert, as part of the journey of love, is a manifestation of the madness which overcomes the lover. The previous chapter introduced in 2.15 the figures of the *cārā-sāz* (curer) and *gham-gusār* (sympathiser), both of whom, while intending to help the lover, misunderstand and ultimately betray him. The same is the fate of the *nāṣeḥ* (advisor), who in one of four couplets explicitly linking *'ishq* with madness, assumes something of the dimensions of a constable or a psychiatrist, again acting wrongly in spite of a professed sympathy for the lover. In this couplet, as in several of Ghalib's verses, the poet is imprisoned in order to be saved from the terrible fate of wandering the desert:

3.37 If well-wishers have imprisoned me, very well—let it be
Do they think this will free me from love's madness [20: 5]

This conceit is quite conventional, but Ghalib's use of antithesis (*tazādd*), combined with the irony of the second line, provides an effective expression of the poet's impatience.

In a complex and obscure couplet, Ghalib describes the result of an insincere lover's feigned madness:

3.38 A pretense of fidelity, a baseless claim of love
And counterfeit madness in the season of flowers is as tumultuous as the day of judgement [207: 4]

Apparently what Ghalib is saying is that the beloved is temporarily deceived by the hypocritical lover's claim of love and his pretended madness, and thus grants him a measure of fidelity (or in another meaning of *muqābil*, confronts—i.e. assumes—his fidelity). However, with the coming of spring—a time when true love manifests itself—the pretender is revealed; in other words, he will be called to judgement by the beloved, and made to suffer for his insincerity.

The previous couplet is typical of Ghalib's outré poesy; the following is an example of his utmost sincerity, as expressed in a *musalsal* (continuous) ghazal apparently written as an elegy on the death (or dying—since he speaks directly to her) of an actual beloved:

3.39 Love still has not captured, Ghalib, the effect of madness
All that was left in the heart was the taste for suffering, alas! alas! [140: 12]

In this *maqṭa'* (concluding verse) of the ghazal, Ghalib laments the inadequacies of his love in an extraordinary outburst of grief: his love was unable to attain the boundless force of desert-wandering madness—instead, all he could do was grieve. Additional impact is given to the final true rhyme (*qāfiya*) by the ambiguity (*īhām*) of the word *k͟hwārī*, which has a secondary meaning, usually in compounds, of drinking—in this case, drinking the bitter dregs of grief.

In an entirely different linkage of madness with love, the poet's tone is sympathetic, yet subtly ridicules the lover's state:

3.40 The labors of the nightingale prompt the flowers' laughter
They say that what we call love is a derangement of the mind [34: 3]

In this couplet the flowers are clearly the beautiful ones or beloveds, and the nightingale is the poet, singing his song of praise and complaint with utter abandon.

In addition to his desert-wandering, another attribute of the lover's madness is his neglect of his house, resulting in its destruction (*k͟hāna-k͟harābī*). Ghalib, in numerous couplets, is sympathetic to this course of action, but in one verse including *'ishq* he expresses a different attitude:

3.41 I have become ashamed at the destructiveness of love
There's nothing at all left in the house but the futile desire for building [115: 6]

This couplet includes two ambiguities that very much heighten its effect; a reading which draws on the secondary meanings of *ḥasrat* and *k͟hāk* would evoke 'grief' as well as 'desire', and 'dust' as well as 'nothing'. Another couplet utilizes *ḥasrat* in its primary meaning of 'grief':

3.42 The grief, O pleasure of destruction, that no strength remained
For malevolent love, a debilitated body is useless [101: 5]

In both these couplets, a pattern emerges which has occurred previously, but never so obviously: in those verses linking two words commonly invoked in the traditional diction of the ghazal, Ghalib often portrays a situation, or evokes a response, that is contrary to the ordinary expectations of the ghazal. Since both *'ishq* and madness are normally seen as positive attributes, Ghalib unites them to form a negative—and hence surprising—statement: he is tired of the destructiveness of love, and of debilitation, and he seeks some constructive action.

To take another example of such a reversal: it is assumed that the lover will honor his obligation to prove (and also display) his love in fits of weeping. Thus the mention of tears (*ashk* or *āṅsū*), crying (*ronā*), or lament (*nāla*) is in itself enough to invoke the lover's state. Using both 'love' and 'tear', Ghalib introduces a relatively novel conceit:

3.43 Again there has been the witness of the love-seeker:
The order for tearfulness is still in effect [165: 12]

The pursuit of love is here brought into a truly courtly context: the lover has been asked to testify, and his testimony confirms that lovers are still expected, by the laws of love, to weep. What the poet clearly implies—but does not say—is that the lover issues his testimony through the act of crying itself.

Water and Fire Imagery in 'Ishq

With the introduction of weeping as a manifestation of love, we come to Ghalib's use of water imagery within the context of *'ishq*:

3.44 From crying, and in love, I became more fearless
I was washed so that I became utterly clean [211: 1]

This is another example of Ghalib's self-assertion, though without the typical exaggeration of the following couplet:

3.45 The destitution of love has brought weeping, Ghalib
To whose house will the flood of destruction go after me
[58: 9]

There can be no question that Ghalib is a peerless lover; his love produces such a flood of tears that he purifies himself, and brings destruction to his own home in the form of a great flood.

If Ghalib is a poet of water imagery, he is also *par excellence* a poet of fire as well; some of his most striking images involve fire, candles, fireworks, flames, sparks, and lightning (Schimmel 1979: 62-95). The following verses demonstrate flame images, linked with *'ishq*:

3.46 There's no forcing love, Ghalib—it's a fire
Which cannot be ignited, nor made to go out [192: 9]

3.47 When the candle goes out, then from it smoke rises
The flame of love wore black, after me [58: 3]

3.48 It is the heat of longing love, that again, like the candle

Wants to drive the flame up the vein to the pulse of the heart [185: 3]

Two further couplets deal with lightning, a force associated with the destruction of the farmer's crops:

3.49 I am entirely pledged to love, and unavoidably in love with life
I worship lightning, and mourn the reward [of my lost harvest] [12: 1]

3.50 The radiance of existence is from house-destroying love
The gathering has no candle, if lightning is not in the harvest [88: 5]

Couplet 3.46 is superbly simple and concise; the four following verses are ingenious, even tours de force—and these are the two alternate approaches that Ghalib brings to traditional images in combination with his use of the unexpected: stark simplicity, and complex ingenuity.

'Ishq—Compression and Ambiguity

Two couplets remain which include the word *'ishq*—and which could only have been written by Ghalib. (This is admittedly the sort of statement, made by Hali throughout the *Yādgār-e-G͟hālib* [1963], which is difficult to substantiate; but it seems reasonable in this case to assert that these verses demonstrate the sort of brilliant and stunning paradox of which Ghalib was a master, along with his inimitable self-confidence and wit.)

The components of the first couplet, given below in transliteration, must be translated several ways in parallel English to capture some of the reverberations present in the original Urdu:

3.51 dil lagā kar āp bhī G͟hālib mujhī se ho ga'e
'ishq se āte the māne' Mirza sāḥib mujhe

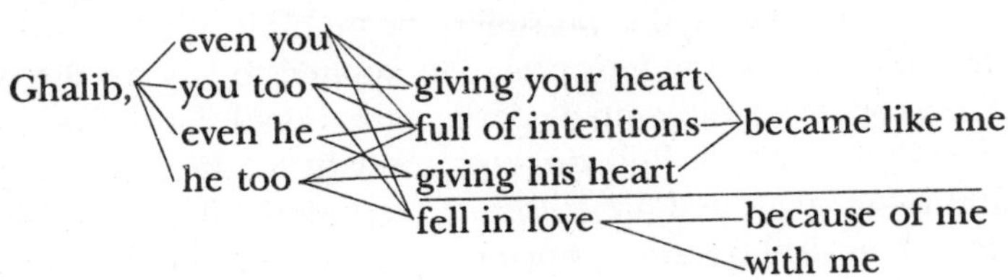

You/He used to hinder me, Mirza Sahib, from loving
[204: 5]

First of all, the phrase *dil lagā kar* is from the verb *dil lagānā*, which means 'to give or apply the mind (to), to intend; . . . to give the heart (to), fall in love (with, -se)' (Platts 1930 : 523); *āp* can mean either 'you' or honorific 'he'; *bhī* can mean both 'too' and 'even'; *mujhī se* can mean 'from me', 'because of me', 'to me', or 'like me'; and the verb *ho ga'e* is indefinite plural in person ('we', 'you', 'they', or honorific 'he'). The second line is less ambiguous, involving simply the question of person ('you' or honorific 'he').

This is an ingenious elaboration on the traditional theme of the poet's confidant becoming his rival (see 4.40); in this case, the confidant is the advisor (*nāṣeḥ*) as well, for he used to come advising him against love. The process was repeated over a period of time ('used to hinder'), and the advisor, in spite of his intentions, was captured by the spell of love.

The ultimate paradox in this couplet—and the source of its effectiveness—is the utter ambiguity of person, particularly since the poet uses his *nom de plume* (*takhalluṣ*) as is conventional in the last couplet (*maqṭa*') of a ghazal, and therefore seems to be addressing himself (though it may be someone else who is addressing Ghalib). In the second line, moreover, 'Mirza Sahib' is addressed—and again, it is not clear whether this is intended to refer to Ghalib. The poet may be describing something that occurred to him (as in his wiser self advising against love), or to a friend directly addressed, or to a friend politely referred to in the third person. The person speaking is ambiguous, the person addressed is ambiguous, and the person spoken of is ambiguous.

Finally, in the last couplet using the word *'ishq*, Ghalib presents a most provocative question to his audience:

3.52 Who is equal to the man-stunning wine of love
The cry is repeated by the lip of the *sāqī*, after me [58: 7]

The ambiguity is less complex than in the previous couplet, and exists primarily in the possibility of multiple intonations in the first line, and in the interpretation applied to 'cry' in the second. The scope for ambiguity is particularly broad if the first line was intended to be recited twice or even thrice in the actual recitation—as suggested by *mukarrar* (repeated). The first line may be a rhetorical question, since the *sāqī* (cupbearer) knows that no one save Ghalib is equal to drinking the wine of love; this would be the case if 'cry' is interpreted as presenting a challenge. The first line may be a taunt thrown to other poets, since the *sāqī* knows that Ghalib is a difficult act to follow; this would be true if *ṣalā* ('cry') is translated as 'invitation'. The taunt could be against Ghalib himself, who did not have the strength to withstand the rigors of love. Finally, if 'cry' is interpreted as an expression of desperation, the essential effect of the first line is a lament for the passing of the greatest of poets.

In the above verses Ghalib writes of love, jealousy, and death; love and grief, struggle, and madness; and love as a game, a journey, as the elemental forces of water and fire. In all these couplets, there is the effect of an even, judicious distribution of words, images and allusions, and tensional relationships—all linked in a consistent but variegated network of connotations. Even when these verses are gathered artificially together, as done here for immediate scrutiny and comparison, they reveal no single theme that becomes intrusive through ineffectual or excessive use. The heart does appear several times (and if any word is overused in these couplets, it is 'heart'), always indicating an area of major concern to any poet, the arena of his emotions—just as the recurrent image of the foot is a powerful symbol of Ghalib's motivation (in whatever state of action or inaction) to wander the wilderness and the world in sublime dementia. What does emerge from these couplets is the prevailing range of tones and shades associated with *'ishq*: in essence, passivity, affliction, and debilitation.

Shauq

For Ghalib, love in its positive and active complexion is best expressed by the word *shauq*, which Platts defines as 'desire, yearning, deep longing, predilection, . . . inclination, love, fancy (for), pleasure (in); taste; ardour, zeal, eagerness, avidity; alacrity, gaiety, cheerfulness; curiosity' (1930: 736). The Persian definition, according to Steingass, is 'filling with desire; desire, yearning, love; affection, inclination, predilection; fancy; pleasure; curiosity; sympathy' (1892: 766). Unlike *'ishq, shauq* seems to have for Ghalib more of the Urdu priority of meanings than the Persian—particularly in terms of 'ardor' and 'zeal', as should be evident from the couplets which follow. Though numerically fewer than those describing *'ishq,* these verses are generally more visionary in their dynamism, and provide an excellent example of one of the ways is which Ghalib tempered and transformed traditional expression for his own purposes.

Of the couplets in which *shauq* is used, only two echo the passive, often plaintive connotations of *'ishq.* In the next major section of this chapter, the *shauq* couplets are arranged in a continuum, progressing from the area of commonality between *'ishq* and *shauq,* as found in 3.53 and 3.54, to an area of meaning in which *shauq* is not only active and hopeful but vigorously—even vertiginously—kinetic and celebratory.

Shauq and Suffering

Only one couplet dealing with *shauq* has the sense of debilitation usually associated with the lover's state in *'ishq:*

3.53 Love has this fault—that at every breath, a lament is drawn out
The condition of the heart is such that one fears to breathe [154: 4]

In other words, the heart has become so weak with the strain of lamentation that the poet fears—since he cannot breathe without lamenting—that every breath will be his last. The sense of this couplet is not ostensibly different from what it would be if *'ishq* were used, except that the description of symptoms here is more dynamic: one feels an almost kinaesthetic sense of holding the breath.

The second relatively passive *shauq* verse has a hint of complaint to the beloved, though it is dominated by the poet's cursing his own naiveté; in this couplet, as in the last, *shauq* is not appreciably different in connotation from *'ishq:*

3.54 Because I am stupid, I am happy at the beloved's vexation
Thinking it means another recitation of love—but it was not so [39: 5]

The poet assumes with a schoolboy's credulity that his beloved's vexation will give him another chance to repeat his story of love, the way a student repeats a lesson for a dissatisfied teacher. But according to convention the beloved is cruel, and will not give him another chance.

Moving on to the more typical usages of *shauq*, we find that the remaining couplets have clearly entered the active realm. There is some reference to the beloved's cruelty in the following verse, but Ghalib staunchly chides his own love for harboring any thoughts of enmity:

3.55 Oh! Oh! God forbid—she and enmity
O love, for shame—what is this idea of yours [142: 4]

The poet clearly has the capacity to bear any degree of injustice, for he has a longing so strong that it cannot be without hope:

3.56 From that lip will certainly come a kiss someday
But extravagant love will be needed, and rakish courage
[189: 2]

This verse expresses an optimism never suggested in the usages of *'ishq*.

The Personification of Shauq

Like the *'ishq* couplets, the *shauq* verses include some examples of personification in which love enters a distinctly active mode. In these instances *shauq* may be addressed directly, or given some quality or power which stops short of full personification ('love has this fault', 'love has opened the knots', 'love's complaint is that . . . ', and so forth). But on two occasions Ghalib makes *shauq* a character in itself. In the first, love assumes the role of a rival:

3.57 Love, in very respect, turned out to be the rival of possessions
Even in the canvas of the picture, Qais turned out to be naked [6: 1]

Involved here are two plays on words; *rang* means both 'case' and 'respect', as well as 'color', and *parda* means both 'curtain' and 'canvas'—so that several words play on some aspect of the word *taṣvīr* (picture). Qais, also called Majnun, is the archetype of the mad lover wandering the desert in the sublime exhilaration and ecstasy of love; unable to bear the restrictions of his clothing (and by extension, of society), he tears his collar in the action of *cāk-e-*

garībān (see 4.100, 6.3, and 6.35) and lets his garment fall as he wanders. What Ghalib is saying is that *shauq* is so jealous of possessions (and the rival always triumphs) that he does not permit the lover to have clothes even in a picture; thus Qais emerges from the protective curtain (*parda*) of modesty to become naked on the canvas (also *parda*) of the picture.

In a less complex and yet fuller personification, *shauq* emerges in the marketplace of love (*bāzār-e-shauq*):

3.58 Again love is seeking a buyer
Having offered the merchandise of mind and heart, and life and soul [234: 9]

This verse illustrates the typical cataloguing and enumeration that sometimes occur in the ghazal—though Ghalib makes sparing use of such devices. In the original Urdu there are only three words in the series, but the last—*jān*—carries connotations of both 'life' and 'soul'. But for Ghalib, the marketplace of love provokes only boredom; he prefers (see Chapter V) the trackless expanses of the desert, and the exultation of a madness far removed from commercial society:

3.59 Who has the leisure for the transactions of love
Where is the taste for the inspection of beauty [86: 2]

The word *z̤auq* (taste, pleasure) is often associated with *shauq*, and here provides an ingenious combination of the faculties of both taste and sight. This verse is somewhat atypical of Ghalib in that, for him, the pleasure of *naz̤z̤āra* (sight, inspection) is one of the prime goals of the lover; but this couplet comes from a ghazal (see 3.33) on the theme of *ubi sunt*, with the *radīf*, *kahāṅ* (where?).

Shauq and Madness

Two couplets on the subject of madness and love (see 3.37-40) introduce the associations of energy and kinetic action to which Ghalib adds the phenomenon of *shauq* (kinetic imagery did occur in such verses as 3.3, 3.36, and 3.44-50, but they comprise only a minority portion of Ghalib's treatment of *'ishq*).

Undaunted by the trials of love, the poet persists in his assertiveness, and even exceeds the requirements of his etiquette:

3.60 For God's sake, give due praise for this madness of love
That at her doorstep, I arrive before the messenger
[177: 4]

The madness of *shauq* seems to save the poet the anxiety he felt (3.4) while telling the messenger his story of *'ishq*; he races towards the beloved's house, perhaps out of simple impatience that she hear his words, or in the certainty that he can represent himself better than the messenger. But even the power of *shauq* does not prevent him from having second thoughts once he has arrived:

3.61 Alas! the madness of love, that at every breath I take
I go there myself, and thus will only be confounded [18: 3]

The poet's perplexity may result from a variety of causes: the sight of the beloved, the realization of the futility of seeking union with her, sheer nervousness at the prospect of being in her presence, or any combination of these. This couplet may also be interpreted in the sense of love for the divine beloved: the mere sight of the world is a source of astonishment for the poet.

Shauq and the Power of Sight

The process of seeing, particularly when involved with a vision of the beloved's beauty, is a common motif in the ghazal. Ghalib makes frequent use of this motif; while the previous couplet merely hints at the stunning impact of a vision of the beloved, another *she'r* speaks directly of the effect wrought by her appearance:

3.62 O improvident heart, show restraint in your love
Who can endure the brilliance of the vision, of the sight of the beloved [54: 2]

The word *tāb*, here translated as 'brilliance', also carries connotations of burning heat and pain, so that the inflammation of the poet's heart, as a result of seeing the beloved, is also suggested. In another ghazal, Ghalib refers once again to the limitations of the human eye in its inability to absorb the full beauty of the beloved:

3.63 Love has opened the knots of beauty's veil
Except for sight itself, no obstacle now remains [42: 5]

The beloved is traditionally veiled, but the capacity of *shauq* is such that it has actively removed the veil; such action is futile, however, for the poet still cannot achieve his goal of union with the beloved. From one perspective, the glance itself is the rival; from another, there is the duality of the observer and the observed.

The two previous couplets strongly suggest a divine beloved (as does 2.20, 'Who can see Him . . . '). On those occasions when the veil actually *is* removed, it is almost certainly an earthly being that the poet sees:

3.64 Wine has unveiled the beauty of the self-adorning one
O love, here is permission to welcome beauty [170: 3]

The beloved *sāqī*, having become intoxicated, has let the veil fall, and the poet—who according to the etiquette of the tavern cannot himself make advances—thirstily drinks in the sight of his beloved's face.

Just as the presence—and particularly the view—of the *sāqī* is the source of indescribable pleasure for the drinker (for only the *sāqī* can pour the wine), so the cupbearer's absence provokes not only the drinkers, but even the vessels themselves into a state of restlessness and anxious boredom:

3.65 Last night, the intoxication of love for the *sāqī* was as great as the tumult of Judgement Day
Even the wine-goblet was a picture-house of uneasy stretching [19: 1]

The congruence here of reflections in numerous goblets with a picture-filled room suggests that the vessels themselves are longing for the *sāqī's* presence, as shown by their stretching and reaching. This image of multiple reflections and pictures is typically Ghalibian, in that it is unusual, precise, and highly visual.

We return to the poet standing stunned in front of the beloved's house (3.61). In spite of the difficulties in seeing the beloved, the poet ponders a solution: since *shauq* is not to be contained, he produces a rather elegant and euphuistic rationalization of this plight.

3.66 Are we afflicted if the door and wall appear before our eyes
To love's sight, the door and wall are like wings and feathers [59: 1]

The power of longing in love's faculty of vision is so great that the doors and walls—apparent obstacles to the unresourceful lover—themselves provide that faculty with the means of elevating itself to a point where the beloved can be seen.

In two verses Ghalib links *shauq* with the traditional garden imagery of the ghazal (the garden represents the abode of the *gul* [rose] as a symbol of the beloved). Both couplets express the lover's exquisite joy in suffering by making an unexpected play on some traditional motif. The first verse refers to the convention that the person picking a rose is in danger of being pricked by the thorns. The devoted lover enjoys any pain resulting from love, but he also knows that he will never be permitted to pluck the rose—i.e. to be united with the beloved—and that it thus seems he will be denied being wounded by the rose's thorns. Ghalib's ingenuity of rationalization, however, saves him from being refused this particular suffering:

3.67 There *are* thorns in the pain of longing for sight
If love does not pluck the flower of contentment's garden, no matter [176: 2]

The thorns may be the pricking of grief—or in a more subtle allusion, the eyelashes, which are also curved and sharp.

The second couplet (from a different ghazal) portrays in the first line what seems to be a miracle: the beloved promises the poet a tour of the garden (*sair-e-gulistān*), which may mean either a glimpse of her face (with its rose-like cheeks) or a literal stroll through the garden in the beloved's company. But the alert reader or listener should know that union in the tradition of the ghazal is never this easy, and that the beloved's promise (see 2.12-13) is never what it seems:

3.68 The promise has come of a tour of the garden—how happy the fate of love
The good news of execution is decreed, though it is not mentioned openly [101: 2]

Ghalib, as we might expect, has the perspicacity to know what the beloved intends in her promise: the object of sight in the garden is the redness of the rose, and for the beloved, the scattering of the poet's blood is like the planting of a rose-bed. The lover, as decreed by tradition, is honored to be slaughtered by the beloved, for his murder 1) proves the dedication of his love, 2) represents at least some bestowal of attention by the beloved, and 3) concludes his long experience of suffering.

Invoking again the power of sight—though here the act of seeing is subordinate to the major conceit in the verse—Ghalib personifies his own restless love in the dagger by which he longs to die:

3.69 The uncontrollable emotion of love should be seen
The breath of the dagger is outside the dagger's breast
[1: 3]

The second line involves a pun untranslatable by any single English word. *Dam* (breath) also means the sharp edge of a sword or dagger, so that when Ghalib says the *dam* of the dagger is outside its breast, he means first, that the dagger's cutting edge (which in its brightness should be seen) is around the perimeter of the dagger's bosom (i.e. the body); and second, that in anticipation of killing the lover, the dagger's breath is outside its breast (i.e. it is breathless with anticipation). This couplet, as Chishti has observed, demonstrates another of the specialities that have made Ghalib so distinctive: the combination of imagination with poetical aetiology, or the fanciful assignment of cause (1959: 238-9).

Shauq and the Kineticism of Elemental Imagery

In Ghalib's depiction of *'ishq* in terms of natural phenomena, he used both fire and water imagery with particular effectiveness. In 3.45 there is a clearly kinetic sense of *'ishq* in the flood, as there is in the flame and pulse of 3.48. Yet the kineticism of 3.49 and 3.50 (with the imagery of lightning and crops) has nevertheless an effect of passivity, for the crops are the victim of the lightning's awesome but momentary power. In the *shauq* couplets invoking fire, Ghalib has portrayed the power of love in a similar mode, as both destructive and creative.

The image of the beloved slaughtering the lover is expressed in one couplet with such ambiguity as to permit a rich variety of interpretations:

3.70 If you strike me, in my longing for sight, on the neck
My vision, as in the trimming or snuffing of a candle, will be scattered from me [191: 7]

In the second line the word *nigāh*—echoing *dīdār* (sight, vision) in the previous line—may mean 'look', 'glance', 'sight', or 'view', thus suggesting both the lover's longing glance at the beloved and his unwavering gaze, both a brief glimpse of the beloved and a more sustained view; the word carries at the same time associations with the beloved's glance, which wounds the lover with arrows of love (eyelashes) launched from the arched bow of her eyebrow. The *gul-e-sham'a* (literally, 'rose of the candle') can signify both the trimming of the candle wick to make it burn more brightly, and the extinguishing of the candle (the word 'snuff' in English carries both meanings, though the present connotation is almost exclusively the latter). The candle is also associated with the poet, and the flame of the candle with the poet's tongue, or power of speech (see 6.24); hence a snuffed candle represents a silenced poet. The word *pareshān* (scattered), finally, carries an elaborate network of associations, most commonly involving the beloved's disheveled tresses (see 6.12 and 6.32) and the poet's scattered sensibilities (see 3.106).

The beloved traditionally kills the poet by striking his neck with a sword, which process in this couplet may be likened to the trimming of a candle wick; but at the same time she is killing him, so that the action may also be read as extinguishing the candle. Smoke scatters from the extinguished candle, just as brightness scatters from the trimmed wick; the poet is thus acknowledging that the beloved may kill him, but he also suggests, with distinctive assertiveness, that the passion of his love of sight (which permits him to see the beloved) cannot be extinguished.

Ghalib's frequent use of fire imagery in an active mode is evident in the following reference to the beloved's departure on a journey:

3.71 When, at the prospect of the journey, the beloved tied the saddle
The burning of love tied a heart to every mote of dust [30: 1]

The image here is striking, though fanciful (since the beloved in most circumstances would have had a servant to prepare the saddle), and evokes the ancient Arabian precursors of the ghazal. In the dust of the desert the beloved prepares to depart from her poet-lover; his grief and agitation at her leaving him are such that his love ties a heart to every mote of dust that her preparations cause to rise into the air, in the hope that some part of the poet may accompany the beloved throughout her journey.

On another Occasion Ghalib describes the consequences of love's burning:

3.72 Why do you ask of the being or non-being of the people of love
They have become the rubbish and trash of their own fire
[211: 5]

The exigencies of love have reduced the lovers to a state resembling that of rubbish, and the fire of their love has consumed this trash, producing (circularly) more trash. This *she'r* presents, in a more unusual statement, the theme of one of the *'ishq* couplets quoted in the previous section:

(3.15) You have asked for news of the arduousness of love's suffering
Those people gradually became anguish from head to foot
[168: 4]

Yet in the *shauq* couplet the destructiveness of fire, instead of consuming the people of true love altogether, allows them to continue burning.

In the three couplets just discussed, Ghalib portrays *shauq* as a candle burning, or as fire; his *Dīvān* also includes four couplets associating *shauq* with ocean or river, and in these verses he draws deeply on a sense of water in motion. The first verse refers again to the process of sight—specifically, the *hasrat-e-dīdār* ('longing for vision', a phrase which occurs in 3.67):

3.73 In the moist eye, from the longing for sight, is hidden
Broken-reined love, which is called a river, an ocean
[230: 5]

Mixed metaphors do not much trouble connoisseurs of

traditional Urdu poetry; the imagistic fusion of horse and river thus poses no problems, though for the English-speaking reader, 'rampant love' would perhaps be a more effective translation than 'broken-reined love'. The word *daryā* has 'ocean' as its primary meaning in Persian, though in Urdu it probably carries more the connotations of a large river.

Using *daryā* elsewhere in the sense of 'ocean', Ghalib writes:

3.74 Love's complaint is that, even in the heart, there is want of space
Though the restlessness of the ocean was annihilated in the pearl [28: 1]

Ghalib states with remarkable compression that while the agitation of the stormy ocean is ultimately tamed and contained in the pearl (a reference to the belief that certain raindrops falling into the ocean were transformed into pearls—see 6.19 and Naim 1965: 192), the restlessness of love is infinitely greater than that of the ocean; the human heart, with all its capacity for suffering and agitation, is unable to contain the vast, turbulent surgings of love. There is here an implicit visual congruence between pearl and heart, as well as an implication of priceless value, in that both have been formed through great hardship and suffering.

Ghalib elsewhere presents a very different, but no less memorable evocation of the enduring and boundless nature of love; speaking to the cautious and skeptical beloved, who fears that union will reduce the poet-lover's ardor, he says:

3.75a If in your heart there is the idea that in union will be love's decline
The wave in the ocean of water strikes, hand and foot, like this [117: 9]

The individual united with the divine beloved is like the single raindrop merged with the ocean; thus, if the individual experiences the transcendence of union with a beloved greater than himself, his passion will simply merge with that of other lovers and become like the waves of the ocean. A less literal translation, but one capturing the sense of the Urdu more effectively in English, would be

3.75b If you think that union will reduce the ardor of love
Just see how the waves in the ocean thrash endlessly
[117: 9]

An effective extension of the previous image, taken from another ghazal, is Ghalib's assertion that

3.76 Love is the means of lordly exaltation for the lowly
The grain of sand becomes the desert, the drop becomes the sea [43: 3]

This verse depends upon the sort of exaggeration (*mubālagha*) and telescoping of perceptions that existed in the earlier couplet (1.3) comparing the sun to a lamp in the wind's path. The double comparison of opposing elements—earth and water—in both their atomic and infinite dimensions is a Ghalibian *tour de force*, by including elemental opposites as well as dimensional opposites, he encompasses the entirety of the intermediate realms. One might say that these two brief lines, like the grain of sand and drop of water, themselves contain the enormity of both the oceans and the deserts of existence. It should perhaps also be noted that though the desert and the ocean are in a sense opposites, they are both composed of infinitely tiny elements, and pass through eternal restlessness and change—though on different scales of time—in the shifting of their waves, and thus, on another logical plane, they are manifestations of the same unity.

Two more couplets from the *Dīvān* illuminate connections between *shauq* and the desert, which for Ghalib is the natural habitat of *shauq*:

3.77 From the smallness of the place, the grief of love has been reduced to dust
If each mote were a net, the vastness of the desert would be the prey [229: 3]

Or again:

3.78 Love has sent me running in the desert, where
The road is nothing but the glance of an eye in a picture
[93: 2]

These couplets, rather obscure as they are, will be discussed at length in Chapter 5 (5.55 and 5.67). Suffice it for the moment to observe that *shauq* is here portrayed in typically visionary kineticism.

Continuing his comparison of *shauq* with natural phenomena—or more precisely, with natural phenomena involving the elements (fire, water, and earth, in the form of love, the desert, and dust)—Ghalib has composed two verses including references to wind. The first is quite simple, and quite effective:

3.79 I am the whirlwind of the road of restlessness
The desert wind of love is my progenitor [184: 7]

As long as the winds continue to blow through the vastness of the desert (the traditional abode of the lover), the poet will be as restless and strong as those winds. The term *bānī*, translated here as 'progenitor', also has connotations of creator and founder, as in the founder of a tradition.

The second verse is more complex:

3.80 Except for flight in the love of elegance, what can possibly remain
Judgement Day is a cold wind blowing over the dust of the martyrs [62: 7]

The image here is of wind as a manifestation of love's insatiability. True lovers, gone to their graves, have long since become dust scattered on the desert winds—through the unceasing restlessness of their love—over such a vast expanse that their dust can never again be gathered, even in the resurrection on the day of judgement. Their love was so great that they escaped mere limitations, and have merged with the infinitude of the desert.

The Journey of Shauq

Of the two remaining *shauq* verses, one (as part of a three-couplet *qiṭa*', or sequence) is difficult to classify. Ghalib, with a rare explicit reference to autobiographical detail, composed this *qiṭa*' with the obvious intention that it be recited during his stay at Lucknow on his way to Calcutta:

3.81 The reason for coming to Lucknow is not evident—that is to say
The passion for travel and spectacle is not important to me

This city is not the final destination in the stages of love
Ali's tomb and the Ka'ba are the journey's goal for me

There is a hope leading somewhere, Ghalib
The road's path is the allurement of kindness—with its long letter *kāf*—for me [124: 9-11]

The predominantly Shi'a audience of Lucknow would of course have been pleased that Ghalib mentioned that city in his recitation, and would not have been at all insulted that he identified it as only one of the caravanserais on his road of love. The ultimate irony of this *qiṭa'*, however, is the fact that Ghalib was not going to Mecca on a holy pilgrimage; he was journeying to Calcutta in a desperate attempt to secure the pension that he felt was due him (see Russell and Islam 1969: 45-50)—and for a man of his pride, such supplication for kindness (*karam*, beginning with the letter ک—*kāf*—long and flat like a road) must have been a painful role.

Finally, after all the visions Ghalib has created in response to *shauq*, it is typical that he should praise the expanse of his love at the expense of his poetry. In a couplet from the last ghazal in the *Dīvān*, he writes:

3.82 The narrowness of the ghazal's straits is not equal to love
I need more latitude to tell my story [235: 8]

Ghalib, it seems safe to say, has not disappointed his audience in his skillful manipulation—and transcendence—of the limitations of the ghazal. Within the scope of eighty-two couplets, he has managed to evoke a wide range of circumstances, characters, locations, moods, and actions, each tending to be consistent with the larger concepts of *'ishq* and *shauq*, and sometimes with both. After a careful, thoughtful perusal of these couplets, it is possible to review some of the features of the mental concordance, mentioned above, that the *Urdu-dān* brings to an appreciation of the ghazal.

In the realm of phenomena and actions associated with love, Ghalib has invoked madness, fame, faith, difficulty, dedication, cruelty, labor, destruction, war, flight, life, and death; sighing, crying, laughing, curing, imprisonment, flight, running, standing, washing, breathing, kissing, inspection, unveiling, stretching, welcoming, touring, thrashing, scattering, seeking, and of course (the list is only partial and random), falling in love.

As characters, Ghalib has summoned beloved, friend, enemy, rival, lover, messenger, patients, master, man, well-wisher, *sāqī*, buyer, and seller; the people of love, lust, and affliction; such luminaries of the ghazal world as Khusrau, Farhad, Hamza, Christ (as curer), and Qais (Majnun, the mad), as well as the assembled martyrs of love; and to provide the cliché that proves the rule, Ghalib has even included one nightingale, one unspecific prey, and a respectable showing of roses.

As settings, Ghalib refers to the beloved's doorstep, Khusrau's palace, a gaming house, bedchamber, road, caravanserai, the lover's ruined house, a court, bazaar, picture-house, execution place, and garden, as well as the sun, the starry sky, the desert (with its sands and winds), and the ocean (with its surging waves); also, the Ka'ba, Najaf, and Lucknow.

Since the ghazal expresses the poetry of love, it is appropriate that Ghalib invokes various portions of the human body, most frequently—as we have come to expect—his own: brains (to be dashed out), heart (in numerous verses), foot, wound, hair and hair-roots, blood, scars on the heart, blister, vein (a particularly evocative word for Ghalib, because of the kinetic image of the pulse), breath (with the sense of breathing), neck, and eye. The beloved seems indistinct, even incorporeal, except for her eye, and only once, her lip; this reticence on Ghalib's part could be from a combination of modesty (in not wishing to embarrass the beloved—or himself—with an unseemly attention to the details of her physical person), pride (at not wanting to use commonplace imagery to describe her beauty), and simple self-absorption (in remaining more concerned with his own state of being than with that of the beloved).

The imagery of these eighty-two verses is selective, and usually captures the reader's attention: the fruitless willow, the personification of love bringing salt-boxes for the poet's wounds, the poet's shroud and collar like the dawn, and the distinctive images of flight, fire, water, wind, and sight; from the paraphernalia of everyday life, Ghalib draws crops, purse, wine, thorns, dagger, saddle, pearl, net, and rubbish and trash.

Finally, there is Ghalib's preoccupation with communication: questions, laments, recitations of story and tale, gossip, transactions, decree, witness, news, cries, pledges, and cajolery. There are the states and moods to be communicated: uneasiness, anger, envy, despair, pride, suffering, joy, anguish, blood-thirstiness, pain, enmity, extravagant love and rakishness, exultation, intoxication, amazement, grief, and madness.

All of these elements reflect a wide range of the features of human life, and a broad skein of relationships among those features that is remarkably complex and evocative for a total of 164 lines of poetry. But what is just as remarkable as all that is included in these couplets, it seems to me, is what is excluded. There is a comparatively small proportion of images in these lines, in favor of a general abstraction that is given to an analysis of relationships, of attractions and conflicts, rather than to the more descriptive types of poetic statement. Those images which do occur are at the very least striking, and usually, stunningly effective, as will be evident in the last chapter, which one again considers the ghazal as a complete sequence of couplets.

This abstraction facilitates an exploration of the states of love, which is almost certainly the most preoccupying and problematic relationship in which an individual may be involved—particularly when love is conceived as inclusive of the religious impulse as well. When such a relationship is described, too much denoted detail is superfluous within the 'bundles of relations' that constitute the individual couplet; it is up to the reader or listener to supply the connotations of that relationship and its components, since most of the elemental relationships of the ghazal will have been experienced first hand, or at least in such a vicarious way for them to become 'real'. In the latter case, a sustained exposure to the topoi of the ghazal will provide for the *Urdu-dān* a semantic field of reference for each of these topoi. For example, *'ishq* (as has been evident in this chapter) tends to be associated in Ghalib with passivity and suffering, though the suffering may be delicious in its own way; *shauq*, on the other hand, tends to be more charged with a longing that draws the poet-lover into action, vertiginous motion, and dynamic madness.

As for the more concrete words and images of the ghazal, and the fact that they are usually Persian in origin—it has been asked more than once whether a Delhi resident who had never seen the sea can respond adequately to an image drawn from the ocean. As Ralph Russell has correctly observed, the fact that most English (or Urdu) speakers would not recognize a nightingale or its song when they encountered it does not prevent their responding to a poetic reference to the bird (Russell 1969: 119); their literary experience, with all its past associations, has achieved a subjective reality no less than that of any other feathered, flying creature—and certainly having a more poetic effect than (for example) a crow. What is important is the fact that a nightingale *sings*; its size, coloration, and the details of its song are of little contributive value to any use in poetry. While there can occur a degree of semantic depletion in the unimaginative poetic use of a word or image, the nightingale in Ghalib's poetry comes distinctly to life through the way he employs it: as a source of amusement (since madness is traditionally either revered or ridiculed) for the entire garden of roses. The nightingale not only sings, but it delivers its song in a laughable state of derangement (3.40).

As a result of encountering, and *learning*, the above verses, the reader can now provide a network of connotations for the words *'ishq* and *shauq,* as used by Ghalib to describe different though interrelated aspects of love. For purposes of comparison, we now turn to the other two words that Ghalib uses for love—*muḥabbat* and *ulfat*—to complete our survey of the denotation of the word love, and the connotations that is has for him.

Muḥabbat

Ghalib periodically uses the word *muḥabbat* (defined by Platts as 'love, affection; friendship' [1930: 1007] and by Steingass as 'love, affection; friendship; esteem, benevolence' [1892: 1182]) for love. While the word occurs with less frequency in the *Dīvān* than *'ishq,* it appears to have much the same range of meaning—except that the beloved herself may engage in *muḥabbat* as a more balanced, mutual form of love, but not in *'ishq,* with its connotations of illness, derangement, and dying.

Of the eleven *muḥabbat* couplets, five refer directly to the beloved. In these cases the word may take on a variety of shadings, though the very fact that the beloved is mentioned indicates that *muḥabbat* is used primarily in the sense of a relationship.

The first verse involves contrast, balance, and implicit paradox:

3.83a In love, there is no difference between life and death
Seeing her alone we live, that infidel for whom we are dying [220: 8]

The second line uses a colloquial expression for death—'for the breath to come out'—which has other meanings evident in an alternate translation:

3.83b In love, there is no difference between living and dying
Seeing her we live, that infidel who takes the breath away
[220: 8]

The Urdu verb *marnā* (to die) involves the same secondary meaning of pining and longing as the English. With the clever manipulation of words, and the not unusual use of *kāfir* (infidel) for the beloved (who is very often also described as an idol worshipped by the poet!), this verse is perfectly competent but not truly exceptional—as is the following couplet, which offers another description of the poet's expiring from love:

3.84 I am struggling in the agonies of my last breath; now,
O love, let us see your power of attraction
I may not be able to say anything—but let her come to
inquire about me [164: 2]

In a literal sense, this couplet is completely serious. The poet's last request is that the beloved at least come to ask about his condition, after all her indifference and neglect. Beyond this is the hope that if she comes, the lover will be able to see her at last, for as in the previous verse (3.83), the sight of the beloved is a source of supreme joy, even life.

I would also suggest a possible ironic reading: that the lover is feigning death (he still has enough breath to speak the verse) in order to trick the beloved into coming.

The poet knows full well that it is fruitless to expect any affection from the beloved. But if he is willing to die in order to bring her to him, he may also try plays of logic to persuade her to pay him some heed:

3.85 We are free from even asking why there is no love
But do something with us—why not let there be hate
[120: 1]

Here again is nimble-witted Ghalib, refusing to accept the humiliation of being totally ignored.

In the following couplet of the same ghazal, Ghalib changes his tone to one of unambiguous complaint, in order to provide some variety in recitation (see Chapter VI). He has tried various devices to provoke the beloved into simply acknowledging his presence, if not returning his *muḥabbat*; and he has clearly failed. He therefore turns his desperate ingenuity to a mere imagistic congruence:

3.86 Weakness has not left me even a shade of familiarity
There's a weight on my heart—why should there not be the print of love [120: 2]

This couplet, though pleasing, is not exceptional. It is the only verse containing *muḥabbat* which refers either to the heart, or to the scars which have been produced there by the pain of love. The effect of this couplet is created largely by the *īhām* (ambiguity) based on the word-play on *raṅg* (whose primary meaning of 'color' is here translated as 'shade') and *naqsh* (picture—here translated as 'print', just as the English *print* includes both meanings of 'picture' and 'impression'); for a similar play of meanings see 3.57.

A more subtle complaint is raised in a verse from another ghazal. Such is the poet's experience of love, that even on those rare occasions when the beloved does seem favorably disposed toward him, or even expresses some affection, he still cannot trust his apparent good fortune; as in 3.85, he simply has no real expectation that she will ever give herself to him:

3.87 Since in every innuendo, every gesture of hers, there is another meaning
Even if she does love us, another doubt arises [63: 1]

The rival puts in a conventional appearance in the *muḥabbat* couplets, though Ghalib's response is ambiguous:

3.88 Do you think I am my own enemy
I'll grant you—though I don't believe it—that the rival loves you [149: 4]

According to Mehr, the only possible meaning, given Ghalib's adherence to poetic conventions, is that the poet will not demean himself by stopping his love, even though the rival may have true devotion to the beloved (n.d.: 491-2). Chishti, on the other hand, suggests that Ghalib, seeing that the rival truly loves the beloved, does not squander his time and effort in loving her further (1959:

659-60). While the first interpretation seems more likely in view of the conventions of behavior in the ghazal, the second does seem marginally possible, particularly in view of the verse (3.5) in which Ghalib refuses to love the beloved when she herself, in choosing not to recognize his truer love, is cruel to the rival rather than to him.

On another occasion, Ghalib laments his folly in confiding his feelings to a companion:

3.89 Our commiserating friend disgraced us; to hell with this love
Whoever cannot bear grief, why should he share my secrets [127: 3]

The friend undoubtedly disgraced the poet by revealing the fact of his love, and perhaps the identity of the beloved, either by telling people of his friend's great grief, or perhaps by falling in love himself with the beloved and going subsequently mad. The use of the phrase *lage āg*, which can mean both 'set fire to' and 'to hell with', is echoed in the second hemstitch by the word *tāb*, which means both 'grief' and 'pain' (see 3.62). Here is another example of Ghalib's fire imagery, though this couplet involves only word-play, and not the sort of dynamic imagery in which the actual process of burning is emphasized.

The lover should learn not to confide in anyone, perhaps on the basis of the sort of experience just described. In another couplet Ghalib invokes the poet's house through the synecdoche (*majāz-e-mursal*) of *dar-o-dīvār* (door-and-wall; see 3.66), which Ghalib frequently uses to mean 'house':

3.90 Don't tell anyone, Ghalib—for in this era there is no
Confidant of the secrets of love, except for the doors, the walls [59: 10]

(In Urdu, unlike English, the walls do not have ears, and are therefore trustworthy.)

We have already discussed one couplet (3.39) from the ghazal in which Ghalib is apparently lamenting the death of an actual beloved. Another verse from this ghazal includes the word *muḥabbat* in combination with *yārī* (friendship, love), an abstract noun formed from *yār* (friend, beloved; see Chapter 5):

3.91 The dignity of the pledge of love has fallen into the dust
The way and code of love have left the world, alas! alas! [140: 8]

Ghalib's beloved was such that, after her death, Ghalib will be unable to love anyone else, nor will any love at all be possible in the world.

In the following couplet, Ghalib combines *muḥabbat* with *tamannā* (longing), a word which Ghalib uses with particular intensity:

3.92 Who breathed into the ear of love, O God
That incantation of waiting that is called longing [230: 3]

This couplet, simple in construction and vocabulary, is a worthy example of *sahl-e-mumtana*ʻ (deceptive ease), for Ghalib has with apparent effortlessness combined a number of powerful motifs: blowing or breathing (with a secondary meaning of giving life, or of inflaming or setting on fire); as personification of love in 'the ear of love'; an invocation, impassioned and desperate, of God; an incantation or spell; the process of waiting (for union with—or even sight of—the beloved); and the psychological state of extreme longing. The process of the vivification or inflammation of love is here called forth with Ghalib's distinctive efficacy, and combined further with the provocative question, 'Who has brought love itself to a state of action?'

In the last of the *muḥabbat* couplets, Ghalib assumes a characteristic posture of debilitation, though in this case from an excess of sensuous experience—not from union itself, but from the torment of being able to enjoy only the fragrance of the beloved, as symbolized by the garden, or the flowers of the garden (by implications, the poet is a nightingale):

3.93 There used to be love for the garden, but now I feel such irritability
That the wave of fragrance from the roses makes me suffocate [11: 2]

The tone of the verse is one of boredom, of saturation with inferior sensual experience, and possibly, of hangover.

These couplets introduce a few additional elements into Ghalib's portrayal of love, most notably the conventional identification of the beloved as the beautiful infidel (with its pleasing tension in connection with the recurrent image of the beloved as idol), and the linking of love with hate in 3.85, probably in an implicit allusion to Satan's preferring God's abhorrence to no attention at all. Yet the word *muḥabbat* is somehow more neutral in these verses than either *'ishq* or *shauq*.

Ghalib's use of *ulfat*, on the other hand, is distinctive, and does add some innovative dimensions to his depiction of love, particularly in the areas of complex imagery and witty logic.

Ulfat

Ghalib uses *ulfat* to denote love in a total of fifteen verses. Platts defines *ulfat* as 'familiarity, intimacy; attachment, affection, friendship' (1930: 76), though in Ghalib's idiom the word seems more parallel to the passive aspects of *'ishq*. Four occurrences of *ulfat* exist in association with words denoting imprisonment, or enthrallment by the beloved; the only previous instance of imprisonment was in 3.37, when the poet's alleged friends sought to restrain his desert-wandering. In one of these verses, Ghalib selects the garden for his setting, while giving the traditional associated imagery a somewhat unusual twist:

3.94 The demand for freedom from love for the rose is wrong
The cypress, in spite of its freedom, is imprisoned in the garden [95: 2]

The cypress is usually seen as inferior to the beloved in stature, just as the blush of the roses is pale in comparison with the beloved's cheek. Here Ghalib employs the rose as a symbol for the beloved, and links the cypress with the nightingale-poet in being immobilized by the beloved's awesome beauty.

Returning to the more direct image of the poet-lover imprisoned by the beloved, Ghalib engages in an ingenious, if ultimately effete, act of rationalization:

3.95 Asad, I am a prisoner of the result of love for the beautiful one
The collar on my neck has become a comforting arm [114: 9]

The main effect of this imagery is from the word *kham*, which means not only 'necklace', but 'noose' and 'curl' as well: the lover is imprisoned figuratively by love for the beloved, by the beauty of her tresses, and by the kindness of her cruelty; he considers his captivity a gift from her, as though his yoke were a decorative necklace.

Ghalib's imagery of imprisonment is more ironic in another verse:

3.96 The helplessness, the claim that we are in love's captivity
As though our hands are pinned by a stone, we are pledged to faithfulness [231: 7]

The poet, of course, agrees to being in the beloved's thrall. This image is so engaging that Faiz Ahmed Faiz named one of his collections of verse *Dast-e-tah-e-sang*, 'The hand under the stone' ([1964]). The charm of this couplet is in the implicit reference to the beloved's heart of stone, which like a literal stone, crushes our hands and prevents our escaping the imprisonment, voluntary though it may seem to be, of love.

In one more couplet Ghalib describes captivation by love, in this instance with absolute simplicity and directness:

3.97 I am imprisoned in love for the hunter
Otherwise I still have the strength for flight [72: 4]

The poet's *ṭāqat* (strength) is important for Ghalib, just as he is frequently concerned with the feebleness and debilitation brought by love. This couplet is in direct opposition to 3.14, in which Ghalib said that he had been a useful man until incapacitated by love; here Ghalib still claims the ability to fly—but it is to the beloved (personified in the hunter) and her even greater ability to enthrall, that the nightingale-poet yields. In presenting his power of flight (a central motif for Ghalib—see 3.66) as latent by choice, the poet praises all the more the beloved's captivating beauty.

Ghalib seems more sympathetic to the beloved in *ulfat*, with its essential connotations of friendly companionship, than in *'ishq* or *muḥabbat* (in *shauq*, as we saw, he is concerned primarily with his own state of being). In one couplet he says

3.98 On her delicate heart I take pity, Ghalib
Don't torture that infidel in a trial of your love [10: 2]

Again the idol becomes the infidel (see 3.83); she is not only not faithful to him, but she has shown him no sign whatever of any love. Yet Ghalib begs himself not to torture the beloved by making her subject him to a trial; because of her delicacy (see 2.13-14) she could never stand the strain of testing him, nor the effort of executing him. This couplet includes not only conventional praise for the beloved's exquisite delicacy, but a tribute to Ghalib's strength and endurance as well.

There is the grief of *ulfat* (*gham-e-ulfat*) for the poet just as there is *gham-e-'ishq* (another area of consonance with *'ishq* as opposed to *shauq*, which has no *gham* in Ghalib). In one rather unremarkable—though perfectly competent—couplet, Ghalib echoes the note struck earlier of the incurability of love's grief (see 3.16-17):

3.99 There has been created, they say, a remedy for every affliction
If this is so, why is there no cure for the grief of love
[120: 4]

In another *she'r*, Ghalib has a more original, more perplexing question of survival:

3.100 There is now in this crowded habitation a famine of love's grief
We yield to this—that we will remain in Delhi; but what will sustain us [20: 7]

There is here a play on the idioms *gham khana* (literally, 'to eat grief'), which means to suffer affliction, and *gham-khwārī karnā* (literally, 'to do the eating of grief'), which means both to suffer and commiserate. The implications here are that 1) there is no beloved in Delhi to cause lovers to suffer, and/or 2) there is no one in Delhi to commiserate with Ghalib, nor anyone with whom to commiserate. In other words, there are neither true lovers in Delhi, nor worthy beloveds. A third possible reading might be that there are so many lovers in Delhi that there are not enough beloveds to go around.

In *ulfat*, as in *'ishq*, the lover is pessimistic about his prospects:

3.101 I did not see the attainment of love, only the breaking of desire
Heart was joined to heart, like lips saying 'sorrow' [40: 3]

The conceit here is that in pronouncing 'sorrow' (*afsos* in Urdu), the two lips of the mouth are rounded, and quite separate. In another couplet relying on visual comparisons, Ghalib writes:

3.102 In the country of love, there is no account of tyranny like this
On whose title page is not a seal imprinted by the eye of the beloved [62: 5]

The beloved knows the effect of her wiles to be the torture of the lover—she sees it with her own eye, which is round like the author's seal on a book; in fact it is she who is the author (though the poet is the scribe) of the lover's tale of woe.

An even more abstruse conceit involves a play on the compound *rag-e-gardan* (vein or sinew of the neck), which has a figurative meaning of pride:

3.103 The danger is this—that the bond of love will not make me stiff-necked with pride
Pride at love is disastrous—don't become my enemy [196: 1]

As a dutiful lover, the poet offers his head to the beloved for sacrifice; but if he becomes proud, and she becomes an enemy of this pride, she will cut the bond of love, as represented in the proud stiffness of the poet's neck. This is another example, albeit more convoluted than usual, of Ghalib's sense of paradox.

The following couplet, which is something of a riddle, moves from purely visual imagery to causal and logical thought:

3.104 Fate wanted me to be 'ruined by the wine of love'
Only 'ruined' was written; enough—the pen could go no further [177: 2]

The answer to the riddle is that fate itself, upon encountering wine (since fate writes not just in words but in events as well), became drunk, and the pen became incapable of writing. The word *kharāb* (ruined), moreover, may be translated also as 'drunk', 'profligate', 'polluted', 'wasted', and so forth, in meanings which parallel many colloquial English expressions for intoxication. (For an extended discussion of Ghalib's calligraphic imagery see Schimmel 1979: 112-36.)

The above verses have included several rationalizations, made by Ghalib with consummate simplicity and irrefutable logic, of the lover's condition. Another is this advice to himself:

3.105 If my sweetheart loves not, let her not love—at least she is my sweetheart
Speak of the smoothness of her gait, the intoxication of her wiles [210: 9]

Ghalib also uses *ulfat* in describing a conspiracy to bring about the lover's madness:

3.106 Love wrote to the tresses a promise from the down on the cheeks
It is absolutely acceptable to us, whatever derangement there will be [193: 5]

There are three fine verbal plays in this couplet. The first is in the expression *yak qalam* (literally, 'one pen'), which is here translated as 'absolutely', but which has a clear association with the process of writing. The second plays upon the double meaning of *kh̲at* as both 'letter' and 'down on the cheek [of the beloved]'. The third is in the traditional association between *ẕulf* (tress) and *pareshānī* (dishevelment); though the apparent meaning of *pareshānī* in the verse is the dishevelment of the poet's heart and life (see 3.70), there is a clear innuendo of the dishevelment of the beloved's tresses (see 6.12 and 6.32), which the poet-lover desires, but will never attain (see 6.18).

Of all the couplets including *ulfat*, the most deeply felt is unquestionably from the elegiac ghazal on the death of Ghalib's beloved (see 3.39 and 3.91):

3.107 From the fear of disgrace, you went and were hidden in the veil of dust
With you, the cloaking of love's secrets is finished, alas! alas! [140: 7]

There is a rich and moving play on the concept of *parda* here. In the first line Ghalib uses a most elegant word—*naqāb*—for veil, in referring to the veil of dust, which is of course death. In the second line, Ghalib uses the term *parda-dārī* (curtaining) to describe his concealment of his love and of the beloved's identity. As in other couplets from this ghazal, the implication is not only that love is finished for Ghalib, but for all lovers as well, with the death of his peerless beloved.

A third important mood or tone (after debilitation and exultant energy) is evident in these couplets: one of wit, of playfulness with imagery, as though the process of 'friendship' is more focused on external concerns than on the greater self-absorption of the other three words for love. There is here the more conventional reference to the beloved's rose-like cheeks, cypress-like stature, and wave-like gait. The beloved appears again in the playful epithet of 'infidel', and the elaborate puns, figures of speech, and complex imagery are distinctly different in character from the other couplets discussed above; at the same time, there is an admirable directness and depth of feeling in the other *ulfat* couplets, particularly in the last, elegiac verse.

What emerges from this chapter's exhaustive survey of Ghalib's denotation of love is a sense of the eminently balanced and crafted effect of the *Dīvān*: no word or image appears in excess, no single aspect of technique, tone, imagery, diction, or mood dominates. These 107 occurrences of the four words for love demonstrate Ghalib's wit, energy, and imagination, as well as the depth, on occasion, of his feelings. The verses surveyed constitute roughly one-fourteenth of the 1468 couplets in the *Dīvān*; yet in only one verse does Ghalib use more than one of the words for love:

3.108 I am entirely pledged to love [*'ishq*], and unavoidably
(3.49) in love [*ulfat*] with life
I worship lightning, and mourn the ensuing loss of my
crops [12: 1]

For a genre whose basic expression is of love, the occurrence of a common word for love with such relative infrequency shows an admirable restraint on the part of the poet, particularly in light of the wide range of love-related relationships and perspectives he has been able to invoke. Yet these couplets by no means represent Ghalib's complete portrayal of love. To explore this portrayal further, through the perspectives of the participants (beloved, rival, and lover), we turn in the next chapter to Ghalib's presentation of the ghazal's central personae.

CHAPTER 4

The Personae of the Ghazal

Not all, only a few, have appeared as tulips and roses
What faces, what figures there must be, hidden in the dust
GHALIB [112: 1]

The spatial restrictions of the individual couplet necessarily limit the number of characters that may be introduced meaningfully into ghazal poetry; yet the presence of a considerable variety of characters should already be evident in the verses discussed above. 'Masters of eloquence' are invoked in chapter 1, along with God, children, and Ghalib as co-worker, fellow drinker, and confidant. Chapter 2 introduces the lover, beloved, healer, friend, advisor, consoler, mystic, and drunkard. Additional figures encountered in Chapter 3 include the rival, messenger, enemy, victim, patients, master, infidel, well-wisher, cupbearer, buyer, seller, prisoner, hunter, and progenitor; martyrs, and the people of love, lust, and affliction; Love and Fate; and Khusrau, Farhad, Hamza, Christ, and Majnun.

A perusal of Ghalib's full *Dīvān* provides an even broader range of actors: doorkeeper, watchman, litter-bearer, mirror-holder, heartholder, and pensioner (among servants); poet, juggler, fireworks master, singer, and minstrel (among entertainers); thief, highwayman, fugitive, murderer, plaintiff, defendant, witness, court official, and executioner (from the world of crime and punishment); laborer, farmer, gardener, flower-seller, rose-gatherer, fowler, pearl-merchant, pharmacist, guide, and boatman (from the various trades); beggar, mendicant, dervish, preacher, teacher, *shaikh*, fairy, *ḥourī* (celestial maiden), and angel (as religious and heavenly beings); and Muslim, Brahmin, Zoroastrian, and Christian (from among the religious communities). Other figures, more vaguely defined, appear as well: complainant, admonisher, novice, corpse, opium eater, toper, profligate, envious one, cruel one, playful one, and so forth—usually as some manifestation of one of the central characters (beloved, lover, or rival) to whom this chapter is devoted.

Among actual individuals referred to in the *Dīvān*, we find the poets Mir, Nasikh, Zuhuri, Vahshat, Shaifta, and Ghalib (as Ghalib, Asad, and Mirza), as well as Ghalib's relatives and friends: Arif, Nayyar, Ali Bahadur, Mirza Yusuf, Tajammual Husain Khan, and the Emperor, Bahadur Shah Zafar. Finally, Ghalib invokers the traditional Islamic figures of Khizr, Gabriel, Jacob, Joseph, Zuleikha, Solomon, Mary, Ali, and Mansur al-Hallaj, along with the legendary or historical Laila, Shirin, Alexander, Jamshed, Faridun, Kaikhusrau, Darab, Bahman, Mani, and Barbad.

Yet however many such figures may appear in ghazal poetry (*sab kahāṅ, kuch . . . numāyāṅ ho ga'īṅ* . . . 'not all, only a few, became manifeṣt . . .'), the eternal triangle—that triad of beloved, lover, and rival—remains the central preoccupation of the ghazal, and represents the primary configuration of characters as they illustrate some aspect of love, or of the poet's quest for his goal.

Once again, the concern of the ghazal is not so much the characters themselves as the relationships between them. The previous chapter examined the network of associations among the words in the *Dīvān* which specifically denote love; the pages which follow will explore the connotations of the words representing the central characters of the ghazal: the beloved (as denoted by the word *yār*, literally, 'frieṇd'), the rival (indicated by *g͟hair* or *raqīb*), and the lover (*'āshiq*).

The Beloved

Ghalib uses several nouns, defined as follows, to denote the beloved (all references, indicated in parentheses, are to Platts 1930):

ma'shūq: 'a beloved object; beloved, love, sweetheart, mistress' (1048).

dost: 'a friend, one beloved; a lover, a sweetheart' (534).

yār: 'a friend; a lover; paramour, gallant; mistress;—companion, comrade' (1247).

k͟hūbān: 'the fair, the beautiful; (as a sing.) sweetheart, ladylove' (495).

but: 'idol, image, statue; a beloved object, mistress (= *māshūq* [*sic*])' (131).

ṣanam: 'an idol, image (syn. *but*);—a mistress, lover, sweetheart' (746).

kāfir: 'infidel, impious, ungrateful;—one denying god, an infidel, an impous wretch;—a Caffre (*met.*) a mistress, sweetheart' (801).

qātil: 'a homicide, murderer, an assassin; an executioner' (786).

While the latter connotes the action of the beloved (in that the lover desires to die, both figuratively and literally, at the beloved's hand), other words describing the beloved's attributes are used as well by Ghalib, often in direct address:

g͟hāfil: heedless one, neglectful one.

sitam-gar: tyrant, oppressor.

shok͟h: 'playful, mischievous; petulant, saucy, bold, daring, hardened, strong; insolent, presumptuous; brazen, wanton, impudent, shameless' (736).

sang-dil: stone-hearted one.

dil-bar: 'heart-ravishing, captivating, attractive, charming, lovely, beloved;—heart ravisher, a lovely person, a sweetheart' (522).

dil-dār: 'possessing or winning the heart, delighting the heart, charming;—having heart, encouraged;—a lover, mistress, sweetheart (syn. *dil-bar*)' (523).

jān: 'the breath of life, vitality; life, spirit, soul, mind; self; animation, vigour, energy, force, stamina; the best part, the essence (of a thing); that which imparts life, or beauty, etc. (to a thing), ornament, grace, beauty; a sweetheart, darling' (372).

Of all the words denoting the beloved, the one occurring most commonly in the *Dīvān* is *yār*, which occurs a total of thirty-eight times (including twice in the plural *yārān*, and at least once in the non-erotic sense of 'companion'); *but* occurs twenty-four times (including seven plurals—*butān*—and two compounds, once each with *k͟hāna* and *kada*, both of which mean 'house'); *ṣanam* three times (including one each in the plural *aṣnām* and in compound with *kada*); *kāfir* seven times for the beloved (as well as four times for the lover and once for the heart); *dost* ten times in the sense of 'beloved'; *k͟hūbān* six times (once ambiguously); *jān* thrice (including twice in the plural *jānān*); *ma'shūq* and *dil-dār* twice; and *dil-bar* once.

While it would ultimately be of some use to make a thorough analysis of all these occurrences, such an effort would expand this chapter to unmanageable proportions. In the interests of economy, therefore, I have limited consideration to *yār*, which is clearly Ghalib's dominant denotation of the beloved, and which includes in its range of associations most of the connotations of the other terms as well.

The Beloved as Yār

In the first *she'r* to be considered, Ghalib acknowledges that the beloved is essential to the lover's existence:

4.1 For one's own disgrace, what efforts can avail
A beloved alone is needed as an agent of chaos [190: 7]

At the same time as admitting the indispensability of the beloved, Ghalib shows to her personality a distinct indifference that goes far beyond the discretion of traditional ghazal etiquette. In poetry describing an actual beloved, the poet would disguise her distinguishing features in order to avoid disgracing her. But here, Ghalib betrays his self interest: he desires his own disgrace and consequent notoriety, and he realizes with some reluctance that without a beloved he cannot exist as a poet-lover. Yet the tone of this couplet is not one of complaint; rather, it accepts a reality, and exults in the exhilaration of the *hangāma* (chaos and tumult) wrought in his own life by love.

The Visual Effect of the Beloved

In six couplets, Ghalib combines rather conventional evocations of the sight of the beloved with a description of the energizing effect that this vision has on the lover (see especially 3.62-7 for earlier statements of the connection between sight and love). These couplets are most significant, given the tradition that love beings.with the first stunning glimpse of the beloved's beauty.[1] Of the traditional height and stature of the beloved (see 3.94), Ghalib observes:

4.2 Until I had seen the elegant sight of the beloved's stature
I did not believe in the torment of Judgement Day [39: 4]

As in the previous verse, Ghalib refers, here obliquely, to the galvanic power of love. Ghalib's pleasure in suffering is clear in the voluntary nature of his resulting torment; at the same time, he makes an implicit play on words by associating height (*qāmat*) indirectly with Judgement Day (*qiyāmat*), for as noted by Mehr, the beloved's heart-ravishing stature is identified metaphorically as the torment of the day of judgement (n.d.: 147).

In another couplet emphasizing the visual effect of the beloved on the lover, Ghalib first employs a somewhat unusual static image (in the *eẓāfa* compound 'style-of-the-print-of-the-foot'), then delivers a subtly kinetic image (again in *eẓāfa*, 'wave-of-the-gait-of-the-beloved') in the second line:

4.3 Just see the enchantment of the style of her footprints
The undulation of the beloved's walk, too—what a riot it started [159: 5]

Ghalib describes his beloved's beauty of face in similar fashion:

4.4 Seeing the rose's cheek, I remember the beloved's face
The fervor of springtime sharpens the desire of longing [201: 3]

4.5 Why wasn't I consumed seeing the radiance of the beloved's cheek
Rather, I burn with envy, seeing the power of my faculty of sight [61: 1]

In the first example, Ghalib employs a conventional comparison of the beloved's face to the rose, heightened by the fact that the face is recalled and not seen, and by the sense of spring roses in a riot (*joshish*, or 'ebullition; heart; fervour; emotion; violent desire' [Platts 1930: 397]) which only increases the poet's inconsolable longing. In the second verse, Ghalib makes a comparable connection between the visual radiance of the beloved's face and the heat in the lover's heart, but he also provides an unexpected turn which removes the beloved even further than mere temporal or spatial separation: the poet's heart burns not with love, nor with the conventional envy of the rival (see 4.42-4), but rather with envy for his own power of sight (see 6.7). As is so often the case for Ghalib, the power of envy transcends that of love.

Elsewhere Ghalib uses not fire, but another elemental image to describe the effect of seeing the beloved. He begins with the conventional scene of the beloved inquiring with feigned concern (when she knows full well that *she* is the cause of the lover's disturbance) after his well-being:

4.6 When my beloved asked me, 'How have the senses left you?'
Seeing my delirium, the wind began to blow, like this
[117: 7]

The lover is so overcome with the sight of his tormentor that he enters a state of *bekhudī* (selflessness, total distraction), while the wind, caught up in the unleashed force of this rapture, proceeds to join the rush of uncontrollable excitement. There is a striking contrast between the two lines, from the neutral potentiality of the first to the surging motion of the second, concluding with the climactic use of *havā* (wind) as the *qāfiya*.

When the beloved resorts to one of her ultimate weapons—a glance, Ghalib resiliently springs into a posture of great assertiveness:

4.7 I have become, for the scimitar of my beloved's glance, a whetstone
May I be congratulated! How auspicious is this difficult life for me [203: 2]

Ghalib's ability to bear all the beloved's attacks serves only to increase her skill in tormenting him—a torture which proves his mettle at the same time as giving her pleasure. In this verse there is an adroit word-play between *girān-jānī,* which means both 'difficult' and 'heavy', and the reference to the sharpening stone.

The Beloved's Eyelashes

The glance of the beloved, seen as a weapon, is sometimes symbolized in her eyelashes which resemble arrows in their length and sharpness. As was evident in the previous chapters (see 2.14, 3.21, and 3.67), Ghalib has a predilection for imagery created around eyelashes, and among the *yār* couplets there are four more such examples.

In the first, Ghalib describes one of his poet-lover's typical states—a debilitation from love in which he is not equal to the challenge of the beloved's total arsenal:

4.8 In the heart there is confrontation with the ranks of the beloved's eyelashes
Though there is not the strength to bear the pricking of even a single thorn [113: 8]

The thorn, always a component of the image of the beloved as a rose (and also the scourge of the desert-wandering poet's blistered feet), is clearly inferior to the magnificent sharpness of the beloved's arrowlike lashes, which like her glances, are launched from the exquisitely curved bows of her eyebrow. In the second *she'r* Ghalib is independent enough to attempt throughout his life to escape her glances, though ultimately he is vanquished by another, unexpected force: predestination.

4.9 The heart fled the beloved's eyelashes up to the moment of death
It has thought the warding off of fate's arrow would be so easy [35: 7]

Elsewhere, Ghalib employs an image reminiscent of his description (3.59) of the transactions of love (*kārobāṛ-e-shauq*):

4.10 I had to give a full accounting of every drop
My heart's blood was a trust from the eyelashes of the beloved [17: 1]

The blood is that flowing from the heart wounded by love's arrows. In another instance, still maintaining his independence, Ghalib says with distinctively self-assertive wit:

4.11 So what the hell if the beloved's eyelashes are thirsty for blood
I should keep some for my own blood-shedding lashes too [235: 2]

The Thought of the Beloved

For Ghalib—cerebral poet that he is—not only the sight of the beloved enthralls his heart, but her imagined image captivates his attention as well:

4.12 Still, a reflection of the idea of the beloved remains
The dejected heart is like the cell of Joseph's prison [10: 9]

4.13 Take care with me, O hopelessness—what a disaster this is
That the skirt of the idea of the beloved is slipping from my hands [206: 5]

Both of these images are highly visual—the first incisive but static, the second more elusive and in motion—and both are quite unusual. Joseph's dark cell is one of the less frequently used stock images of the ghazal (see 6.28), and Ghalib's likening it to the lover's dark heart (which contains the image of the beloved, brilliant like Joseph) is novel, as is his clothing the idea of the beloved in a garment, when the word *dāman* (skirt or hem) is usually associated with the lover's own long shirt, whose border is conventionally soaked with his tears. The implication is that if the mere reflection of the idea of the beloved is a beautiful as the peerless Joseph, how much more ravishing her actual beauty must be.

The Beloved's Other Attributes

Four couplets remain in which the *yār* is evoked in conjunction with some description of her traditional characteristics, and in each case Ghalib achieves some reversal of conventional expectations. In a description of the fragrance of the beloved's tresses, Ghalib creates a subtle and ingenious exaggeration:

4.14 In that place where the wind combs the locks of the beloved
The brain of the deer of Tartary's desert is like a bag of musk [229: 1]

An appreciation of this imagery depends upon the knowledge that musk is said to be extracted from the navel of the Tartary deer; the beloved's locks are so fragrant that their scent, wafted on the wind to the nostrils of the deer of Tartary, collects in the creature's brain with a concentration of fragrance—even after such a distance—that is equal to that of the deer's navel itself (the word *dimāgh*, translated here as 'brain', has secondary meaning in Persian of 'palate' and 'nose', as well as 'intoxication' and 'desire'—see 6.32—so that this verse is particularly rich in sensuous reverberations).

The beloved's extreme and deliberate cruelty (another traditional attribute) is evoked in a Ghalibian reversal of expectations:

4.15 Ah, alas! that the beloved drew her hand back from torture
When she saw me greedy for the pleasure of pain [61: 6]

Once again (see 2.14 and 3.18-19) Ghalib longs for the delicious pain that the beloved can inflict directly on him, and is ready to bear any amount; but here he is devastated when she refuses, with exquisite malice, to bestow any pain whatsoever.[2] the beloved's disposition (*k͟hū-e-yār*) is elsewhere responsible for the poet's relegation to a veritable hell of torment:

4.16 In this burning, the flames resemble the beloved's disposition
I would be an infidel, if I did not find satisfaction in punishment [98: 1]

This reversal plays upon the idea of the poet's fidelity to his beloved rendering him an infidel to the god of conventional religion (see 5.10)—hence his banishment to hell; there is also a hint of the infidel as fire-worshipper (*ātish-parast*), and an additional resonance created by the fact that the poet often refers to his beloved as an infidel (see 3.83 and 3.98).

Finally, Ghalib achieves a pleasing alteration of the traditional imagery of lip and tooth (*lab-o-dandān*), usually associated with the beloved's matchless beauty, in the following *she'r*:

4.17 The longing-smitten heart was the tablecloth for the savor of pain
Friends have taken whatever they could, according to the discrimination of their lips and teeth [6: 4]

The implication is that the friends' (or beloved's; *yārān* is in this context ambiguous) lips and teeth—in other words, their power of 'taste' as well as articulation—will be the only limitation in their capacity to feast on the poet's suffering, through the excellence of their ability to recite and savor his verses in their full flavor.

Union and Separation

Up to this point there has been no explicit discussion of the two primary states of being for the poet-lover—states which are the elemental concern of his existence: union (*vaṣl, viṣāl*) with the beloved, and separation (*firāq, furqat,* and *ḥijr*) from her. Clearly, on the basis of the couplets already discussed, the lover invariably finds himself in a state of separation, while he aspires desperately to attain union. In five of the couplets including the word *yār,* Ghalib refers explicitly to one of these two conditions, and implicitly suggests union in two other verses.

In the two couplets speaking of separation from the beloved (*firāq-e-yār* in the first, and *ḥijr-e-yār* in the second), Ghalib describes the intolerability of the state in which he finds himself:

4.18 I am not mad, Ghalib, but in His Majesty's words
'If there is to be peace in separation from the beloved, how can it be?' [126: 10]

4.19 What can I say about the heart's condition in separation from the beloved, Ghalib
That from restlessness, every thread in my bedding has become a thorn [195: 6]

Each of the above couplets concludes its respective ghazal, as shown by the poet's use of his *ta͟kh͟halluṣ* (pen name), and thus strives for a certain decisive impact as a means of closure. In the first, Ghalib quotes a line from Bahadur Shah 'Zafar' (Mehr n.d.: 436), in what we may assume is a gesture of respect to the Emperor; it is also probable that this ghazal was recited at a *mushā'ira* at which the emperor was present, so that this *maqṭa*' (concluding verse of the ghazal) constitutes an ingenious and most appropriate return of the poetic candle to the *maḥfil's* host, who may well have been Zafar himself.

The second couplet relies for it impact upon the rhyming of *k͟hār* (thorn) with *tār* (thread) in the phrase which conclude the ghazal, *har ek tār-e-bistar k͟hār-e-bistar hai* ('every thread of the bed is a thorn in the bed'). The effect here is dependent upon the unusual *radīf, -e-bistar* (of the bed), to which may be attached only a limited number of appropriate words ending in the *qāfiya -ār*; by the end of the ghazal, Ghalib has no doubt cast far and wide to find rhyming words which may be associated with *bed,* and the *tour de force* of including two in a single line is certain to have pleased the audience. It is impossible to duplicate such an effect in English, but the admittedly lame translation

4.19a Restlessness makes every thread's line in the bed a thorn's spine in the bed

begins to convey Ghalib's rhyming portrayal of the lover's torture as he lies pining (no pun intended here) on his bed. The lover's pain in separation, finally, is underscored by the use in both verses of rhetorical questions whose answers everyone in the audience knows: in 4.18, the answer is that there is no possible way to find peace in separation, while in 4.19, the obvious response is that any attempt, no matter how ingenious, to describe separation must fail to capture fully the lover's excruciating agony.

Three additional couplets associate *yār* directly with some word for union; a fourth links the beloved with the word for guest (*mehmān*); and a fifth portrays the lover in the extraordinarily rare posture of being at the beloved's pillow. It is significant that in his evocation of the much-desired state of union (or its explicit absence), Ghalib employs a witty conditional statement in the second line of each of the first two couplets, and describes some aspect of fire—the source of many of his distinctively kinetic images—in the second lines of the next three verses.

The *maṯla*ʻ (beginning couplet) of one of Ghalib's most beloved ghazals has already been analyzed (see 2.11); it uses the phrase *viṣāl-e-yār* (union with the beloved):

4.20 This was not our fate—that there be union with the
(2.11) beloved
If we had lived longer, there would have been this same waiting [21: 1]

The *maqṯa*ʻ (concluding couplet) from another of Ghalib's famous ghazals employs the term *vaṣl* for union:

4.21 Let the beloved's provocations continue, Asad
If there isn't union, at least there is longing [149: 10]

Ghalib, while preferring the actual experience of union, is still capable of savoring the pain and torture of separation in the experience of *ḥasrat* (longing).

The association of fire imagery with union is typical of Ghalib in his representation of love as an elemental force (see 3.46-50 and 3.70-6):

4.22 In the heart, the passion for union and the memory of the beloved did not remain
Fire, in this abode, has so struck, that what there was, burned [5: 2]

4.23 It's been a long time since making the beloved a guest
Since, from the cup's boiling passion, making the assembly a rack of lamps [234: 1]

4.24 It burns, seeing me on the pillow of the beloved
Why shouldn't this scar be on my heart—of the suspicion of the candle [76: 7]

Each of these verses has a particular density of highly evocative words. The first consists of a typically Ghalibian description of the destructive effect of love's fire (see 3.72) in the heart (*ghar*, literally, 'house', which as we shall see in the next chapter, is a favorite setting for Ghalib). The second is a brilliantly visual and kinaesthetic reminiscence of some past assembly of the beloved, following a first line which is equally simple and poignant—and utterly non-visual; the word *cirāg̲h̲ān* ('lamps; lights; a display of lamps, a general illumination' [Platts 1930: 428]) is one which Ghalib has made distinctively his own, and which appears here in a double poetic aetiology in which both the cups, and the literal and metaphoric (the cups become a *cirāg̲h̲ān*) rack of lamps, reflect the turbulence of the lover's heart (see Chapter 6 for a discussion of this entire ghazal). The third verse betrays Ghalib's preoccupation with rivalry (see 4.5 and the central portion of this chapter) in his extension of the connotations of envy (in the verb *jalnā*—'to burn') to the candle, which is usually a sympathetic and illuminating companion to the beloved and the lover during their rare moments of union (if they occur at all); there is also here a faint tone of betrayal, since the candle is sometimes seen as a symbol of the poet (see 3.70 and 6.24), with the tongue of flame linked to the poet's own power of speech.

In two additional couplets Ghalib discusses the lover's capacity for envy:

4.25 Asad died from the joy of the beloved's message
I envied the messenger the questions and answers [153: 7]

4.26 Put aside any discussion of capacity for hating the rivals
Here, in the heart, from weakness, there's not even lust for the beloved [113: 6]

The first is the only example in the *Dīvān* of an explicit linkage of the words *yār* and *qāṣid* (messenger), and the second is the only instance of a joint occurrence of the words *yār* and 'rival' (in this case the plural *aghyār*, from *ghair*). The probable explanation for the rarity of such explicit combinations is that Ghalib's poetic skill permits him to exploit the associative possibilities of any single actor in the personae of the ghazal, so as to invoke a second figure by implication and connotation, thereby rendering a second denotation not only heavy-handed, but redundant as well. In light of this explanation, it is not surprising that both of these verses are quite conventional, without any particularly distinguishing features.

The Beloved's Abode

As we shall see in the next chapter, Ghalib's poetic vision has a very strong sense of physical location. In seven couplets *yār* occurs in *eẓāfa* compound with words indicating some place associated with the beloved: *dīvār* (wall), *āstān* (doorstep), *dar* (door), *kū* (lane) and *rāh* (path); two other verses refer to the abode of the lover. As might be expected (on the basis of the couplets surveyed thus far), Ghalib accentuates his own presence, rather than that of the beloved, in these places.

In one case, Ghalib succeeds both in glorifying the beloved and in calling attention to his own status as well:

4.27 He who sits in the shadow of the beloved's wall
Is the sovereign emperor of Hindustan [139: 6]

In comparison to the glory of the beloved, all of Hindustan is but a shaded area along her wall. But the lover (and, we assume, Ghalib) is thinking of himself as the master of that ground, and hence no less than the Emperor.

Ghalib's reluctance to leave his post is evident:

4.28 Though a wave of blood should engulf my head
I cannot leave the doorstep of the beloved [47: 5]

In 3.3, Ghalib, though distracted in love to the point of dashing out his brains, is still too proud to use the beloved's door-step as an instrument of his self-destruction. Here, in a different posture, the poet is committed to his fate, and even if he is in danger of being drowned in waves of blood (from his own tears, or his own slaughter, or the slaughter of other lovers), he will not be deterred from his devotion.

Ghalib, ultimately, expects little to result from his attendance upon the beloved—such is the convention of the ghazal. In the following *she'r*, he begins with a rather pedestrian complaint to the beloved's doorkeeper (another stock character in the ghazal), who has persisted in ignoring his entreaties, and ends with an unexpected comparison:

4.29 After a life of abstinence, he would have admitted me at last
Would that the gatekeeper of Paradise were himself the beloved's doorman [32: 3]

The reference is to Rizvan (which as a noun means Paradise itself), the guardian angel at the heavenly entrance, and the equivalent of St. Peter at the Pearly Gates. Rizvan would certainly recognize Ghalib's observance of his obligations throughout his life and would admit him without question, whereas the beloved's gatekeeper is more selective and cruel, like the beloved herself. The implicit comparison of the beloved to God is here twofold: first, in the connotation of the word *vara'* (here translated as 'abstinence') suggesting fear of God; and second, in the implication that to be in the presence of the beloved would be a greater joy than to enter Paradise, i.e. the presence of God Himself.

The three verses set in the *kū-e-yār* (the lane of the beloved —a powerfully evocative setting for Ghalib) will be discussed in detail in Chapter 5. It will suffice for the moment to note Ghalib's typical preoccupation with kinetic or paradoxical imagery:

4.30 My dust floats about the lane of the beloved
At last, O wind, the lust for wings and feathers is gone
[59: 4]

4.31 In the beloved's lane, I couldn't remember the code of living
The astonishment of the footprint became a mirror-holder and showed me, like this [117: 8]

4.32 Again, in distraction, I forgot the way to the beloved's lane
Otherwise I would have gone one day to search for myself [100: 8]

In a fourth verse, referring not to the beloved's lane, but simply to her path (*rāh*), a faintly kinetic sense of the beloved passing in a scattering of dust is overshadowed by the poet's own boast of his capacity for, and fondness of, suffering:

4.33 The dust of the beloved's path is a source of pride for the heart's wound
Otherwise, where in the world would enough salt be created [78: 2]

There is no apparent justification in the first line for associating dust with a wounded heart's pride, though the lover's heart might be proud of his beloved for the awesome spectacle of the dust raised by her passing. Only in the second line does Ghalib explain his juxtaposition: dust resembles salt, which poured on a wound increases pain (see 3.21), and as Ghalib frequently makes clear, he is usually equal to any degree of torture that the beloved can devise, and the more the better. The exaggeration here in the quantities of dust and salt, combined with the question, 'where in the world?', is reminiscent of the earlier couplet (4.27) comparing the shaded area near the beloved's wall with all of Hindustan.

The Beloved and the Lover's Abode

While Ghalib appropriately associates the beloved with her own haunts, in only two verses does he link his own abode directly with his *yār*:

4.34 It's not a shadow—for upon hearing the glad tidings of the beloved's coming
A few steps forward moved my door and wall [59: 3]

4.35 With what face to you complain of being abroad, Ghalib
Don't you remember the unkindness of the beloveds of the
motherland [102: 10]

In the first, the beloved has sent the extraordinary news that she is coming to visit Ghalib—probably, as convention would have it, because Ghalib is dying (see 4.36, and 4.94-95). The significant word her is *sāya* (shadow), which also has connotations of 'apparition' or 'spectre'. Read alone, the first line might seem to imply that the beloved's coming is no apparition—it will be real! In the second line Ghalib clarifies his meaning: not their shadow, but the door and wall themselves advanced in anticipation and welcome of the beloved; thus *sāya* in this context may mean both 'apparition' and 'shadow'. Not only is Ghalib's visual ingenuity at work here, but he is again (see 4.27) playing upon the traditional associations of the shadow where the lover stays within the shade of the beloved's wall.

In the second couplet above, the general reference, taken out of the actual context of Ghalib's life, is to the lover's *ghurbat* (exile), which has resulted from his wandering in madness, or from the disgrace of having his love revealed, or from a destitution which has forced him to go elsewhere in search of sustenance. But in fact this ghazal was recited in Banda, when Ghalib was on his way to Calcutta in pursuit of his pension (Mehr n.d.: 103), and thus the intended meaning of the couplet is clear: *yārān* means 'friends' (though it could also be taken to mean 'beloveds' in the sense of individuals from whom Ghalib sought patronage), and Ghalib is complaining that no one in his own land—i.e. Delhi—appreciated him properly, so that there is no reason for him to feel homesick.

The Friends of the Poet

In the four remaining *yār* couplets (as in the previous verse), the primary connotation of the word seems to be 'friend' or 'companion'. In the first, the poet-lover's comrades have failed him:

4.36 The eyes, in spite of trying to stay open, are closed
Friends brought her to my pillow, but at what time [53: 1]

Whereas the beloved's pillow is the ultimate destination of the lover's quest (see 4.24), the beloved herself does not visit *his* pillow until the time of his impending death, when she is brought by his friends, perhaps out of mere curiosity or vengeful cruelty, to see him dying—or perhaps out of genuine grief when she realizes the true nature of his love. In any case, the beloved's motives hardly matter; for Ghalib, it is too late.

Speculating about the reaction of his friends (and perhaps of his beloveds) after his death, Ghalib asks:

4.37 What, after telling my story, will my friends cry
Except for this raving tale of mine [184: 3]

There is an ambiguity in the first line, for Ghalib may be asking either what his friends will cry, or simply whether they will cry. The answer, given in the second line, is that his friends will indeed be weeping, and will repeat his verses, the distracted narrative of his life. (The word-play between *bayān*—'narration'—in the first line and *āshafta-bayānī*—'distracted/lovelorn narration/speech'—in the second is only hinted at in the translation.)

The final *yār* couplet is also the last couplet of the final ghazal in the *Dīvān*:

4.38 With especially elegant performance, Ghalib has become a singer of subtleties
The challenge is open to discriminating friends [235: 14]

Ghalib concludes his ghazals with this invitation to other poets to follow his example, in which there is no lack of elegant subtleties. This couplet itself involves a rich ambiguity of meanings that is appropriate in a conclusion to the *Dīvān*; to begin to perceive these meanings it is necessary to reproduce the original couplet, then discuss the various possible interpretations of the individual words:

4.38 adā-e-k͟hāṣ se G͟hālib hai nukta-sarā
ṣalā-e-'ām hai yārān-e-nukta-dān ke liye [235: 14]

The first word, *adā*, has connotations of 'grace, beauty, elegance; . . . charm, fascination; . . . amorous signs and gestures, coquetry' that are usually associated with the beloved, as well as of 'completion, perfection; performance, fulfillment; accomplishment' (Platts 1930: 32). The second word, *k͟hāṣ*, means 'distinguished (from others): . . . special, distinct; private; kept for private use (of a king or master), personal, own, properly;—choice, select, choicest, best; pure, unmixed, unadulterated; excellent, noble' (Platts 1930: 484). *Nukta*, used in both lines, means 'a point (of wit); a quaint saying; a pithy sentence;—a subtle or quaint conceit; a nice or metaphysical distinction; a mythical signification' (Platts 1930: 1147), while the suffix *sarā* means 'singing or trilling' (Platts 1930: 650), so that a *nukta-sarā* is one who sings all these things—in other words, a poet.

The word *ṣalā* (see 3.52), which begins the second line, means 'calling or inviting (beggars, etc.), to receive or partake of food; invitation; annunciation; proclamation; voice, call, cry (of an auctioneer, or salesman, etc.); shout, challenge (of a foe)' (Platts 1930: 745), and is modified by the adjective *'ām*, or 'common, general, universal; public; vulgar, popular, plebeian; ordinary' (Platts 1930: 758). *Nukta-dān*, finally, means 'understanding subtleties of mystical meanings, sagacious, discerning, nice, of penetrating intellect' (Platts 1930: 1147).

The parallels and contrasts within the couplet should be readily apparent: the 'special' (with all its connotations of excellence) performance of Ghalib is contrasted by its position at the beginning of the first line with the 'ordinary' invitation or challenge at the beginning of the second; again, by position, Ghalib is juxtaposed with the *yārān* (friends, beloveds) who are *nukta-dān* (discerning) of his *nukta-sarā* (singing of subtleties). Ghalib is a poet-lover of distinction who nevertheless has some of the attractive qualities (*adā*) of the beloved, and his invitation (to beggars? no—actually it is to discriminating friends) or challenge to savor his *khāṣ* singing is *'am* (universal—to everyone, beggars, friends, and beloveds of taste alike). He is both praising his audience, friends, and beloveds, and challenging them, with a faint tincture of ridicule (from the words *'ām* and *ṣalā*, in contrast to the complimentary tone of *nukta-dān*), while at the same time succeeding in making clear his not inconsiderable opinion of himself and his poetry.

These *yār* couplets, in short, provide not only a sometimes compelling picture of the beloved and her capacity to enthrall the poet-lover, but an opportunity for Ghalib, using the beloved primarily as a point of departure as well as a catalyst, to assert himself, and to explore the effects that the beloved, and his love for her, have on his mind and heart. The states in which he portrays himself are almost as numerous as the couplets themselves: envy, delirium, pride, combativeness, debilitation, ignorance, flight, selfishness, hopelessness, eagerness for punishment, restlessness, impatience, rationalization, longing, passion, nostalgia, recollection, forgetfulness, death, lust, exhilaration, courage, dedication, persuasiveness, satisfaction, learning, searching, complaint, and dementia. Since all these states involve a relationship with the beloved—and by extension, with any desired object or goal—the possibilities of their serving the personal interpretations of individual listeners or readers are enormous, and hardly repetitive. Yet all these conditions and relationships follow the conventions of the ghazal, so that they may be understood easily, in all their complexity, on the basis of those conventions.

The Rival

After the beloved (and apart from the central figure of the poet-lover himself), the rival is the most important character in the stock personae of the ghazal, and appears specifically denoted as *g̲hair* or *raqīb* in fifty-one verses in the *Dīvān.* The rival, as mentioned previously, appears in a triangular configuration with the lover and beloved, and serves as a foil to the lover and a touchstone for the perfection of the latter's necessarily superior (because more genuine and profound) love. The cruel beloved invariably showers her affections and attention on the rival and neglects the true lover, whose capacity to suffer this neglect is the measure of his devotion to the beloved. As in the case of the beloved, the rival may be represented both on the plane of earthly love, and on the level of mystical love, in a variety of guises (see Chapter 2 for a list of triadic variations as suggested by Narang).

Ideally—or so it would seem—the lover's attitude toward the rival should be one, if not of magnanimity, at least of noble patience and understanding. He realizes that anyone who may encounter the beloved is a potential rival, for the beloved's beauty is such that no one can resist it. In two famous verses, Ghalib assumes such a posture, realizing in the first couplet (*maṭla*ʿ) of one of the ghazals that the messenger through whom he communicates is particularly susceptible:

4.39 If he gave her his heart, he's human—what's to be said
If he became a rival, let it be—he's a messenger, what's to be said [202: 1]

Here Ghalib seems sympathetic to the condition of the messenger, even though the latter has now become his rival. In the *maṭla'* of a second famous ghazal, Ghalib's discovery of his own role in creating yet another rival comes to him as something of a surprise:

4.40 The mention of that fairy-faced one—and then, too, my description
He became my rival, finally, who had been my confidant [44: 1]

The conversion of confidant to rival is by no means novel in the ghazal, but in this verse Ghalib makes it clear (with typical, though understated, self-congratulation) that it was the power of his description that captivated the confidant, and not the actual beauty of the beloved.

While the ideal stance of the poet-lover toward the rival might be expected to be inherently sympathetic (after all, he too is suffering), the usual posture adopted in rivalry is one of suspicion, envy, enmity, quarrelsomeness, and complaint, and in this Ghalib is no exception. For him the rival, once a rival, cannot presume to occupy the position of confidant:

4.41 The rival asks thus after my health, in separation from her
Intimately, as though he were a friend, a sympathetic friend [54: 6]

There is no naiveté in Ghalib's indignations, for the chances are overwhelming that the rival is merely shamming sympathetic behavior, while in fact harboring only ungenerous motives in his heart.

Envy for the Rival

In another couplet from the same ghazal, and in four additional couplets, Ghalib explicitly associates the rival with states of envy and enmity:

4.42 In love, it was the ruthlessness of envy for the rival that
(3.8) struck me down
I am finally the victim of my enemy, though I was stricken
for my friend [54: 4]

In this case *dost* (friend) clearly refers to the beloved, and Ghalib realizes with characteristic acumen the debilitating effect of envy on his love. In another verse, the rival himself falls victim to excessive jealousy, as Ghalib describes with obvious relish:

4.43 Enmity for me lost all for the rival
The extent to which he is an enemy should be seen
[190: 6]

The rival, having become obsessed more with envy than with adoration of the beloved, loses her favor. Ghalib comments elsewhere on the dangers of blind envy:

4.44 Envy says: the rival has her affection, alas
Wisdom says: whose friend will that unkind one be [43: 1]

The poet knows that the beloved will never be kind to a true lover; hence, her apparent affection for the rival is only counterfeit, and temporary at that, for the beloved must ultimately be cruel to everyone (as demonstrated by the wave of blood, from other slaughtered lovers, that threatens to engulf Ghalib in 4.28). At times, even for Ghalib, the cruelty of the beloved is beyond tolerance:

4.45 Put aside any discussion of capacity for hating the rivals
(4.26) Here, in the heart, there's not even lust for the beloved
[113: 6]

But at his wisest, Ghalib has enough self-respect to maintain the dignity and dedication of his love:

4.46 Do you think I am my own enemy
(3.88) I'll grant you—though I don't believe it—that the rival
truly loves you [149: 4]

Ghalib knows that however authentic the rival's love may seem to be, he would certainly bring about his own downfall by succumbing to envy for the rival. Better that the rival—and not he—be the enemy, and that he continue his dutiful love.

The Bazm and the Rival

One of the two settings in which the rival most commonly appears is the *bazm* or *maḥfil*—the convivial gathering with the beloved; (the other setting—*vaṣl* or union—has already been discussed in connection with *yār,* and will be examined presently in its association with the rival). Both words have rich and evocative associations in Urdu, with connotations of pleasant company, celebratory mood, some element of performance (as of singing, dancing, or poetic recitation), witty repartee, elaborate decoration of the setting, and possibly the drinking of wine. In five couplets in Ghalib's *Dīvān,* the rival is explicitly associated with the words *bazm* or *maḥfil,* invariably to the detriment of the poet-lover. In four of the verses, the latter is clearly excluded from the gathering:

4.47 Having heard of the decoration of the *bazm,* the heart is afflicted
As though the rival's intent has found its mark [154: 7]

(The rival's intent is twofold: to ingratiate himself into the presence of the beloved, and to aggrieve the heart of his rival, the poet-lover.)

4.48 The rivals take, in the *maḥfil,* kisses from the cup
I remain thus, with lips thirsting for a message [181: 1]

(The message for which the poet hopes is an invitation to join the assembly.) In both verses above, to be sure, the poet is lamenting his state of exclusion, but in the next two couplets his loneliness and envy are complicated by extraordinary anxiety:

4.49 Why does she drink so much wine in the rival's *bazm*
Just today she intends to test us
Just today she intends to test herself [44: 2]

(The grammatical form of *apnā* suggests the latter reading, but as associated ambiguity from other couplets of the ghazal permits the former as well [Mehr n.d.: 141]. In the first reading, the beloved would appear in a state of wild intoxication on the lover's doorstep, causing him acute embarrassment on her behalf as well as his own, and arousing his jealousy with the fact that she has been with the rival. in the second reading, hardly less anxiety-producing for the poet, the beloved tests her ability to maintain her composure and respectability in the rival's presence, and the consequences of her becoming intoxicated beyond control are equally humiliating and disturbing for the poet.) The fourth *bazm* couplet involves an even more convoluted picture, typical of Ghalib in the complexity of its imagery:

4.50 The sighing of the heart, last night, was without effect
It became the evil-averting incense of the *bazm* of union with the rival, though it was restless [16: 1]

Literally, the sigh acts as does wild rue when burnt to avert the evil eye; a simile is made between the audible palpability of restless sight (produced from the heat of the heart) and the rustling sound of rue burning, with its scented smoke spreading restlessly through the room where the beloved and the rival are united in dalliance. The sigh's effect, therefore, is opposite from that intended by the poet: instead of arousing the sympathy of the beloved, it acts as a protective enhancement of the rival's conquest.

The fifth couplet linking the rival with the *bazm* is more light-hearted, though again the poet's intention meets with an unexpected reversal as he tries to reason with the beloved that the presence of a rival disturbs the assembly:

4.51 I said: 'The *bazm* of elegance should be free of the rival'.
Hearing this, that genius of tyranny put me out, saying 'Thus?' [117: 6]

Two more couplets from the same ghazal also mention the rival:

4.52 At night, drunk with wine, bringing the rival along
May God let her come here, but may He not let it be thus [117: 3]

(The couplet is reminiscent of 4.49, in which the poet dreads the appearance of the drunken beloved.)

4.53 'What happened that night with the rival?' When I said this, now just see
She came and sat in front, and said: 'Now see, thus!' [117: 4]

'Now see, thus' may be interpreted in two ways: the beloved is outraged at the poet's presumption in asking her; or she simply sits saucily in front of him, demonstrating the familiar manner in which she had treated the rival. In either case, the poet is distressed by her response.

The Rival in the Lover's Conversation

The principle of discourse with the beloved, whether in the context of the *maḥfil* or elsewhere, is an important aspect of Ghalib's treatment of the rival. For without some sort of verbal exchange, no matter how petty or querulous, the lover seems to have no prospect of advancing his cause:

4.54 The rival's sweet-talk has had its effect
(3.6) She doesn't even suspect us mute ones of love [104: 1]

The desirability of verbal exchange with the beloved, of whatever sort, is underscored in another verse, in which Ghalib uncharacteristically praises the beloved in the same breath as questioning the rival:

4.55 How sweet are your lips, that the rival
Receiving your curses, did not find them distasteful [27: 4]

The Lover's Complaint of the Rival

The idiom of complaint, as we have seen previously, is common in conversations between the lover and the beloved, and between beloved and rival as well. Seven of the verses which mention the rival involve a tone of protestation, whether verbal, or through such expressions as sighs. Ghalib takes the statement of his complaints against the beloved very seriously, and in a couplet from the ghazal just referred to, he protests when the beloved calls others to relish his suffering:

4.56 Why do you gather together my rivals
It would be a show, not a genuine session of complaint
[27: 2]

The logic of complaint becomes even more convoluted when Ghalib objects to the beloved's mention of the rival, even in a negative complexion, because his jealousy cannot bear any attention that the beloved might grant to his competitor:

4.57 I complain of your mentioning the rival
Even though it be in the form of a complaint [120: 3]

The beloved can be no less peevish, to Ghalib's great pleasure:

4.58 The mention of me, even in abuse, she couldn't accept
If the rival's talk spoils her mood, nothing is lost [101: 1]

Ghalib takes the conventional complaint of the beloved's tyranny through several permutations. In one verse, he adds his protestations of the rival's injustice to the rival's complaints of the beloved's injustices:

4.60 She was faithful to us, so that the rival called it oppression
So it continues: that they call us good ones evil [87: 1]

(Ghalib, as we might expect, includes both himself and the beloved in the category of good people.) In another instance, however, it is Ghalib who complains to the beloved about her beneficence to the rival:

4.61 Your style, your habit—we know what it is
If you're kind to the rival, then what is tyranny [217: 2]

Continuing the tyranny demanded by the etiquette of love, the beloved reserves her greatest cruelty for Ghalib, whom she knows to be a true lover:

4.62 Just see the irony in the efficacy of faithful love
(3.7) The rival sighed, but she was angry with me [29: 2]

Ghalib himself knows the pointlessness of the rival's sighs:

4.63 Upon seeing the rival, why should not the heart be calmed
I used to sigh—but I was also seeking some effect [37: 7]

As has been evident in numerous verses, reversals of position, as well as of logic, are a common feature of Ghalib's portrayal of the lover's association with the beloved. A gesture, a phrase, an act are interpreted with the opposite meaning of that intended, and the result is often embarrassment and shame:

4.64 Her beauty, and her high opinion of herself, have preserved that lustful one's reputation
She has confidence in herself—why should she test the rival [116: 6]

Had she tested him, Ghalib says, she surely would have found him wanting. In another case, Ghalib rises uncharacteristically to his competitor's defense:

4.65 How can she, O Lord, forbid the rival from being presumptuous
If she were also modest, then she would be too embarrassed [154: 3]

The beloved, says Ghalib, can neither criticise the rival for being presumptuous (lest she herself demonstrate presumptuous behavior), nor simply be modest (and say nothing), for his presumptuousness would be an affront to her modesty.

The Rival and the Lover's Pain

Not only words and sights, but glances too are part of the *suḥbat* (conversational exchange) of the *bazm*. Even looks of anger toward the rival are more than Ghalib's jealousy can bear:

4.66 You—and towards the rival, sharp, sharp glances
I—and pain, from your eyelashes long [13: 3]

The jealousy is twofold: at the simplest level, Ghalib simply envies any attention shown to the rival; but in a subtler reading, we know that Ghalib is jealous of any suffering the rival may feel from the beloved's reproaches, for he always represents himself as an expert sufferer who is eager for the pain of love and the beloved's cruelty.

In another context, Ghalib's joy in bearing the pain of love's wounds is completely misinterpreted by the rival:

4.67 From having the wound stitched, I'm blamed for seeking a remedy
The rival thinks there's no pleasure in the wounding of the needle [88: 6]

Ghalib's ingenuity in devising new sources of pain is underscored by the alternative meaning of *ta'n*—used here in the sense of blame—as 'stab'. Even when the rival becomes concerned about Ghalib's state, Ghalib is still preoccupied with demonstrating his capacity to withstand suffering:

4.68 I will not tolerate the rival's courtesy, in order to increase the pain
The wound is like the smiling of the murderer: entirely salt [78: 5]

The murderer is conventionally the beloved, who delights in her role with a wound-like smile, and as there is relish in her smile, so there is for Ghalib the relish of salt in wounds (see 3.21 and 4.33). Even if the beloved is ultimately not responsible for the poet's death from his suffering, she is implicated in the act:

4.69 You are not saved from the accounts-calling of Judgement Day
If the murderer is the rival, then you are a complicit witness [125: 2]

Though envy of the rival was the cause of his death, Ghalib does not absolve the beloved for her part therein.

The Beloved's Meeting with the Rival

The beloved, by her very nature, will continue to be wanton and presumptuous, and this fact drives Ghalib nearly to distraction:

4.70 You said: 'Why is there, in meeting with the rival, disgrace?'
You're right, you're absolutely correct: 'Tell me again—yes—why is there?' [127: 10]

'But of course', says Ghalib, raving with sarcasm, 'you're quite right to ask what disgrace there is'—when the answer is perfectly obvious: the beloved is compromising herself by consorting with someone not (like the poet) a true lover, and is exposing herself to the possibility of discovery and disgrace. Yet the beloved persists, and Ghalib asks, trying still another avenue of attracting at least some attention from her:

4.71 You know what practices you have with the rival
If you were simply to go on asking after my health, what would be the harm [125: 1]

After such great indiscretions with the rival, what can be lost by so small an indiscretion as asking poor Ghalib about the state of his distracted heart?

Beyond the distressing thought of the beloved being with the rival in the *bazm* or *maḥfil*, there is the intolerable idea of her being in physical intimacy with him, as indicated by such words as *vaṣl* (union—often in the sexual sense), *ba<u>gh</u>al* or *ā<u>gh</u>osh* (embrace), or *bosa* (kiss) in six of the rival couplets. We have already seen the hallucinatory intensity of the lover's distraction:

4.72 The sighing of the heart, last night, was without effect
(4.50) It became the evil-averting incense of the *bazm* of union with the rival, though it was restless [16: 1]

His envy, in another verse, drives his ingenuity to a similar degree of strangeness:

4.73 The picture of the wiles of the mocking idol, in the embrace of the rival
The drawing of the pen of Mani requires a peacock's foot [185: 1]

The sight of the beloved in intimacy with the rival is so loathsome that only an instrument as ugly as a peacock's foot can serve, even in the hands of a painter like the great Persian Mani, to capture the distastefulness of the occasion.

Whereas these two couplets, relying as they do on abstruse imagery, are not particularly effective, other verses capture with greater immediacy the lover's state of mind:

4.74 In the rival's embrace today, you are sleeping somewhere—otherwise
What is the reason, having come to me in a dream, for your secret smiles [10: 10]

There is a rich logical resonance here: the beloved appears in the poet's dream (whether sleeping or waking is ambiguous) smiling mysteriously, and the poet has to assume that the only reason for her smile is that she is happy in the arms of the rival, and wishes to torture the lover by appearing to him, smiling at her enjoyment, in his own dream.

In another couplet, Ghalib describes with both eroticism and wit an argument with the beloved:

4.75 How fine! You did not kiss the rival
Enough, keep still! I too have a tongue in my mouth
[139: 5]

The latter statement has two interpretations: the poet has some undeniable proof that the beloved did kiss the rival, and need only speak (with his tongue) to divulge this proof; the poet himself, moreover, is capable of testing, by taste, whether or not the beloved has kissed the rival.

The Poet's Suspicion in Union

Even on those rare occasions when Ghalib is united with his beloved, he is haunted by the thought of his rival. He is unable, for example, to accept the beloved's kisses as tokens of genuine affection, quite possible with good reason:

4.76 In the rival's company, did this habit not emerge
She has begun to give kisses, without being implored
[152: 7]

In another verse, he realizes that his fear of interruption by the rival has caused the beloved to doubt his love, so that he must explain to her:

4.77 *I'm* anxious in union, in dread of the rival
What suspicion is it that has made *you* so restless [98: 7]

The words *vahm* (suspicion, doubt) and *pīc-o-tāb* (restlessness) also appear in another *ghair* couplet, but here the 'rival' is used in a Sufistic sense as anything that distracts from the Divine:

4.78 To this extent am I remote from my own reality
To the same extent that, from suspicion of the other, I am consumed with restlessness [99: 5]

Similarly, in another couplet, *ghair* refers to someone other than the poet:

4.79 Freedom does not justify isolation
Do it from yourself, not from someone else—why should there not be madness itself [120: 8]

In other words, the loss of self is the most effective manner of obtaining freedom, in the form of sublime madness.

The Rival and the Secret of Love

Returning to an earthly plane, we find that whereas dread of the rival (in 4.77) prevented the poet from becoming totally absorbed in the beloved's presence, a similar dread compels him to refrain from indulgence in the sublime dementia of the lover; such a demonstration would reveal the secret of his love to the rival, who would certainly turn such a revelation to his own advantage:

4.80 From dread of the rival, I cannot take leave of my senses
I am compelled to this degree, O control—alas! [77: 1]

Yet the rival, inferior to the true lover, has no such compunctions:

4.81 The rival wanders about, holding your letter thus
If anyone should ask what it is, he cannot hide it [192: 3]

As for the beloved herself—the ingenuity of her cruelty has provided her with complete freedom from worry about disgrace:

4.82 In a veil is her secret friendship with the rival
The veiling of the truth is this—that she does not care
[199: 2]

The beloved is so open about her ties to the rival that no one would suspect her of having those ties. Ghalib laments this openness bitterly:

4.83 I had to go to the rival's door a thousand times
Would that I didn't know your path [100: 3]

Yet he knows that the rival's door is the one place he may be certain of catching a glimpse of the beloved, who in going to the rival does not even attempt to conceal herself.

Ghalib's Rival in other Forms

The remaining rival couplets are typical of Ghalib in their ingenuity, and avoid the cavilling tone characteristic of most poets, and found also in the previous verses. In one case, conflicting aspects of Ghalib's personality assume the roles both of lover and rival; his eye is intent upon the sight of the beloved, whereas for his heart, the mere thought of the beautiful one is enough to provoke a state of sublime madness (see also 4.5):

4.84 They have become, then—my heart and eye—rivals
Having made sight and thought their appurtenances
[234: 7]

Elsewhere Ghalib, ever watchful for possible rivals, finds one in the flower's scent which, as part of her daily self-adornment, surrounds the beloved:

4.85 Spring invents it for you
My rival is the breath of annointing fragrance of the flower
[81: 5]

(An additional delicacy to this verse is the fact that *nafs*, from the same root as *nafas*—'breath'—also means envy, so that there is an undercurrent of envy in Ghalib's description of the flower's fragrance.) The narcissus itself might seem to be a rival as well; but knowing that the flower is both literally and emotionally blind, Ghalib does not feel threatened:

4.86 Towards you with longing, the narcissus is staring
May the heart and eye of the rival be blind: drink on
[57: 4]

As seen in the third chapter, Ghalib in one instance assigns to *shauq* the role of a particular sort of rival, in a couplet having an allusion to the legendary Qais (also called Majnun—the mad one), who wandered the desert naked in sublime dementia:

4.87 *Shauq,* in every respect, turned out to be the rival of
(3.57) possession
Even in the canvas of the picture, Qais turned out to be naked [6: 1]

Finally, in two particularly effective couplets, Ghalib endows the concept of the rival with positive attributes, in a stunning reversal of the traditional presentation. In the first verse, he refers to the story of Yusuf and Zuleikha, in which Zuleikha gathers some of the women of Egypt for dinner, then asks the slave Yusuf to appear to them: all are so transfixed by his unearthly beauty that when his appearance interrupts their slicing of lemons, all the women cut their fingers, thus giving Zuleikha a particularly sweet revenge:

4.88 All are unhappy with rivals, but with the women of Egypt
Zuleikha is happy, that they became entranced by the Moon of Canaan [112: 5]

In a shrewd warning to the beloved, Ghalib points out that she cannot continue to occupy her position of tyranny—made possible primarily by her beauty—forever:

4.89 I tolerate these tyrannies, for I have my reasons: there are beautiful ones in love with you
Let me speak plainly: I'll find a rival like you one day [66: 1]

In short, the figure of rival serves two essential purposes for Ghalib. First, it enables him to vent his pettiest emotions, however ingeniously, against the beloved, or simply against the vicissitudes of existence. Secondly—and much more distinctively—the conventions associated with the rival serve as a point of departure, and often reversal, for Ghalib's logical and imagistic inventiveness, as in the six couplets just discussed. In either case, the vagueness of the rival as a character is almost always greater even than that of the beloved (at least we have a few general details about her height, gait, complexion, the color of her hair and cheeks, and the thinness of her waist). The rival is merely a symbolic figure *against* whom Ghalib is able to react, paying no attention whatsoever to specific traits or distinguishing features, so that the focus of attention remains on Ghalib himself, as on most other poets as well.

The Poet-lover

As the first two major sections of this chapter have demonstrated, the lover himself is the central preoccupation for Ghalib, more than the beloved herself, and more than the rival, both of whom serve primarily as reagents upon the personality and world-view of the poet-lover. It is therefore not surprising that the twenty couplets from the *Dīvān* which use the word *'āshiq* (lover) or its plural *ushshāq*, while fewer in number than those referring to the beloved or rival, are nevertheless generally of a consistently higher quality in terms of conciseness, and of ingenuity in logic and imagery.

The Beloved as Lover

The couplet which concludes the previous section presents, with irrefutable reasoning, the likelihood of the beloved herself falling in love one day—just as the poet's messenger or his confidant fell in love with the beloved (4.39-40); again:

4.89 I tolerate these tyrannies, for I have my reasons: there are beautiful ones in love with you
Let me speak plainly: I'll find a rival like you one day
[66: 1]

The verse is wittily ambiguous in its intention: either the lover will find a rival who is as beautiful as the beloved, or he will fall in love with one of the rivals whom his erstwhile beloved loves, so that *she* becomes his rival.

In another couplet more elegant and less facile in Urdu than it seems in English, Ghalib describes in the beloved those same lover-like symptoms that he himself has experienced—weakness, loss of color—but manages with considerable deftness to turn those symptoms to the beloved's favor:

4.90 She became a lover—that fairy-faced one—and became delicate
The more color she lost, the fairer she became [154: 8]

Warning elsewhere of the danger of beloveds' losing their vanity in sympathy for the ordeals of the lovers tortured by their exquisite beauty, Ghalib says:

4.91 Let not there be grief for lovers, lest these idols learn simplicity
How desolate would be the mirror-house, because of me
[191: 4]

The Fraternity of Lovers

Ghalib sometimes uses the plural of lovers, as he did in the previous verse, to invoke the honorable brotherhood of those stricken with love and thereby underscore the fact that love is a universal experience—though of course all lovers are not up to Ghalib's mark. Another such couplet depends for its impact upon an untranslatable pun, with the word *ghubār* sharing its primary meaning of 'dust' with the word *khāk*, yet being used here in the sense of impurity, rancor, and grief, the last two meanings of which it shares with the word *ranjish*, which also means offense:

4.92 It's absurd to suspect us of having indignation [*ranjish*] in our hearts
In the dust [*khāk*] of lovers, there is no rancor or impurity [*ghubār*] [171: 4]

(With the common association of *khāk* and *ghubār* as 'dust', the second line has the initially paradoxical meaning of the English 4.92b. In the dust of lovers, there is no dust.)

The 'dust of lovers' probably means 'in the bodily clay of lovers', though there is a powerful suggestion of dust as being all that remains of the true lovers of the world (see 3.80). The main sense of this verse, word-play aside, is that true lovers harbor only the most dignified of motives and feelings in their hearts.

The third couplet speaking of lovers in the plural refers, as in 4.91, to the beloveds as 'idols':

4.93 Just see what bounty lovers find from the idols
A Brahmin has said that this year is good [175: 6]

Here Ghalib makes the novel association between the idol-tending Brahmin (a conventional figure in the ghazal, though not particularly common in Ghalib) and the Brahmin as astrologer. The idols, it must be remembered, are beloved and hence almost always cruel and untrue to their word, so that any promise to lovers of the year being auspicious, no matter how alluring the idea may be, is fraught with the probability of unfulfillment—as hinted by the tone in which Ghalib uses the polite imperative, *dekhiye* ('please see') and the exclamatory *kyā faiẓ* ('what bounty!').

The voice in the previous verse is ironic and basically good-humored in its treatment of the beloved. It is a measure of Ghalib's self-confidence as a poet-lover that only two of the '*āshiq* couplets have tones of unrelieved bleakness:

4.94 Why do you fear the dejection of lovers
Here no one hears another's lamentations [187: 3]

This fourth couplet using 'lovers' in the plural is universal in its complaint of human suffering and loneliness; 'here' refers to the world, and the poet is addressing a beloved who may be either earthly or divine. In another verse, Ghalib laments that

4.95 The eyes, open so determinedly, have closed, alas! alas!
You've come at a fine time to this sick lover [73: 3]

The beloved, with typical cruelty (see 3.84 and 4.36), only comes to visit the lover after his death, granting the vision of her beauty to his eyes only when they are sightless, after having been perpetually open in life.

In the fifth couplet invoking the fraternity of lovers, Ghalib's tone is more typically self-assertive:

4.96 We will write letters, even though they have no meaning
We are lovers, after all—of your name [181: 3]

The poet claims the right to write the beloved's name endlessly, we would say, with the determination of Sisyphus. This assertive tone is also to be found, with a remarkable degree of intensity, throughout the remaining *'āshiq* couplets. Of the lover's dedication to suffering at the hand of the beloved, Ghalib observes (see also 3.21, 4.33, and 4.68):

4.97 To go and leave the ravaged body of the lover is unjust
The heart seeks more wounds, and the vital organs demand salt [78: 6]

The lover, moreover, is adaptable in his love, through which he is reduced to poverty:

4.98 In the trade of begging, Asad, I did not desert merriment
Becoming a beggar, I became a lover of the merciful ones [168: 10]

The Lover and Madness

For Ghalib, madness—even more than the dedication to love described in the last few couplets—is an end in itself:

4.99 Who made any claim of perseverance
What's the good of patience in the lover's heart [22: 11]

Desperation is more the order of the day, in Ghalib's thinking, and it is with full admiration that he writes:

4.100 Alas, the fate of these inches of cloth, Ghalib
In whose lot it is to be the lover's collar [18: 9]

The true lover, in his impatience and distraction, rents his collar (which represents the strictures of society) in an attempt to cast away the entire garment of convention (see 3.57, 6.3, and 6.35); elsewhere as well, Ghalib ridicules mere convention:

4.101 Union is as good as separation in the world of dignity and restraint
A wanton beloved and a deranged lover are needed [181: 9]

In another verse linking *'āshiq* (lover) and *ma'shūq* (beloved), Ghalib makes the ultimate assertion of his supremacy as a lover, in a reference to the legendary Majnun and his beloved Laila:

4.102 I am a lover, and beguiling the beloved is my work
Laila derides Majnun before me [209: 10]

The Elemental Imagery of the Lover's Symptoms

Having surpassed even Majnun in madness, Ghalib is capable of the most visionary portrayal of his love:

4.103 If, from the place of the lover's martyrdom, for miles the henna grows
How much, O Lord, was it the slaughter of the longing to kiss the beloved's feet [40: 2]

The reddish color of the pulverized henna plant is associated both with the color of blood and the decoration of the beloved's feet; the extent to which the plant has grown is a measure of the lover's unsatisfied longing. In another couplet with brilliant color in its imagery—though perhaps more coherent in its novelty—Ghalib describes the lover's perseverance throughout trials as elemental as nature itself:

4.104 Grief, in the embrace of calamities, nurtures the lover
My blazing lamp is like the coral in the ocean of the dust-storm [227: 5]

The intensity of the poet's love burns in his stormy life as spectacularly and unwaveringly as the bright reefs of endless coral in the thrashing sea.

Continuing the elemental imagery of love, Ghalib observes that

4.105 Every atom of the lover's body is a sun-worshipper
Even after it turned to dust, the passion for the sight of elegance did not die [69: 4]

The metaphor is enhanced by the implicit play on *havā*, which here means 'passion', but also has a primary meaning of 'air', joining with the fire of the sun and the thirst of the lover's passion (see also 3.71 and 4.30).

Ghalib makes a similarly effective use of auditory imagery in portraying the lover's madness by again evoking the wind—here as the lover's audible sigh—in a description of the lover's longing to be smitten by the beloved's eye:

4.106 Don't ask the lover's breast about the edge of the glance's dagger
From the wound-like niche in the door, only air rushes out [228: 3]

The effect of the comparison is underlined by the word-play between *havā* (air, wind) and *āb*, whose primary meaning is 'water', but which here means 'edge', as of a sword. The lamentation of the fraternity of lovers is elsewhere likened to the music of the spheres when the stars are in dissonant conjunction:

4.107 The bodies of lovers are the instrument of discordant fortune
As though their lament were the sound of the motion of the planets [148: 2]

Here too there is rich word-play, as in the contrast between *sāz* (instrument) and *nā-sāz* (discordant, or without a *sāz*), and the use of *tāli* (star, destiny) and *sayyāra* (planet). The suggestion of celestial music as the combined lamentations of all the lovers in the universe is a breathtaking evocation of the suffering and discord of life.

Finally, the crying of the demented lover, like his sighing, has for Ghalib the dimensions of a major natural phenomenon:

4.108 The monsoon of the lover's crying should be seen
Like the flowers themselves, the wall of the garden burst open [95: 1]

Not only have the lover's tears, like ceaseless rains, brought the flowers of the garden into bloom, but they have also caused the masonry of the garden walls to burst with the moisture, in a fine evocation of *k͟hāna-k͟harābī* (destruction of the house), which is an aspect of the traditional behavior of the lover tormented by sublime madness.

The lover, as the above couplets demonstrate, *can* be efficacious, in spite of the beloved's indifference or cruelty, and despite the apparent victory of the rival in the quest for the beloved's affections. Having been stricken with love at the sight of the beloved, smitten with the sharpness of her glances and the arrows of her eyelashes, ravaged with the longing for union and the grief of separation, consumed with envy for the rival, and humiliated with defeat and failure, the poet-lover must find some strategy for survival, or submit to inevitable debilitation and death. Though Ghalib is at times tempted into assuming an idiom of complaint, whether petty or ingenious, in an exchange where he may score small victories in logic but will surely lose in action, his strongest inclination is to adopt a mode of action in which the superiority and power of his love will be manifest, and to choose the arenas in which he wishes to compete.

For it should be evident by now that competition is one of the essential features of love in the ghazal, and a primary motivation in the relationships that Ghalib establishes among the personae of his ghazals. Though the beloved rarely submits to the stratagems and attempted persuasion of the poet-lover, neither does Ghalib's poetic alter-ego yield to the eternal frustration of his quest, but instead develops a sort of martial art of *'ishq* and *shauq* in which he turns the disadvantages of his position into sources of strength: in *'ishq,* passive suffering becomes a professional skill as the poet evolves into a connoisseur of pain and grief, while the irrepressible and dynamic madness of *shauq* creates epic events and scenes of true spectacle that are no less worthy of being *seen* than the beloved herself (see 4.108 above, and 5.44, 5.63, and 6.40 below). The rival remains, meanwhile, a necessary but faceless foil for the lover's action, and a galvanic force for his love.

As noted at the beginning of this chapter, Ghalib has chosen *yār* as the word which most fully captures the essence of his ideal beloved. One cannot compete in any true sense with a *but* (idol—

the next most frequently occurring word for the beloved), while there is an implicit dynamic of bilateral exchange in *yār* (the most common term of direct address in colloquial Urdu banter, whether good-natured or hostile), which in its connotations of *friendship* permits the broadest possible scope for exploring a relationship that is both competitive and fundamentally affectionate in nature.

Since competition demands an arena, we turn next to the proving-grounds Ghalib has selected for a demonstration of his love in its various manifestations. The following chapter will continue to examine and identify the connotations of a third group of central words and images (which denote particular settings in which the ghazal's personae interact in love) in an exhaustive discussion of all the occurrences of these topoi in the *Dīvān*, in order to expand further our understanding of Ghalib's use of the ghazal tradition as a vehicle for his own distinctive voice and vision.

NOTES

1. The importance of sight in the love-process is evident in Nykl's English translation of Ibn Hazm's eleventh-century Arabic treatise on love, *The Dove's Neck Ring*; Chapter Three is entitled 'Falling in love in sleep', Chapter Four, 'Love from description [of the beloved],' and Chapter Five, 'Love at first sight' [1931: 26-33].
2. One is reminded of the old definition of a sadist as someone who refuses to hurt a masochist.

CHAPTER 5

The Landscape of the Ghazal

We are in that place from which, even to us
Comes no news at all of ourselves

GHALIB [162: 8]

If the beloved, rival, and lover represent the central triad of characters in the ghazal, the lane of the beloved, the lover's house, and the desert comprise the primary settings in the landscape of Ghalib's ghazals, though we shall see at the end of this chapter that the *Dīvān* includes numerous other settings as well. As has been the case with other topoi in Urdu poetry, each setting will acquire a general range of connotations which the poet may explore, and to which he may add in order to show his own particular nature and manner of viewing life and its myriad relationships.

The Lane of the Beloved

Following traditional Indo-Muslim architecture, the beloved's house is situated behind a high wall, and may be approached only by way of a lane. In poetic convention, this lane is one of the likely haunts of the distracted poet-lover who, often with his rivals, waits in the hope of a fleeting glimpse of the beloved, and perhaps even of some brief discourse with her.

For the poet with true humility, the lane of the beloved is a place of great wonder, a place to lose oneself utterly in the contemplation of indescribable beauty, or at least in the hope, however vain, of such contemplation. In his typical versatility, Ghalib is fully capable of assuming such an attitude. In couplets treating the beloved's lane in specific words (*kū-e-yār,* or *kūca*), or her house (*ghar*), Ghalib does assume an unassertive and purely devotional posture. In the first, he seems in the initial line to avoid the usual exaggeration of comparison so common in Urdu poetry:

5.1a In splendor, Paradise is no less than your lane

But he returns to the second line with a surprise exaggeration proving that even Paradise is inferior after all:

5.1b The setting is the same, but Paradise is not so populated [102: 9]

The beloved is complimented by being said to have such a multitude of lovers, and further flattered by the subtle but unmistaken comparison to God (see 4.29).

A second *she'r* begins with a compliment of uncertain sincerity, but again Ghalib recovers to deliver another well-wrought offering of praise:

5.2 So cheap, so abundant has become the wine of splendor
That intoxicated in your lane is every door and wall

Nothing—not even the wood and stone of doors and walls (in synecdoche for the beloved's house, and perhaps the houses of others)—is able to resist becoming drunk with the beloved's beauty; the implicit chiding (that the beloved is perhaps too free in letting herself be seen) simply makes more piquant the effect of the compliment.

In a verse of further ingenuity, Ghalib suggests that even the sun in all its splendor is eager for a glimpse of the beloved (see also 3.71 and 4.105):

5.3 Gathered together are all the elements of the glance of the sun
Those are not dust-motes in the windows of her house's walls [88: 3]

The proud sun cannot admit to this eagerness, with its tincture of jealousy; it disguises its faculty of sight as dust motes suspended in the window-chink of the beloved's house. Or again, perhaps it is humility that prompts the sun to disguise itself as dust, the lowliest of substances:

5.4 If the rose's fragrance has no lust for your lane
Why is it, that it became the dust of the road in the eddies of the eastern breeze [49: 8]

The incomparable bouquet of the rose itself seeks exposure to, and enrichment from, the beloved's fragrance, and with true *adab* (etiquette) assumes the humble status of dust, in order not to betray its concupiscence. Ghalib reveals the same desire, which he finds satisfied only after his death:

5.5 My dust floats about the lane of the beloved
(4.30) At last, O wind, the lust for wings and feathers is gone
[59: 4]

When the lover actually catches a glimpse of the beloved, the effect on him is overwhelming:

5.6 How could I remember, in the lane of the beloved, the code of living
The astonishment of the footprint became a mirror-holder and showed me, like this [117: 8]

The footprint is immobilized with amazement at the impact of the beloved's beauty, and occupies the most humble of positions, under her feet.

On some occasions, Ghalib's fondness for wit and striking imagery begins to call more attention to his poetic ingenuity than to the beloved's beauty:

5.7 Again, in distraction, I forgot the way to the beloved's lane
(4.32) Otherwise I would have gone one day to inquire after myself [100: 8]

This verse, reminiscent of 2.8, is a fine description of the paradoxical effect of the state of selflessness (*bekhudī*) that results from true love. Just as astonishment and selflessness are two of the effects of love, so is debilitation, as described in numerous verses in Chapter 3.

5.8 From my weakness, the ant's footprints are a yoke around my neck
Where is the strength for me to run from your lane
[124: 3]

It is love that brings the lover to such a pass of unimaginable weakness, and the beloved is well complimented in this verse—but is the poet not more praiseworthy for fashioning such a superb example of the weakest possible form of binding?

Moving from ingenious imagery to logical banter, Ghalib accomplishes a deft juxtaposition of opposites that continues to highlight his cleverness, rather than the beloved's charms:

5.9 Like this he has lived, in season after season, so that now, of the lane of the friend
If you do not say it is the home of the enemy, what is there to say [202: 3]

'He' is certainly the rival, who by his presence transforms the beloved's lane into the enemy's abode. Or again, in discourse with his friends who have come to advise him to abandon his love, Ghalib makes the unchallengeable observation that:

5.10 Very well, she doesn't worship God. Go away! If she is faithless, so be it
Whoever loves his religion and his heart, why should he go to her lane [116: 8]

Ghalib declares his own apostasy from faith and reason in his decision to worship the beloved, and thus he easily defuses the force of his companions' advice:

5.11 The heart again has gone on pilgrimage to the lane of reproach
Having made desolate the idol-house of proud thought [234: 8]

The poet is resigned to being abused for his love by his friends, or by the reproachful beloved, even though he has abandoned everything—his house, his pride, his love for other beautiful ones—in his devotion to her, and returns again and again, as though on pilgrimage, to her lane.

Even in his devotion to the beloved, Ghalib is jealous—and in some respects his jealousy is greater than his love:

5.12 Envy did not permit me to take the name of your house
I ask everyone: where should I go [100: 2]

Ghalib faces a dilemma, for the revelation of the beloved's name or address would bring about scandal. Ghalib makes clear that it is fear of sharing the beloved with others that forces him to remain separate from her; in this verse there is none of the magnanimous praise by that side of Ghalib which saw even the doors and walls drunk with the beloved's beauty.

The beloved, for her own part, refuses to visit Ghalib, giving as her stock excuse that she does not know the way to his house—an answer, perhaps, to his not knowing, and not asking, the way to hers. His response to her aloofness is ultimately to make her doorstep his abode, and to make fun of her 'ignorance' (which is in actuality mere cruelty) by asserting his own superior knowledge:

5.13 When I made my home at your door, without your permission
Even now, you won't know my home without my telling [60: 1]

Ghalib brings his assertiveness to the fore in the three remaining couplets set in the beloved's lane; he begins with wit and ingenuity, as just seen, and the essentially complimentary nature of the verses gradually gives way to skillful boasting, which however delicately stated, can turn into outright braggadocio:

5.14 O inhabitants of the lane of the beloved, watch out
If you should meet somewhere Ghalib of the distracted head [160: 7]

The 'inhabitants' are the rivals, and the poet warns them to beware of Ghalib, for he is certainly something beyond their experience. The verb *dekhnā* (see!) at the end of the first line seems to suggest the possibility of a glimpse of the beloved, but that hope is dashed when it turns out to be the spectacular Ghalib who is to be seen.

Another typical example of Ghalib's pride echoes 3.2, in which Ghalib's madness is proposed as the source of the beloved's fame:

5.15 Don't bury me in your lane after killing me
Why should people find your house through knowledge of me [160: 2]

The fame of Ghalib—the poet with the distracted mind—has come to exceed that of the beloved, so that he begs her to inter him anonymously so that his *pata* ('address', as well as 'knowledge') will not betray her existence to the rivals.

Finally, just as Ghalib glorified the beloved by comparing Paradise unfavorably with her lane, he turns such a comparison to his own great advantage:

5.16 Oh, we've heard of Adam's departure from Paradise,
(1.9) however
It was truly disgraced that, from your lane, I departed
[220: 3]

Even Adam is a lesser sinner than Ghalib, who offended the beloved with his incomparable persistence more than Adam had offended God. Again, with fine wit, Ghalib has compared the beloved to God.

The previous couplets as a group tend to display Ghalib's wit and ingenuity as much as his passions, and his absorption with himself as much as his adoration of the beloved. When we consider those verses referring to the poet's own abode, Ghalib's sense of self emerges even more clearly, as demonstrated by the greater number of couplets (34) treating the subject and the greater passion in that treatment.

The Lover's House

The words Ghalib uses to denote the poet-lover's abode are *ghar* and *k͟hāna*, as well as the occasional phrase *dar-o-dīvār* (door and wall) as a synecdoche for the entire house (see 3.66, 3.90, and 4.34). One of these words may occur in compound, as in *g͟ham-k͟hāna* (grief-house—see 5.26) or *mātim-k͟hāna* (mourning-house—see 5.22); *k͟hāna* also occurs in the *Dīvān* in other compounds with *mai* (wine) or *ā'īna* (mirror), but these do not refer directly to the lover's house, and so are not discussed here.

Ghalib's portrayal of his house is one of the vehicles for the expression of his state of mind, which invariably depends upon the nature of his relationship with the beloved. As is the case with Ghalib's reference to the beloved's abode, the lover's house is rarely described in particular detail—there is no mention of roof, different rooms, the materials of construction, or similar features. Rather, the house is important in providing 1) a potential setting for the lover to meet his beloved in some degree of privacy, away from the many rivals, or much more frequently, 2) the setting for the lover's expression of grief at being rejected and scorned by the beloved, or in a related state, his delirious madness, which in Ghalib is more frequently positive than negative in its connotations.

In only one couplet is Ghalib's mention of his house in essentially neutral tones:

5.17 If anyone has to write a letter to her, then have it written by me
It's morning, and from the house I come out, pen behind my ear [220: 5]

This strange little verse reflects a carefree optimism found nowhere else in the entire *Dīvān* in quite this way. Otherwise, his house is for Ghalib the scene of some elevated state of hope, suffering, or dementia.

The Beloved's Coming to the Lover's House

The previous chapters have shown the beloved's scorn for the poet's love in favor of that of the rival, so that the poet has little hope of achieving the much desired state of *viṣāl-e-yār* (union with the beloved). Sometimes, to taunt the lover, the beloved will promise to come to his house (see 4.34, 4.36, and 5.13); Ghalib is skeptical, for he is familiar with her *nāz-o-andāz* (wiles), *taghāful* (neglect and indifference), and *ẕulm* (tyranny):

5.18 She will come to my house? How should that promise be regarded, Ghalib
In these fresh tribulations is our test by the ancient heavens [205: 10]

Ghalib tells himself that the stars have existed for eons; they know what will happen, and yet they test us. Ghalib's particular wit is here exemplified in his asking two purely rhetorical questions when he is fully aware of the answers, and in his attribution of his troubles to a rather senile and doddering Fate's witless repetition of the same old challenges; Ghalib has been around for a long time, and he wonders how naïve the beloved, and the heavens as well, can be in expecting him to believe her promise. Or again:

5.19 Honor your promise of coming! What sort of style is this
Why have you entrusted the watchmanship of my own house to me [203: 7]

Both couplets represent facets of the same attitude: Ghalib is proud, witty, and indignant, and he is beginning to lose patience.

It is not appropriate for him to be reduced to the status of his own watchman, yet by not honoring her promise to come, the beloved gives him no other choice but to wait, looking for her arrival.

There is no doubt that the poet-lover's house would be brightened by a visit from the beautiful one:

5.20 The life of the house is an eyesore without you
I cry always, seeing the door and wall [59: 7]

In one of the two ghazals in the *Dīvān* which are elegies for actual persons (67 for his nephew Arif, and 140—see 3.39, 3.91, and 3.107—for a beloved mistress), Ghalib laments the loss, through Arif's death, to the brightness of his home:

5.21 You were the moon-of-the-fourteenth-night of my house
Then why did you not remain that adornment of the house a few days more [82: 1]

The comparison of the beloved's face to the moon is conventional in ghazal poetry; yet the reference here to his nephew as the *full* moon of his house is rich in poignance and grief. In another couplet, Ghalib makes an aphoristic statement on the effect of grief—or at least, poetic grief:

5.22 Grief, to the free, is no more than a moment's breath
With lightning we illumine the candle of our house of mourning [82: 1]

The reference to lightning (one of Ghalib's favorite kinetic images—see 3.49-50) indicates not only the brevity of mourning, but its intensity and potential destructiveness, which the resourceful poet turns to his own advantage.

Ghalib assumes the guise of a *darvesh* (holy beggar) who worships the beloved, in an attempt to persuade her to visit him:

5.23 Give your alms-portion of beauty, O radiant one, like the sun
That the beggar's bowl may be the lamp of the *darvesh's* house [25: 3]

This lambent use of sun imagery is just as effective in its own way as the brilliance of the lightning imagery. As though in response to Ghalib's request in *darvesh* guise, the beloved, perhaps rewarding his devotion, or possibly indulging in a simple exercise of her infinitely resourceful cruelty, sends a message that she will visit him:

5.24 The news is hot of her coming
Today of all days, in my house, I haven't even a burlap mat [27: 5]

He had been so certain, in his devotion, of her inattention that he had failed to make any arrangement for hospitality in the remote possibility that she might actually come to his home. Miraculously the beloved arrives, but again (as in 5.6 and 5.7) the power of astonishment leaves him disoriented:

5.25 She came to my house! It is the power of God
Yet I can only look, sometimes at her, sometimes at my house [107: 2]

He fears that something is wrong, that it is not really the beloved who has come, or that he is not in his own house. With utterly simple diction and structure, Ghalib conveys a sense of complete bewilderment through his description of a joyous but stunned lover incapable of any action but staring.

The Destruction of the Poet-lover's House

The occasions when the beloved will visit the lover in his house, or even promise such a visit, are rare; consequently it is grief rather than hope that is the predominant emotion in the lover's abode. As a result (according to the conventions of the ghazal), the poet lets his house fall into a state of desolation and ruin as a reflection of the state of his heart:

5.26 When the fate of my house of grief began to be recorded
Fate wrote, among the causes of its desolation, me [203: 4]

Just as the poet needs a beloved as an agent of madness and has no choice at all in the matter (see 4.1), the lover is also under obligation by the etiquette of love to destroy his house, both figuratively and literally, either passively (through neglect) or actively (through the heat of his grief and the profusion of his tears). Yet there is no doubt in the poet's mind about the ultimate agent of his house's ruination:

5.27 How is this affliction less than the destruction of a man's house

Whomever you befriend, why should his enemy be the sky [127: 8]

Granted that fate plays its part in the poet's downfall—but it is really the effect of unrequited love that creates all the poet's troubles. As the English saying has it, 'with a friend like you, who needs enemies?'

On the purely figurative level, the terms *k͟hāna-k͟harābī* (house destruction) and *k͟hāna-vīrānī* (house-desolation) may stand simply for the poet's wretched state, as in a more literal translation of 3.7/4.62:

5.28 Just see her trust in the house-destruction of love
The rival sighed, but she was angry with me [29: 2]

In many respects, the actual destruction of the lover's house is intended to reinforce the sense of his separation from conventional life and society, and his lack of concern for material possessions (see 5.24) and the routines of everyday life.

In five of the couplets dealing with the lover's abode, the destructiveness of love is seen as essentially negative; in two of these, Ghalib laments all that he has lost through love:

5.29 I have become ashamed at the destructiveness of love
(3.41) There's nothing left in the house but the desire for building [115: 6]

5.30 What was in the house, that grief for you might have ruined
All that I had—the longing to build—is still there [136: 1]

The effect of both verses is heightened by the ambiguity in the word *ḥasrāt* (longing, desire, grief) in the phrase *ḥasrat-e-ta'mīr* (*ta'mīr* meaning 'construction' or 'building'), and by the use of the word *g͟hārat* to indicate destruction, in a clear sense of pillage and plunder at the hands of love and, by implication, at the instigation of the beloved. Elsewhere Ghalib repudiates this desire, citing the dangers of indebtendness, which will only distract the poet from his dedication to madness:

5.31 The wall is bent from the burden of obligation to the laborer
O you whose house is ruined—don't accept any kindness [131: 3]

There will certainly be no kindness from the beloved, nor sympathy for the loss of his dwelling-place:

5.32 So—she also says, 'This man is a vagrant!'
Had I known this, I would never have destroyed my house
[100: 5]

The poet-lover, hoping to impress his beloved with the single-mindedness of his love (and we shall see presently the extent to which he will go to destroy his house with the appropriate ostentation), has only managed to secure once more her predictable scorn.

True independence, it seems, is far preferable:

5.33 Go now and live in some place where no one would be
No one to speak with, and no one to know your tongue

You should build a house as though without doors and walls
That has no one as neighbor, and none to keep watch

If you should fall ill, there would be no one to comfort
And if you should die, there would be no one to mourn
[128: 1-3]

(Only the middle verse contains the word *ghar*, but the entire sequence is descriptive of the poet's ideal abode.) Ghalib desires neither ease, nor understanding, nor companionship, nor esteem, any more than he desires the attainment of his ultimate goal:

5.34 I would have been able to set my sights on some loftier place
Would that this side of Heaven my dwelling had been
[44: 3]

Even having reached the *'arsh* (the Empyrean realm, the ninth sphere, where the divine throne is said to exist [Platts 1930: 760]), Ghalib is dissatisfied, for he longs to have a still higher goal. Yet there is no place higher than *'arsh*, and so Ghalib laments his attainment, and wishes for a return to the quest, with its exhilaration and challenge.

Elemental Imagery in the Destruction of the Lover's House

If the beloved is infinitely resourceful in her cruelty, Ghalib is no less so in portraying the ruin of his house, for the degree of his devotion to the beloved is manifest in the extent of desolation in his dwelling: the greater the love, the more extensive the destruction. Even when the process is essentially passive (through neglect) Ghalib introduces the element of spectacle:

5.35 Everywhere in the house greenery has sprung up, showing spectacular ruin
Now, digging grass has become the task of my doorman
[10: 7]

In most cases, Ghalib himself is the catalytic agent for the process of desolation; the ruination through simple neglect is accelerated by the fire of love, or the water of tears:

5.36 In the heart, the passion for union and the memory of the
(4.22) beloved do not remain
Fire, in this abode, has so struck, that what there was, burned [5: 2]

The abode may be the poet's heart, or his house—the net result is the same. In another eloquent verse invoking the inevitability of loss in this world, Ghalib observes that:

5.37 The luster of existence is from house-destroying love
(3.50) The gathering has no candle, if lightning is not in the harvest [88: 5]

He exults in the very process of loss and ruin, if not by fire, then by water:

5.38 The destitution of love has brought weeping, Ghalib
(3.45) To whose house will the flood of destruction go, after me
[58: 9]

While Ghalib seems in the first line simply to be crying abjectly, in the second line he introduces (not unexpectedly, given his penchant for exaggeration in self-praise) the image of a flood from his tears, which must seek in vain to find another lover whose house would be worthy of such enormous desolation.

In an extension of Ghalib's predilection for elemental imagery, two verses explore, in an entirely novel way, particular aspects of the flood created by his weeping:

5.39 Forbidden is the pleasure of seeing the house's ruination
The froth of the flood remains, cotton-colored, in the windows [114: 2]

5.40 From the coming of the flood, what a song of joy is in the heart
The house of the lover, then, is an instrument of water sounds—a *jaltarang* [16: 2]

Both images are certainly rare, and probably Ghalib's own. The exaggeration of the poet's weeping to a flood, complete with the froth of actual floodwaters, is typical of the *sabk-e-hindī* (Indian style of Persian poetry) with its tendency to extend the detail of its imagery to extremes; the second couplet, which explores the auditory aspects of the flood of tears, is more successful. The comparison of a flooded house to the peculiarly Indian instrument the *jaltarang* (a series of bowls filled with different quantities of water—literally, the word means 'waterwave' [Platts 1930: 320]) is particularly striking, and contains interesting possibilities for comparison. The *jaltarang* depends upon the bowls being filled with water to produce the individual notes, just as the rooms of the poet's house must be filled with floods of tears to express the oxymoronic joy of his grief. There is also a secondary sensuous effect in this verse in the comparison of the sounds of rushing water to the rush of joy in the heart's song—an unlikely reaction to a flood for anyone but a lover. For Ghalib, activity and tumult, whatever the source, are important above all:

5.41 The luster of the house depends upon an uproar
Let it be the wailing of grief, if not the melody of joy [176: 5]

In the last couplet of one of Ghalib's finest ghazals (discussed in its entirety in the next chapter), the flood of Ghalib's extraordinary capacity for weeping leaves the singularity of any individual dwelling and moves out to threaten whole populations:

5.42 If Ghalib continued to cry like this—then, O people of the world
You would see these cities desolated [112: 16]

Ghalib cries out, warning the entire world of the force of his love, and the power of lamentation expressed in his verses. The sense here of potential energy, of the creative—or destructive—capacity of love, is very much Ghalib's own; and however effectively the couplets on his house demonstrate this energy, it is in his desert verses that he gives full rein to the kineticism of his poetic style.

This kineticism is not entirely of his own making, of course—it is inspired by love. In two couplets set outside the lover's house, in *his* lane, he learns from the beloved the power of speed in motion:

5.43 When, in a palanquin, she passes through my lane
She doesn't even give the bearers a chance to change shoulders [145: 1]

In a *she'r* from another ghazal, he describes his amazement in the aftermath of her appearance (see also 5.6):

5.44 Just see the havoc wrought by astonishment
I am like a footprint in the wake of her passing [54: 3]

In the first verse, the beloved's cruelty affects not only the lover, but others as well. Both couplets have the sense of motion that is so characteristic of Ghalib's desert poetry, but the second has as well a rich and complex internal logic that is typical of Ghalib's best poetry: he is left, stunned and stock still, like the footprint after her passage. The use of *k͟hāna-vīrāṅ-sāzī* (which I have translated as 'havoc', though it means 'house-ruination') in the previous line suggests also that he is not only like a footprint, but like a footprint in the dust swept away in the wind and rush of her passing; he is both created and obliterated, at least metaphorically, in a single instant. Seeing such power in motion, Ghalib is himself drawn out into the dust of the desert, where he finds a particular sense of being at home in a realm of limitless expanses.

The Desert as the Lover's True Abode

It is not surprising that Ghalib finds in the desert the greatest scope for the expression of his love: historically, the desert was the birth-ground of Arabic love poetry, out of which Persian, and later

Urdu, poetry evolved, as well as the legendary dwelling place of Majnun, who wandered its trackless enormity in sublime madness in his love for Laila. The extremes of the desert—in size, heat, cold, and (so important to the lover) desolation—provide ample scope for Ghalib's imagination. In numerical terms, his desert verses (using the words *dasht*, *ṣaḥarā*, and *bayābān*, as well as one occurrence of *jaṅgal* for 'wasteland'—totalling 36) predominate over those couplets treating the beloved's lane or house (16) and the lover's house and lane (34, including six couplets which use both 'house' and 'desert'). In the desert, the richness and complexity of his imagery, the wit and ingenuity of his logic, the breadth of his vision, and—most of all—his irrepressible energy, come into full play:

The association of the desert with the poet's house occurs in a total of six verses:

5.45 It is no less in desolation, but its dimensions are known
In the desert I feel such joy that my house is forgotten
[102: 3]

5.46 No loss in madness—to hell with it! Let my house be ruined
In exchange for a hundred yards of land, the desert is not expensive [92: 9]

5.47 My house, even had I not wept, would have been ruined
The ocean, had it not been an ocean, would have been a desert [32: 1]

5.48 Weeping has sought the ruin of my house
It makes the doors and walls to drip, to become a desert
[18: 2]

5.49 This—a desolate place, perhaps
At the sight of the desert, my house comes to mind [36: 9]

5.50 Verdant on the doors and walls, things are growing, Ghalib
I am in the desert, and in my house, spring has come
[157: 1]

Each of the above couplets has its particular virtues, and though there is a thematic connection linking the three pairs, there is no effect of duplication or repetition. (It is important to be reminded here that the bringing together of these verses is an artificial exercise intended to replicate, to some extent, a few of the associations in the mind of the person well-acquainted with Ghalib's *Dīvān*; the question of duplication is more general, and relevant to an evaluation of the *Dīvān* as a whole.)

In the first pair of couplets, Ghalib shows his preference for the desert over any house, whose dimensions are known and limited—perhaps to a mere hundred yards. The second pair of verses plays on the association between water and the aridity of the desert (the word used in both cases is *bayābāṅ*, 'waterlessnesses,' occurring as the *qāfiya*); the careful construction of a house will ultimately be undone until it becomes like a desert, whether simply by time and wind, or by the contrasting element of water, in the form of the lover's tears (such clear juxtapositions of elemental opposites in Urdu poetry are particularly pleasing to the audience). The third pair of couplets involves a greater complexity, with an exploration and reversal of the expectations of the poet's house. In the first of the two verses (5.49), the poet discovers that the desert, after all, is really rather inferior in desolation to his house, where the power of his love has had its fullest expression. The conciseness, and the exquisitely delicate irony of the verse (*ko'ī vīrānī sī vīrānī hai*—very loosely, 'well, I suppose you could call this rather desolate . . .') provides a superb example of poetic boasting at its best. The second of the two couplets (5.50) involves a perception that again surprises the poet; drawing on the manifestation of the house's ruin through vegetation (as in 5.34) to suggest the coming of spring, the poet reminds himself of the beloved—*who has not been mentioned in any of these six verses*, so absorbed has Ghalib been in his own madness—and of the possibility that she might appear (metaphorically) as a rose, since spring is the season of flowers (see 3.38). Again, the poet should have trusted his own abode, and its desolation through his love, to be adequate to his needs.

In another verse, Ghalib finds the desert to be lacking in some of the essentials for the conduct of his life:

5.51 At the hands of madness, the head is the bane of the shoulders
In the desert, O God!—there's not even a wall [113: 5]

In an amusing reversal, Ghalib cannot find in the desert any means of dashing out his brains, as on the walls of his own house, if not the step of the beloved's door (see 3.3).

Motifs Associated with the Desert

If the desert does not have walls, it does have several associated poetic motifs. It is partly for the thorns that the lover wanders the desert: the pain they bring to his unshod and blistered foot will further test his mettle (with nettles as well), and for the true lover like Ghalib, this pain is experienced as pleasure:

5.52 I am sitting with my foot in my lap, since I am a desert-wanderer
The thorns in my feet are the striated polish of the mirror on my knee [173: 1]

Ghalib stops to contemplate the thorns in his feet, and perhaps to remove them; putting his foot sole up in his lap, he finds the grain like patterns of the myriad thorns resembling the striations in a steel mirror. There is also a reference to the Sufi idiom of putting the head on the knee as an act of reflection (Mehr n.d.: 56). In a further mystical allusion, Ghalib describes elsewhere his contemplation of the beauty and splendor of God, and the hope of annihilation in Him:

5.53 My heart trembles with the difficulty of the sun's heat
I am that drop of dew upon the thorn of the desert [62: 1]

The desert deer is another motif that Ghalib employs, as already discussed in the previous chapter:

5.54 In that place where the wind combs the locks of the
(4.14) beloved
The brain of the deer of Tartary's desert is like a bag of musk [229: 1]

The desert as a setting is here unimportant except for the exotic color it provides in reference to Tartary. The exotic visual effect of the desert, with its innumerable grains of sand, is evoked in another verse from the same ghazal which refers in metaphorical terms to the act of hunting (though there are ghazal couplets in which the desert deer is actually hunted):

5.55 From the confines of the place, the grief of love has been
(3.77) reduced to dust

If each mote were a net, the vastness of the desert would be the prey [229: 3]

Making a play on the dual meanings of *ghubār* as dust as well as grief or vexation, Ghalib states that his love and passion are so great, that even when they are ground to dust, if each mote were to become a net, each net would have as its desired prey the entire desert. In a similar use of the individuation of grains of sand, Ghalib describes the trials of his wanderings:

5.56 The waves of the mirage in the desert of faithfulness?—don't ask about them
Every grain of sand is like the edge of a whetted dagger [17: 4]

The full effect of this verse depends upon the word *āb-dār*, which means, literally 'water-bearing', though it is always used in its figurative sense in such a context to mean 'bright' or 'sharpened'. This results in a play between the shimmering, wavy image of the mirage, which only appears wetted, and the waves in the steel grain of the dagger's blade, with the brightness of its whetted edge. Here, as in numerous couplets, Ghalib uses the rhetorical request *na pūch* or *mat pūch* (don't ask) to signal a situation of such calamity that it cannot be described.

In an additional couplet exploiting the opposition of desert and water (see also 5.47-8), Ghalib says:

5.57 Love is the means of lordly exaltation for the lowly
(3.76) The grain of sand becomes the desert, the drop becomes the sea [43: 3]

It is the power of love alone that enables the individual to attain mystical union with the infinite (thought this verse could be interpreted just as well, though anachronistically, as expressing the possibilities of the oppressed masses rising, united, to achieve their goals—see Naim 1967).

Majnum and the Desert

Majnun, the deranged lover of Laila, is the archetypal wanderer of the desert; also known as Qais, he appears in the *Dīvān* in a total of seven couplets associated with a word for the desert, and is clearly one of the central legendary figures in Ghalib's poetry (see 3.57/4.87):

5.58 Except for Qais, no one else came equal to the task
Perhaps it was that the desert was as narrow as the envying eye [3: 1]

Majnun's love was so great that, not only was he unchallenged as a lover, but the desert itself was envious of his powers of traversing it so as to reduce the entire expanse to a space as narrow as the eye slitted in envy. Majnun's breath, moreover, was so inflamed with love that:

5.59 The breath of Qais—the eye, the lantern of the desert
If it was not the candle of Laila's dark house, no matter
[176: 4]

If his breath could illumine the breadth of the desert, there was no loss that it could not brighten the interior of Laila's tent, which like her hair, was ebony in color.

Like Ghalib (see 5.18 and 5.23), Majnun—or at least the listener to the story of Majnun—is amazed when Laila intends a visit:

5.60 It was like Doomsday: having heard that Laila would come into Majnun's desert
He spoke, astonished: 'This too can happen in such days?'
[105: 1]

The verse is pleasantly ambiguous in its statement, so that the speaker may be interpreted as Majnun himself, or a contemporary bluenose expressing amazement at the idea of a beloved visiting a lover, whether in those days or these. But when Laila does embark in search of Majnun, she has a distinct advantage over any lover:

5.61 Who is to stop Laila's wandering in wildness
The house of Majnun, the desert-wanderer, was doorless
[19: 3]

It is of course the whole desert that is Majnun's home:

5.62 Every house reflects the rank of its master
With the death of Majnun, the wasteland is desolate
[141: 6]

But such desolation occurs only after his demise, for during his life, he found not only desert-wandering an obligation, but gardening (with his tears) as well:

5.63 Just see the power of Majnun's blood-raining eyes
The entire desert has become a splendrous carpet of flowers [148: 3]

Or referring to the story of Laila's bloodletting (Mehr n.d.: 548-9), Ghalib observes that:

5.64 The dust of Majnun's desert would spring up in flowers from the vein of Laila
If—in place of grain—the tip of the lancet were by the farmer sown [167: 2]

If such a verse is exaggerated to the point of losing its poetic effectiveness, Ghalib assesses in another verse the difficulty of such desert-gardening with a distinct sense of realistic complaint, if not of realistic imagery:

5.65 From the pieces of my heart, the fibre of every thorn becomes a rose's stalk
How long must I nurture such gardens in the desert [215: 6]

The Desert-wandering of the Poet Lover

But it is desert-wandering, not gardening, that provides the most memorable expression of Ghalib's passion. In one *she'r* Ghalib evokes the difficulty of wandering the desert by speaking of the dilemmas involved in the questions of ontology:

5.66 The desert-wandering in the notions of existence is futile
There are still highs and lows in your imagination [69: 2]

Any hope of direction, or a sense of existential location, is inappropriate for the true lover:

5.67 Love has sent me running in the desert, where
(3.78) There is no road but the glance of an eye in a picture [93: 2]

Since it is impossible for the eye in the picture to have the power of sight, it is equally fruitless for the lover to expect a clear path in the desert where he roams. He is compelled so to wander as long as his energy sustains him, even when his friends attempt to suppress his intense restlessness:

5.68 My companions could not cure my wildness
Even in prison, my imagination wandered the desert [7: 6]

5.69 The forbiddance of desert-wandering is of no use
My feet are bound to wander, even in chains [93: 1]

(The pun in English is fortuitous). Once he has entered the wilderness, Ghalib's passion has spectacular consequences:

5.70 Hidden in dust is the desert, because of me
Grovelling is the ocean on the clay, before me [209: 4]

5.71 From the turmoil of madness, nothing is visible, Asad
The desert is a fistful of dust in our eyes [222: 3]

Ghalib's passage across the desert not only obscures the ordinarily visible world; it gives meaning to the world of ultimate realities:

5.72 With but one step of madness, the tome of possibility fell open
The path was the back-stitching for the pages of the two-world desert [19: 2]

As striking as the above image is visually (the train of foot-prints in the dust resembling the individual stitches in the book's binding), it is in a sense of motion, of that distinctly Ghalibian effect of kineticism, that the desert is most clearly manifest.

In the first instance, the action of the poet's wandering is in the immediate past, though the traces still remain:

5.73 From the imprint of my blisters, the road of the desert of madness
Has become a string of pearls, a chain of lamps illumined by me [191: 5]

The image is essentially static, with the lambence of blisters producing the lustrous pearl-like prints, so that the kineticism is essentially frozen, with an additional flicker of fire in the image of the *cirāghān* (firework, rack of lamps), created by the brightness of his blood, or the heat of his pace. The implicit evocation of that pace is made clearer elsewhere:

5.74 Like a charred paper is the page of the desert
In the footprints, the glow of the hot pace remains [70: 2]

The entire desert, in all its vastness, is for Ghalib but a page in size (see 5.72 above); even that is reduced to ashes by the fierceness of Ghalib's love and the fiery flight of his madness, which has the capacity to incinerate merely by the force of imagination:

5.75 Whom can I tell where the heat of the essence of thought is
Even the thought of madness—and the desert burned [5: 4]

In another of his finest couplets, Ghalib draws our imagination into even more vigorous imagery, presenting an incomparable evocation of the sheer vertigo of his *shauq* (for it has been *shauq*, not *'ishq*, that has driven Ghalib into the wilderness). Moving from fire to water imagery, he says:

5.76 Even in exhaustion, my passion is no less than the desert itself
The bubble of the surging wave is my foot's print [11: 1]

He achieves the necessary connection between his single footprint and the individual bubble of the breaking wave, then leaves our perception to the multiplication of his running footprints into the infinitude of bubbles in the wave. But there is more happening here as well. He creates a sense of exhaustion, as well as of relief and exhilaration, in the image of the wave (though it is most unlikely that Ghalib ever swam in the surf, he was still able to imagine the experience). The water-wave imagery is superimposed over the visually consonant but temporally dissonant image of waves of dust or sand in the desert, with the result that there is a major shift of time referents, almost as though by the acceleration of a film. In short, the tension between these two images leaves the reader-listener's perception in a state of shimmering ambiguity.

This ambiguity is brought to an extraordinary degree of paradox in one of Ghalib's remaining desert couplets:

5.77 At every step my distance from the goal is evident
The desert runs from me with my own swiftness [191: 1]

One can hardly imagine a more palpable, even nightmare-like

evocation of the impossibility of achieving one's most challenging goals. Imbedded within these few words is an entire approach to experience, with the implication that a slower pace means a slower receding of the goal, and yet the inevitability of the faster pace brings a corresponding, tortuous continuation of separation from the goal. We are left with a sense of Ghalib's love as large as the desert, and of a dizzying but persistent sense of the elusiveness of his destination.

The Desert and Death

Ultimately, like Majnun (5.62), the poet-lover must succumb to exhaustion from his efforts:

5.78 The tears of desert-wandering madness are taken to the bosom of my shirt's hem
The disabled heart is fallen into the embrace of the bed
[195: 2]

The *dāman*, or hemmed border of the lover's garment, is expected by poetic tradition to be wet with tears; as the lover's strength subsides, he can no longer produce floods of tears, but at least he is capable of providing his *dāman* with its beloved moisture (see 4.13). Stranded, perhaps, in a foreign land, or perhaps already in his grave, Ghalib asks that both his friendlessness and the desert itself be obliterated:

5.79 Upon my head, from the rush of pain at being lost from home, pour
That fistful of dust we call the desert [230: 4]

After all his efforts, and the spectacular demonstration of his lover, the desert itself becomes insignificant.

When the end has come, Ghalib is still not *maghlub* (conquered):

5.80 May God grant such passion for desert-wandering, that after my death
My feet may yet move by themselves, within the shroud
[122: 5]

He remains, even in death, the poet-lover driven and consumed by a lofty and noble passion. In the arena of action he has chosen (the arena of *'ishq* and *shauq*) he is, like his *ta<u>kh</u>allus* 'Asad', a lion (see Schimmel 1979: 9); he remains, entirely, '*<u>gh</u>ālib*': 'overcoming, overpowering, victorious, triumphant, prevailing, predominant . . . superior, surpassing, excelling' (Platts 1930: 768) in the ultimate competition of love.

We have seen above the ways in which Ghalib employs three of the ghazal's traditional settings to express particular aspects of his love. The first verses presented most of the essential features of the beloved's lane and house, where Ghalib first learned the power of love, and the difficulties of its pursuit: he is unable to pass her doorstep or gate (guarded by the doorkeeper) in order to attend her *bazm* or *maḥfil*, decorated with flowers, perfumed with incense, the spirit gladdened by wine (see 447-53). The lover can only hope for some glimpse of her through the chink or window of her wall (see 4.105, 5.3, and 5.5), or she may appear on the balcony, roof, or parapet (see 6.12); yet when the poet does see her, her lane becomes a place of astonishment. This locale, in short, reflects different aspects of Ghalib's passive love—his waiting, his frustration and longing—though the beloved is not unaffected by his presence; she may become famous because of it (5.15-16).

The lover's house, in contrast, is the instrument through which Ghalib expresses his pain in the evening of grief (*shab-e-<u>gh</u>am*) and the night of separation (*shām-e-firāq*). It is in a state tending to ruin; it has no need of a keeper at its door or gate—unless it is Ghalib himself who watches for the beloved (5.19). The house is filled with lamentations and wailing (5.41); or it is a *darvesh's* house, empty of possession (5.24) except perhaps a beggar's bowl (5.23), or some wretched, thorny bedding (4.19) on which the poet tosses and turns, sleepless; or perhaps a pillow, on which he dies (a pillow which almost certainly will never be visited by the beloved except at his death, as in 4.76). Yet the lover's house is a place which may be transformed through Ghalib's passion into a manifestation of enraptured devastation (5.35-38): it is a house whose windows (except for the doors and walls, an occasional fireplace, and a niche—6.26—the only detail of the building's construction) have the primary function of permitting a *view* of destruction (5.39), just as the window of the beloved's house might allow a *glimpse* of her; a house whose rooms become the chambers of a musical instrument filled with the sounds of water and flooding from the poet's tears (5.40). The lover's house, then, becomes the external and objective manifestation of his inner state. If he cannot be efficacious in winning the beloved's favor, he can in many ways transcend any need for that favor, by turning the pursuit of this love into an end in itself, in which the spectacular demonstration of that love brings him an ecstasy that is no small thing in itself. He is able to prevail by seizing his misfortune, and transforming it into victory by immersing himself—paradoxically—in the destructive element in order to create the proof of his love's incomparable power.

The desert, finally, is the setting of Ghalib's greatest virtuosity in love: vast, trackless, strewn with thorns, beset with mirages and dust-storms, seemingly unconquerable—until Ghalib reduces it to insignificance.

The above network of images, however, represents only a few of the available topoi of location or setting to which the ghazal poet has access. Drawing again on the entire *Dīvān,* we can construct an artificial city of images, some of which represent an extension of the beloved's house (a picture-house, a house of mirrors, a house or temple of idols—all involving some element of beauty, vanity, or worship), or of the lover's abode (a mourning house, or house of chains—in which the poet is bound by his friends to prevent him from desert wandering or other disgraceful displays of madness). Or the poet may be imprisoned in a cell, after a trial in the court of love—which may represent either the judgement of love, the beloved, or society at large—or his sentence may be carried out at the gallows (with an echo of Hallaj, the martyr of mystical love), or at some less definite place of slaughter by the beloved's sword. After his death, the poet must be buried in some grave or tomb—settings which hold, as we have seen above, a particularly intense fascination for Ghalib.

This city of images also has commercial and financial districts, with bazaars of love having stores of beauty and transactions in the currency of heart, mind, life, and soul (see 3.58). There is a factory—the 'workship of existence' (*kār-gāh-e-hastī*)—presumably a metaphorical reference to the world itself as the forge and mill of the human spirit; and there are also occasional furnaces, most probably in the same connection. There is a 'trust-house' (*vadī'at-khāna*), a sort of Bank of the Heart in which the poet has been forced to deposit every drop of his blood as proof of his dedication to the beloved (whose eyelashes, of course, assist in the preparations for that deposit [114: 3]). The Imperial Treasury even appears once in the *Dīvān*, in connection with the opening of an Office of Verses as an extension of the Royal Court [14: 1].[1] At the opposite end of the spectrum from the Imperial circles is the gaming house of love (3.33), where the poet goes to play at chance in life and love.

Closely related to this last is the broad network of imagery built up around the opposition between the tavern and the mosque, or in other configurations, the mosque and the church, temple of idols, and fire-temple, with the associated personae of the *rind* (the poet as rakehell and toper), *sāqī* (cupbearer), *shaikh* (pious hypocrite, as a representation of the orthodox religious establishment), Brahmin, and fire-worshipper (with whom the poet often identifies himself). As often noted in writings on the ghazal (Persian as well as Urdu), the wine depicted in such verses may be intended to be taken on one (or both) of two levels of meaning: wine as wine, a superior intoxicant for the spirit, and opiate for the pain of life and love; and wine as gnosis, the knowledge of the divine reality, a metaphorical concealment of the basic message of Sufism. Contiguous settings referred to occasionally include the school of manners (see 6.33), the *madrasa* or religious school, the *khānqāh* or monastery, and the *'īdgāh* (a special category of mosque for the celebration of *'īd*, as a metaphor for the place from which the lover looks for the first glimpse of the new moon of the beloved's [moonlike] face, which signals the joyous holiday at the end of the month of fasting—i.e., from being deprived of the sight of the beloved).

Probably the setting most frequently alleged, by the critics of the ghazal, to have become a cliché, is the garden. Here, however, is an excellent example of how the process of connotation can charge a single word with numerous implications: the mere mention of *bāgh* or *caman* or *gulistān* will inevitably suggest the symbolic apparitions of the beloved (as rose) and the poet (as nightingale)—the *gul-o-bulbul* of which so much fun has been made. Between these two there may be many types of relationships which may be explored; but the nightingale and the rose also exist in relationship to the other personae of the garden—the hunter and the *gul-cīn* ('plucker of flowers,' through whose personage the role of the rival assumes a new significance). Specific garden settings include the rose-bed, tulip-bed, and the grove of cypress, in connection with the beloved, and the *āshyāna* (nest) of the nightingale; a mention of the latter would always invoke the implicit threat, if not the actual occurrence of the lightning which will destroy that nest. In other cases, the nightingale may be imprisoned in a cage (*qafas*), which in itself suggests a possibility of the most desirable medium of communication with the beloved—the breeze (*bād* or *nasīm*). As with the tavern-mosque network, this group of images is worthy of a fuller description and more detailed analysis than is possible within the scope of the present work.

The last major network of locations of the ghazal is based upon the process of travel, either in some explicit pilgrimage (as in the path of Sufism—see Schimmel 1975b: 98-186), or in the demented wandering of the desert by the poet. In this network one finds references to roads and paths (of the wind, of love, or annihilation), the desert (e.g. of the two worlds), valleys (as of thought), stages, tents, caravanserais, and the goal, while the poet travels from his native land into some foreign realm. In related connections in the *Dīvān* there are allusions to Delhi, Lucknow, Hindustan, Tartary, Najaf (the location of Ali's tomb), the Ka'ba and the Well of Zamzam in Mecca, and Mt. Sinai; in a voyage back through time to Persian legend and to the events of the Qur'an, Ghalib refers to Laila's tent, Majnun's house (the desert), Nakhshab (famous for its magical moon—see Platts 1930: 1126), Khusrau's pleasure-palace, Joseph's prison, Canaan, the ancient Assyrian city of Nimrud, Egypt, and the Throne of Solomon.

The landscape of the ghazal is not exclusively urban, but includes numerous references to nature, even beyond those of the cultivated and tamed poetic garden, or the metaphorical desert of madness. The farmer's fields, and particularly his harvest (like the nightingale's nest, always at threat from the lightning) appear occasionally in the *Dīvān*, as do mines as sources of precious substances. Beyond the more cultivated regions, Ghalib also refers to canebrakes, and to entire, jewelled fields of morning dew on meadows or on patches of thorn (see 5.53 and 6.22).

In a larger perspective, there is the world itself, with its mountains and wilderness valleys, its rivers, seas, and oceans with their banks and shores, and (again, for Ghalib a highly evocative image) their whirlpools. Moving into the sky, one finds certain representations of the firmament as a bowl, dome, or dustbin, and various references to celestial bodies: the sun, moon, planets, single constellations (see 6.27), and galaxies of stars (3.36). In the spiritual realm, there is hell as well as heaven, Paradise, and the Empyrean. Numbers themselves assume an effect of mystical or magical significance: the two worlds, the six directions (signifying the whole universe), the seven seas and the seven heavens, and indeed, creation itself (*āfrīnash*—see 1.3), with its infinitude of wonders.

The limitations inherent in the traditional settings of the ghazal—like those of ghazal's personae—should not pose an insurmountable challenge for the capable poet; the poet who is truly accomplished, like any great artist, uses the ordinary materials of his medium to express his unique vision. When Ghalib does desire novelty, for example, he may introduce fields of brilliant henna running to the horizon of the desert (4.103), or vast reefs of coral blazing in the ocean as a metaphor of the poet's lamp burning in the dust-storm of the desert (4.104). But in general, it is through the inspired and innovative recombination of images already charged with meaning and associations that the ghazal poet achieves his aim: the expression of his own perspective through an established genre understood by almost everyone within the Urdu-speaking world.

NOTE

1. One setting which defies classification—the Royal Bath (*ḥamām*)—appears [181.6] in congratulations to the King for recovering from an illness, and having his first bath thereafter.

CHAPTER 6

An Analysis of Three Selected Ghazals

When you read these lines, think of me
and what I have not written here.

ADRIENNE RICH (1969: 61)

The poetry of the ghazal, as should now be clear, is a poetry of exclusion: the poet must discard all that cannot be said within two lines. The first chapter above described some of the processes of compression necessary for an effective poetic statement within the confines of the individual couplet. The four chapters which followed were designed to illustrate, using examples from the *Dīvān* of Mirza Ghalib, how networks of associations may accumulate around the central phenomena, characters, and settings of the ghazal, in order to facilitate the process of compression; these chapters attempted the artificial formation—albeit from the work of a single poet—of the sort of accretive concordance (of connotations around selected nuclear ideas) which a literate Urdu speaker would intuitively form through years of enlightened exposure to the entire tradition of Urdu poetry. In this concluding chapter I will make a few additional remarks about the structure and context of the ghazal, then turn to three of Ghalib's most eloquent ghazals in a summary analysis of the ways in which these various devices, techniques, and topoi come together in the full ghazal poem.

In the last stage of our attempt to understand the tremendous appeal that the ghazal has in Indo-Muslim culture, it is useful to turn once again to Huizinga's writings on poetry:

> In archaic culture the language of poets is still the most effective means of expression, with a function much wider and more vital than the satisfaction of literary aspirations. It puts ritual into words, it is the arbiter of social relationships, the vehicle of wisdom, justice and morality. . . . But as civilization increases in spiritual amplitude, the regions where the

play-factor is weak or barely perceptible will develop at the cost of those where it has free play. Civilization as a whole becomes more serious—law and war, commerce, technics and science lose touch with play; and even ritual, once the field *par excellence* for its expression, seems to share the process of dissociation. Finally only poetry remains as the stronghold of living and noble play.

The playfulness of poetic language is so obvious that there is hardly any need to illustrate it with examples. In view of the enormous importance attached to the practice of poetry in archaic culture it will not surprise us to find that its technique is brought there to the highest pitch of strictness and refinement. It is based on a meticulous code of rules absolutely binding but allowing an almost infinite variation. The system is preserved and passed on as a noble science. [1955: 134]

I am not suggesting from this that the ghazal is an exclusively archaic poetry, but rather that it maintains some of the characteristics of such poetry, and thus has continued to be 'a stronghold of living and noble play' throughout periods of cultural change and advancement.

The 'noble science' of the ghazal requires a complete suspension of normal temporal and spatial perspectives. Like the world of chess, the realm of the ghazal possesses a reality unto itself. Like chess, the ghazal appears to the uninitiated spectator to consist of a fixed number of agents whose options for action in the conventional settings seem terribly restricted. The connoisseur, on the other hand, sees a fascinating and complex network of associations, conflicts, challenges, precedents, strategies, actions, consequences, and implications, the contemplation of which—or even more, the participation in which—can absorb the mind utterly for hours altogether. Just as the appeal of chess lies in the challenge of making the most resourceful use of a limited number of options, so the appeal and challenge of the ghazal lie in its presentation of traditional images and motifs (limited in number and recurring in almost all ghazals) in new perspectives and relationships which, by permutation and combination, are potentially infinite in number.

Yet whereas chess has but one ultimate aim—the capture of the opponent's king—and thus concentrates on the mode of warfare, the ghazal can function in several modes. As Huizinga observes, 'all poetry is born of play'; but he might as well be writing specifically about the ghazal when he continues: 'the sacred play of worship, the festive play of courtship, the martial play of the contest, the disputations play of braggadocio, mockery and invective, the nimble play of wit and readiness' (1955: 129). Up to this point, I have tried to demonstrate the ways in which the ghazal can function in these differing modes.

Variety in the Complete Ghazal

Writing about the European troubadours, Frederick Goldin remarks that 'the special distinction of the troubadour lyric is that it depends for its coherence and effect on a live relation between the poet, or the singer, and the attending audience. The troubadour technique of composing for an audience required the singer to strike many different attitudes in the course of the song' (1973: 6-7). The ghazal poet reciting to a live audience is faced with much the same challenge; as Ralph Russell has written, he must resort to variety in order to maintain the attention of this audience, and will often make use of 'padding' (mediocre but formally correct couplets) to heighten the effect of the two or three best couplets of a ghazal (1969: 121).

Within the microcosm of the ghazal—formal as it is, and bound with an etiquette that allows an ultimate transcendence of all rules—a myriad variety of relationships are created and examined. All are based upon some elemental association, usually on attraction, and most express a response to that association or attraction; some are static and formal, others (particularly in Ghalib) are dynamic, either in equilibrium or in a state of continuing activity and transformation.

Beyond the particular relationships examined in the individual couplet, there is also a wide variety of techniques and devices used (these were summarized in the first chapter), as well as a broad range of grammatic or semantic structures: verb tenses (past, past conditional, present, subjunctive, and future); expressive moods (declarative, interrogative, imperative, and exclamatory); subjects of address (beloved, friend, advisor, self, God, an undefined listener, etc.); tones (complaint, lament, boast, astonishment, challenge, praise, irony, ridicule, skepticism, paradox, and so forth); and sensory invocation (sight, sound, taste, smell, temperature, pressure, and kinaesthesia). In the linking of these various elements, there may be processes which function together to a degree found along a continuum running from extreme simplicity to extreme complexity.

Of the content of the ghazal, it is frequently observed that the genre addresses itself primarily—though by no means exclusively—to love. According to Hali, the two main themes of the ghazal are erotic (*'ishqīya*) and anacreontic (*k͟hamriyāt*), with the latter including both wine-bibbing and its concomitant, the abuse of the orthodox element in Islam (n.d.: 126-7). Sadiq, writing in English, distinguishes the erotic and bacchic strains (1964: 27), and adds a third which he identifies as gnomic (which he also calls *tams̤īliya,* or exemplary), whose object is 'to give the charm of the imagination to ethical or philosophical truths stated in the first hemistich and illustrated by an apt simile in the second' (1964: 30). Sayyid Fayyaz Mahmud divides the themes of the ghazal into three groups: the amatory, the mystical, and the rational (1969: 124). But as Hali observes, the ghazal has in practice become the organ of expression for whatever comes into the poet's mind (n.d.: 132).

To consider these questions of classification and variety, I will now turn to three of Ghalib's best-known ghazals: *muddat hū'ī hai yār ko mehmān kīye hū'e* (234), *āh ko cāhiye ik 'umr as̤ar hone tak* (79), and *sab kahāṅ kuch lāla-o-gul meṅ numāyāṅ ho ga'īṅ* (112).

Ghazal: muddat hū'ī hai . . .

This ghazal, on the basis of the structural and thematic considerations of the previous chapters, should be essentially comprehensible without additional commentary. The most remarkable aspect of this sequence of couplets is the cumulative effect they produce, though some of the individual verses are unusual and capable of standing alone with particular distinction. Like the second ghazal in chapter II (*yeh na thī hamārī qismat . . .*), this ghazal has a definite, internally logical continuity. In this case, the continuity is created by a variety of techniques: repetition; the use of synonyms; the expansion of an idea in subsequent verses; limitation of subject and image; and exaggeration.

6.1 muddat hū'ī hai yār ko mehmāṅ kī'e hū'e
josh-e-qadḥ se bazm cirāg͟hāṅ kī'e hū'e

6.2 kartā hūṅ jama' phir jigar-e-lak͟ht-lak͟ht ko
'arṣa hū'ā hai da'vat-e-mizhgāṅ kī'e hū'e

6.3 phir vaẓa'-e-iḥtiyāṭ se rukne lagā hai dam
barsoṅ hū'e haiṅ cāk-e-garībāṅ kī'e hū'e

6.4 phir garm-e-nālahā'e-sharar-bār hai nafas
muddat hū'ī hai sair-e-cirāghāṅ kī'e hū'e

6.5 phir pursish-e-jarāḥat-e-dil ko calā hai 'ishq
sāmān-e-ṣad hazār namak-dāṅ kī'e hū'e

6.6 phir bhar rahā hai khāma-e-mizhgāṅ ba khūṇ-e-dil
sāz-e-caman-ṭarāzī-e-dāmāṅ kī'e hū'e

6.7 ba-ham dīgar hū'e haiṅ dil-o-dīda phir raqīb
naẓẓāra-o-khayāl kā sāmāṅ kī'e hū'e

6.8 dil phir ṭavāf-e-kū-e-malāmat ko jāe hai
pindār kā ṣanam-kada vīrāṅ kī'e hū'e

6.9 phir shauq kar rahā hai kharīdar ki ṭalab
'arz-e-mata'-e-'aql-o-dil-o-jān kī hū'e

6.10 dauṛe hai phir har ek gul-o-lāla par khayāl
ṣad gulistaṅ nigāh kā sāmāṅ kī'e hū'e

6.11 phir cāhtā hūṅ nāma-e-dildār kholnā
jāṅ naẕr-e-dil-farebī-e-'unvāṅ kī'e hū'e

6.12 māṅge hai phir kisī ko lab-e-bām par havas
zulf-e-siyāh rukh peh pareshāṅ kī'e hū'e

6.13 cāhe hai phir kisī ko muqābil meṅ ārzū
surme se tez dashna-e-mizhgāṅ kī'e hū'e

6.14 ek nau-bahār-e-naz ko tāke hai phir nigāh
cehra furogh-e-mai se gulistāṅ kī'e hū'e

6.15 phir jī meṅ hai keh dar peh kisī ke paṛe raheṅ
sar zer-e-bār-e-minat-e-darbāṅ kī'e hū'e

6.16 ji ḍhūṇḍta hai phir vahī furṣat keh rāt din
baiṭhe raheṅ taṣavvure-jānāṅ kī'e hū'e

6.17 Ghālib hameṅ na cheṛ keh phir josh-e-ashk se
baiṭhe haiṅ ham tahīya-e-ṭūfāṅ kī'e hū'e [234: 1-17]

6.1 It's been a long time since I made the beloved my guest
(4.23) Since, from the cup's boiling fervor, making the assembly a
display of lamps

6.2 I gather again the pieces of my heart
It's been an age since I invited her eyelashes to feast

6.3 Again, from caution, my breath has begun to be stifled
It's been years since I tore the collar of my shirt

6.4 Again, hot with spark-scattering sighs is my breath
It's been a long time since I went to see the fireworks

6.5 Again, love has gone to inquire after the heart's wound
(3.21) Taking as its luggage a hundred thousand salt-boxes

6.6 Again the pen of my eyelash is filling with my heart's blood
Making the flower-emroidery on the hem of my shirt

6.7 They have become then—my heart and eye—each other's
(4.84) rival
Having made sight and thought their appurtenances

6.8 The heart again has gone on pilgrimage to the lane of
(5.10) reproach
Having made desolate the idol-house of proud thought

6.9 Again, love is seeking a buyer
(3.58) Having offered the merchandise of mind and heart, and life and soul

6.10 My thought again has run toward every rose and tulip
Providing a hundred gardens for my sight

6.11 Again I want to open the letter of my sweetheart
Having given my soul to the spell of its address

6.12 Again, my desire longed for someone on the edge of the balcony
Scattering her black tresses across her face

6.13 Desire has again wished for someone to confront me
Having sharpened with antimony the daggers of her eyelashes

6.14 At a coyness like new spring has my sight again stared
Having made the wine-inflamed face a garden

6.15 Again, it is my heart's desire to remain lying on a certain one's doorstep

Leaving my head at the mercy of the doorkeeper's kindness

6.16 My heart searches for that same leisure, that night and day
I could sit in rapt imagination of my beloved

6.17 Ghalib, don't annoy/tease me—for again, with a boiling fervor of tears
I am seated in preparations for the deluge [234: 1-17]

The central concern of this ghazal is clearly the state of the lover in separation from his beloved—a separation made all the more agonizing by the memory of some past time, invoked in the first *she'r*, of the nights when he used to meet with the beloved; each subsequent verse explores some facet of this process of recollection, or of re-enactment in the present of the lover's remembered condition in the past.

These processes of recollection and re-enactment are underscored by an unusual degree of repetition throughout the ghazal. At the most obvious level is the conventional repetition of the *radīf*, or repeated rhyme, in both hemistiches of the first *she'r* and in the second hemistich of each succeeding verse; the *radīf* here is, like many *radīfs* (as those in the two following ghazals), a verbal phrase, *kī'e hū'e* (*did, had done, having done*), which reinforces the effect of memory and re-enactment. There is also the conventional recurrence of the *qāfiya*, or true rhyme (in this case the syllable *-āṅ*) before the *radīf*; yet in this ghazal of seventeen verses Ghalib uses each of three different *qāfiya* words twice: *cirāghāṅ* ('lamps, lights; a display of lamps, a general illumination' [Platts 1930: 428]) in 6.2 and 6.4; *sāmāṅ* (luggage, paraphernalia) in 6.7 and 6.10 (and elsewhere in 6.5); and *mizhgāṅ* (eyelashes) in 6.3 and 6.13 (and once more in 6.6). This repetition of a *qāfiya* word within a single ghazal is rather unusual for Ghalib, and it provides a rare opportunity to observe him employing the same rhyming word in two different verses with identical metric structures. It is unlikely that Ghalib felt any difficulty in finding enough suitable rhyming words for so long a ghazal, since in the third ghazal below (6.25-41), he uses in a sequence of sixteen verses an additional twelve different *qāfiya* words (also ending in *-āṅ*) without any repetition at all. Rather, he probably wanted to display his virtuosity, and surprise his listeners with several examples of an imaginative duplication of a *qāfiya* word.

Another unusual technique in this ghazal is the repetition of the word *phir* (again, then) somewhere in the first hemistich of every couplet after the first; instead of creating an effect of monotony, the skillful use of this word reinforce the modalities of memory and re-enactment throughout the ghazal, and provides an interesting structural balance to the repetition of the *qāfiya* and the *radīf* in the second hemistich of each verse.

Further repetition establishes at least two distinct subsequences within the ghazal. The first four couplets are linked by the phrases *muddat hū'ī hai* (6.1), *'arṣa hū'ā hai* (6.2), *barsoṅ hū'e hain* (6.3), and again, *muddat hū'ī hai* (6.4), which evoke a range of time words (long time, age, years) and grammatical diversity (feminine singular, masculine singular and plural) to make more varied the facets of a single theme: time has passed. A second sub-sequence is created by the appearance of *dil* (heart) in 6.5 through 6.9, and *dil-farebī* (enchantment) and *dil-dār* (sweetheart) in 6.11. Less obviously, two words for breath (*dam* and *nafas*) occur in parallel position at the end of the first hemistich in 6.3 and 6.4; the word *kisī* (someone, a certain one—oblique form) recurs in 6.12, 6.13, and 6.15; synonymous parallel phrases

[māṅge
cāhe] hai phir kisī ko . . . [havas
ārzū]

('Desire has again wanted someone . . .') occur in 6.12 and 6.13; *jī* (heart, desire, wish) is the first word of 6.15 and the second of 6.16; and *baiṭhe* (seated, sitting) is the first word of the second hemistich of both 6.16 and 6.17. A general sense of closure is achieved in the last verse through the repetition of *josh* (boiling, fervor), after its initial use in the first couplet.

This degree of repetition alone is enough to make this ghazal more unified in tone than most of the others in the *Dīvān*. But Ghalib further enhances the sense of unity by limiting each couplet to a description of some aspect of the lover's state of mind; in examining this state at length in a single ghazal, Ghalib in effect provides a catalogue of topoi associated with the behavior of the lover languishing in separation from his beloved.

The lover's emotions are seen both as *'ishq* (6.5) and *shauq* (6.9), though here there is no distinction of the sort discussed in Chapter III. Closely related states of mind and heart are denoted by *havas* (desire, lust), the last word of the first hemistich of 6.12, and by *ārzū* (desire, longing), which follows in parallel position in 6.13.

In a majority of the couplets, the lover is presented in one of his conventional postures (many of which have already been discussed at length in the preceding chapters): preparing his heart for the butchery of the beloved's eyelashes (6.2); tearing his collar to escape the strictures of society (6.3); sighing sighs inflamed with the heat of his grief (6.4); savoring his suffering (6.5); weeping in order to maintain his shirt-hem in the required state of dampness (6.6); dedication to contemplation of the beloved's matchless beauty, whether in actual vision or in his mind's eye (6.7, 6.10, 6.12, 6.14, and 6.16, in a sequence to be discussed presently); commitment to achieving the destruction of his house (here, idol-house of pride) in order to make a pilgrimage to the lane of the beloved (6.8); offering himself to the beloved for sale (6.9), enchantment (6.11), and sacrifice (6.13); establishing his residence on the beloved's doorstep (6.15), and again, weeping—or preparing to weep with the spectacular turbulence of a storm (6.17). In one reading this last verse is a fitting and dynamic conclusion to the ghazal, in an expression of the poet's total dedication to his cause, and the power of his love. But in another interpretation this verse may be read as an ironic comment on the preceding verses, with the ever skeptical 'Ghalib' threatening to tease the poet, whom he has seen going through this elaborate sequence of antics so many times before, always self-serious, and always failing.

Of all of the postures in this ghazal, that of contemplating the beloved is dominant. We have already discussed numerous verses describing the importance of sight to love (e.g., 3.62-69, and 3.83), and of the lover's overwhelming desire to see the beloved (e.g., 4.2-7), or if that is impossible, to keep the thought of her foremost in his mind (4.12-13). This distinction is explored in some depth in this ghazal, being established in 6.7 with the identification of the heart and eye as rivals—the former intent upon the thought (*khayāl*) of the beloved, and the latter yearning for an actual vision (*naẓẓāra*) of her (see 3.59). In a subsequent verse, the thought (again *khayāl*) of the beloved sends the lover running after 'every rose and tulip', whose color reminds him of the vision (here *nigāh*—see 3.70) of the 'hundred gardens' (*ṣad gulistāṅ*) in the luster of her superior complexion (6.10). In 6.12, his desire (*havas*) longs to see 'someone' (*kisī ko*) on the 'lip' (*lab*) of the balcony, with her black tresses (see 3.106) scattered (presumably by the wind—see 5.54) across her face (*ru<u>kh</u>*). In a parallel construction in 6.13, the poet's desire (here, *ārzū*) yearns to see (literally, 'confront', as in a battle) 'a certain one' (*kisī ko*), with her arsenal of long, dagger-like lashes sharpened by the application of antimony (the metallic powder used cosmetically on the eyelids to enhance the enchanting power of the eyes and their lashes). Vision (*nigāh*) returns in 6.14 to stare at 'a coyness like new spring' in the beloved's face (here, *cehra*), whose color has been inflamed by wine into a garden (*gulistāṅ*—again, as in 6.10, the *qāfiya*). Finally, in 6.16—as if the previous vision were not enough—Ghalib desires nothing less than to sit night and day in pure contemplation (*taṣavvur*) of the beloved, in a seeming victory of thought over sight in the rivalry established in 6.7.

The connections among these sight/thought verses are strengthened by the linkages between *sāmāṅ* (appurtenances) of sight and thought as the *qāfiya* word in 6.7, and the hundred gardens 'provided' (*sāmāṅ kī'e hū'e*—again, as the *qāfiya* in 6.10) for his sight; and between these hundred gardens (*gulistāṅ*) in 6.10 and the face like a garden (again, *gulistāṅ*) as the *qāfiya* of 6.14. These linkages are further enhanced by the previous appearance of *sāmān* (as the 'luggage' of love) in 6.5, and of *caman* in the compound *caman-ṭarāzī* (the 'garden-embroidery' of the lover's shirt-hem) in 6.6. The element of numerical exaggeration, finally, occurs both in the hundred thousand (*ṣad hazār*) salt-cellars as *sāmān* (luggage) in 6.5, and the *ṣad gulistāṅ* (hundred gardens) of the poet's sight in 6.10.

In a separate network of references, Ghalib explores some of the connotations of the poet-lover's heart. His *jigar*, in 6.2, is fragmented, though it is not clear whether the poet is the one who cuts his heart into pieces in order to provide morsels for the *da'vat* (feast) of the beloved's eyelashes, or whether the sharp, arrow-like lashes are themselves responsible for the sundering of the heart (see 2.14, 3.67, 4.8-10, and 4.66). In any case, the heart is wounded by the arrows of Love, who in personification brings massive quantities of salt (see 4.33 and 4.68) to heap upon the wound, thus increasing the lover's delight in suffering (6.5). The poet uses his heart's blood to fill his eyelash pen for the decoration of his shirt-hem (6.6), presumably in the process of blotting his eyes (see 5.78), which in this case are moist with tears of blood (see 4.11). The concept of the rival is cleverly introduced, without distracting from the examination of the lover's state, in the rivalry between the heart and the eye (6.7). The heart, apparently becoming a good Muslim, lays waste the idol-house of prideful thought, and goes in pilgrimage (*ṯavāf*—a word also with connotations of the circumambulation of the Ka'ba in Mecca) to the 'lane of reproach'—i.e. of the beloved (6.8). Along with his mind and his life/ soul (*jān*), the poet offers up his heart for sale, presumably to the beloved (6.9), then later gives his soul (again, *jān*) to the heart-enchanting power (*dilfarebī*) of the address on the letter from his sweetheart (*dil-dār*—literally, 'owner of the heart') in 6.11. The final resolution of the heart-soul sequence occurs in the resonance of *jānāṅ* (the plural of *jān*, used here for the beloved) in the *qāfiya* of 6.16.

In this demonstration of a *musalsal* (continuous) ghazal, Ghalib has moved competently over conventional ground with his typical capacity for novelty and surprise. Unfortunately, the first couplet is probably also the best, with the complete simplicity of the first line balanced by the synaesthetic kineticism of the second. The comparison of the wine-filled cup with the individual lamp of the *cirāg̲h̲an* in terms of shape, color, and warmth is ingenious. The choice of the word *josh* ('boiling, ebullition; effervescence; heat, excitement, passion, emotion; lust; fervour, ardour, zeal; vehemence; enthusiasm; frenzy' [Platts 1930: 397]) gives the couplet—and by extension (to the last verse with its repetition of *josh*), the entire ghazal—a high degree of energy. The process of compression, moreover, is facilitated here by a particularly frequent use of the *eẓāfa* (33 times) and the Persian *va* ('and'—5 times) and *ba* ('with'—twice), all of which, in combination with a highly Persianized diction, lend the ghazal a distinctively elegant flavor. While many of the couplets are merely witty, or pretty, the use of kinetic and elemental imagery (fire, wine, salt, blood, antimony, and the turbulence of the storm)—along with the exaggeration of wine to fire, sighs to fireworks, a hundred thousand boxes of salt and a hundred vivid gardens, tears to blood, and the poet's weeping to a typhoon—does create some memorable verses in the context of a larger poem, which is in itself remarkable for the internal richness of its cross-references and unified effect. Yet one finds here only periodic flashes of that eloquence and universality which characterize the best of Ghalib's poetry; he tends to achieve these ends in ghazals which are less discursive, and which allow a mixture of the erotic (as in the above ghazal) with what Sadiq calls the gnomic (1964: 30), and Fayyaz Mahmud calls the mystical and rational ([1969]: 124).

Ghazal: āh ko cāhiye ik 'umr . . .

The second ghazal from among Ghalib's masterworks has a less obvious sense of unity, created largely by a few repetitions in addition to its *qāfiya* (*-ar*) and *radīf, hone tak* (until . . .), which in recent editions has replaced the archaic *hote tak:*

6.18 āh ko cāhiye ik 'umr as̤ar hone tak
kaun jītā hai terī zulf ke sar hone tak

6.19 dām-e-har mauj meṅ hai ḥalqa-e-ṣad kām-e-nihaṅg
dekheṅ kyā guzre hai qat̤re peh guhar hone tak

6.20 āshiqī ṣabr-t̤alab aur tamannā be-tāb
dil kā kyā raṅg karūṅ k͟hūn-e-jigar hone tak

6.21 ham ne mānā keh tāg͟hāful na karoge lekin
k͟hāk ho jā'eṅge ham tum ko k͟habar hone tak

6.22 partau-e-k͟hūr se hai shabnam ko fanā kī ta'līm
maiṅ bhī huṅ ek 'ināyat kī naz̤ar hone tak

6.23 yak naz̤ar besh nahīṅ furṣat-e-hastī g͟hāfil
garmī-e-bazm hai ik raqṣ-e-sharar hone tak

6.24 g͟ham-e-hastī ka Asad kis se ho juz marg 'ilāj
shama' har raṅg meṅ jaltī hai saḥar hone tak [81: 1-7]

6.18 A sigh needs a lifetime to have an effect
Who can live until your tresses are vanquished

6.19 In the net of every wave is a skein of a hundred crocodile mouths
Just see what has befallen the raindrop, until it becomes a pearl

6.20 Loving demands patience, and longing is restless
How can I distract my heart until my liver consumes itself in blood

6.21 I believed that you would not neglect me, yet
I'll have turned to dust before you hear the news

6.22 From the splendor of the sun's ray, the dew learns of annihilation
I too exist only for a single glance of favor

6.23 The time of existence is no more than a glance, O neglectful one
The fervor of the assembly is but a dance of sparks

6.24 For the grief of existence, Asad, what cure is there but death
The candle burns in all events until the dawn [81: 1-7]

Here, in contrast to the previous ghazal, there are only three explicit cross-references between the verses: *naẓar* (glance) in 6.22 and 6.23; *hastī* (being) in 6.23 and 6.24; and *raṅg* (color) in 6.20 and 6.24; a fourth connection exists between *taghāful* (neglect) in 6.21 and *ghāfil* (neglectful one) in 6.23. In addition, there is a certain consonance in the water imagery of the wave and the water-drop (6.19) and the dew (6.22); and the fire imagery of the sun (6.22), the dancing sparks (6.23), and the burning candle (6.24). Given Ghalib's fondness for elemental imagery, it is not surprising that he refers to the two remaining elements as well—air in the lover's sighs (6.21), and the dust of the forgotten lover (6.21), supplemented by the pearl of the transformed droplet (6.18), and the blood of the dissolved liver (6.20). Yet in their preoccupation with time and existence, with survival and transformation, these verses transcend the essential conventionality of those of the previous ghazal.

The impact of the first verse is created largely by the idiom *sar honā,* which means both 'to be conquered' and 'to reach the end of'; thus *terī zulf ke sar hone tak* refers to the lover's attainment of his goal—to reach the beloved's tresses, or more precisely, the *sar* (end, tip) of her tresses (as would be available only in their dishevelment in love-making)—as well as to the conquest of those wild, scattered tresses (see 6.12 and 6.32). Yet the impossibility of attaining this goal is emphasized through the noun *'umr* (age, lifetime) and the verb *jīnā* (to live), which in some ways prefigure the concern with existence in *maiṅ bhī hūṅ* ('I too exist') in 6.22 and the *hastī* (existence) of 6.23 and 6.24.

The second verse (6.19) contains one of Ghalib's most visionary images, based on the popular belief that pearls are formed during one month each year when droplets from that month's first rain fall into open oyster shells, where they become pearls—with the corollary that the same droplets would become venom if they were to fall into the open mouth of a serpent or reptile, such as the crocodile (Naim [1965]: 192).

To reach its goal of being transformed into a pearl, in Ghalib's image, the raindrop must make the virtually impossible passage to the oyster through the concave, net-like scallops of each surging wave (*mauj*—one of Ghalib's favorite motifs), which are likened to the gaping mouths of a hundred swarming, thirsty crocodiles.

The next three couplets return explicitly to the lover and his concern for his own being, with an awareness of the necessity for distracting (*raṅg karnā*—literally, 'to color') his impatient heart (*dil*) with its desire for the thought of the beloved, while the liver consumes itself, turning to blood, with longing (6.20); a realization of the impossibility of the beloved's taking any notice of him, or his love, or even his death (6.21); and the utterance of a yearning for a total loss of self in the experience of a glance (*naẕar*) of recognition from the beloved, earthly or divine (6.22).

Returning to his favored fire imagery in the last two verses, Ghalib reminds his beloved, whom he addresses as *g̱hāfil* ('heedless one', echoing the verb *tag̱hāful karnā*, 'to neglect' of 6.21), of the brevity of existence; it is no more than a mere glance (again, *naẕar*), or a single flare of sparks—perhaps from a guttering candle—in the heat of the *bazm* (assembly—see 4.47-51). Whereas in the previous verse the beloved's sunlike glance would bring the instant annihilation that the poet desires, in this *she'r* the word *naẕar* is somehow devaluing in its effect.

Continuing the final verse in the same setting, Ghalib (who has earlier felt a sense of understanding for the raindrop and the dew as symbols of the man seeking salvation through transformation) identifies himself with the candle of the assembly, in an expression of the need to survive whatever life may bring until it is time to die. The candle, like the poet (for whom it is often a symbol, with a tongue of flame representing the poet's own power of speech—see 3.47-8 and 3.70), is a source of illumination and comfort in the *maḥfil*, and must prevail throughout all of life's conditions and reversals (*raṅg*, literally 'color'), responding with its own reflection of these events ('the candle burns in every *raṅg*') until the conclusion of the assembly (of life) with the coming of the dawn, when the candle is extinguished, or burns itself out in an exhaustion of its resources.

While this ghazal is less conventional, and more eloquent, than the first, it does not quite attain that major sense of sweep and virtuosity to be found in the last of the ghazals to be considered in these pages.

Ghazal: sab kahāṅ, kuch . . .

Comprised of sixteen verses, this is one of the longer ghazals in the *Dīvān*, and one of the best known and most widely quoted. The *radīf* is *ho ga'īṅ* ('became'—feminine plural), which like the *radīfs* in the two ghazals in chapter II, limits the gender and number of possible subjects for the verbal phrase. The *qāfiya* words, like those of the first ghazal in this chapter, end in the syllable *-āṅ*, with the only rhyme words common to both ghazals being *pareshāṅ* (scattered) from 6.12; *mizhgāṅ* (eyelashes) from 6.2 and 6.13; *cāk-e-garībāṅ* (rending of the collar) from 6.3; and *darbāṅ* (doorman, watchman) from 6.15.

6.25 sab kahāṅ kuch lāla-o-gul meṅ numāyāṅ ho ga'īṅ
khāk meṅ kyā ṣūrateṅ hoṅgī keh pinhāṅ ho ga'īṅ

6.26 yād thīṅ ham ko bhī raṅgā-raṅg bazm ārā'īyāṅ
lekin ab naqsh-o-nigār-e-ṭāq-e-nisyāṅ ho ga'īṅ

6.27 thīṅ banāt-un-na'sh-e-gardūṅ din ko parde meṅ nihāṅ
shab ko un ke jī meṅ kyā ā'ī keh 'uryāṅ ho ga'īṅ

6.28 qaid meṅ ya'qūb ne lī go na yūsuf kī khabar
lekin āṅkheṅ rozan-e-dīvār-e-zindāṅ ho ga'īṅ

6.29 sab raqīboṅ se hoṅ nā-khush par zanān-e-miṣr se
hai zuleikhā khush keh maḥv-e-māh-e-kan'ān ho ga'īṅ

6.30 jū-e-khūṅ āṅkhoṅ se bahne do keh hai shām-e-firāq
maiṅ yeh samjhūṅgā keh shama'eṅ do farozāṅ ho ga'īṅ

6.31 in parī-zādoṅ se leṅge ham khald meṅ intiqām
qudrat-e-ḥaq se yahī ḥūreṅ agar vāṅ ho ga'īṅ

6.32 nīnd us kī hai dimāgh us kā hai rāteṅ us kī haiṅ
terī zulfeṅ jis ke bāzū par pareshāṅ ho ga'īṅ

6.33 maiṅ caman meṅ kyā gayā goyā dabistāṅ khul gayā
bulbuleṅ sun kar mire nāle ghazal-khwāṅ ho ga'īṅ

6.34 voh nigāhen kyoṅ hū'ī jātī haiṅ ya rabb dil ke pār
jo mirī koṭāhī-e-qismat se mizhgāṅ ho ga'īṅ

6.35 bas keh rokā maiṅ ne aur sīne meṅ ubhreṅ pe-ba-pe
merī āheṅ bakhiya-e-cāk-e-garībāṅ ho ga'īṅ

6.36 vāṅ gayā bhī maiṅ to un kī gālīyoṅ kā kyā javāb
yād thīṅ jitnī du'ā'eṅ ṣarf-e-darbāṅ ho ga'īṅ

6.37 jāṅ-fazā hai bāda jis ke hāth meṅ jām ā gayā
sab lakīreṅ hāth kī goyā rag-e-jāṅ ho ga'īṅ

6.38 ham muvaḥid haiṅ hamāra kesh hai tark-e-rusūm
millateṅ jab miṭ ga'īṅ ajzā-e-īmāṅ ho ga'īṅ

6.39 ranj se khugar hū'ā insāṅ to miṭ jātā hai ranj
mushkileṅ mujh par paṛīṅ itnī keh āsāṅ ho ga'īṅ

6.40 yūṅ hī gar rotā rahā Ghālib to ae ahl-e-jahāṅ
dekhnā in bastīyoṅ ko keh vīrāṅ ho ga'īṅ [112: 1-16]

6.25 Not all—a few appeared as tulip and rose
In the dust, what faces, what forms must be hidden

6.26 We too recall the variegated, festive decorations for the assembly
But now they have become the adornments of the niche of oblivion

6.27 The Daughters of the celestial Bier were in daylight veiled
At night, what entered their hearts, that they became naked

6.28 In prison, Jacob did not ask after news of Joseph
But his eyes became the windows in the wall of the cell

6.29 (4.88) All would be unhappy with rivals—but with the women of Egypt
Zuleikha is happy, that they became lost in the moon of Canaan

6.30 Let a river of blood flow from my eyes, for it is the night of separation
I'll think that two candles have been set burning

6.31 On these fairy-born, in Paradise, we'll take revenge
By the power of God!—if they become Houris there

6.32 Sleep is his. Pride is his. The nights are his
On whose arm your tresses lie scattered

6.33 I had hardly entered the garden, when it was as though a school had opened
The nightingales—hearing my laments—became singers of ghazals

6.34 Those glances, O Lord—why do they penetrate my heart
Glances which, by the constriction of my fate, became the lashes of her downcast eyes

6.35 To the extent that I suppressed them, they pushed ceaselessly up within my heart
My sighs became the stitching of my collar

6.36 Even if I went there, what answers could I give to her abuse
As many blessing as I could remember were used up on the doorkeeper

6.37 Wine is life-increasing, for in whose hand the goblet has come
Every line of that hand, it seems, has become the life-vein

6.38 We profess the unity of God; our creed is the renunciation of ritual
Religions, when they are obliterated, become the elements of faith

6.39 When man becomes accustomed to grief, grief itself disappears
So many difficulties have befallen me, that they became easy

6.40 If Ghalib were to remain weeping thus, then—O people of the world
See these cities—how they would have become desolated
[112: 1-16]

Before discussing this ghazal as a complete entity, a brief elucidation may be required for each verse in the form of the following notes:

6.25. An expression of *ubi sunt* (see 3.33 and 3.59), a lamentation of what has been irretrievably lost. Contrasts between all and few; flowers (and flower-like faces) and dust; and manifestation and concealment.

6.26. Again, *ubi sunt*, with a more personal tone: now we have become old, but we *too* (*bhī*) remember. . . . Word-play on *nigār* as 'a picture, painting, portrait, effigy, an idol;—a beautiful woman, beauty; mistress, sweet-heart' (Platts 1930: 1150). Contrasts between then and now; youth and age; activity and its cessation (the first *miṣra'* is palpably in motion, the second—motionless, almost like a scene in a mosaic, or a cinematic stop-frame); and memory and oblivion.

6.27. A reference to the constellation of the Big Dipper or Great Bear—the four stars in rectangular configuration are the bier, and the three other stars (the handle of the dipper) are the carriers (sons) of the bier, with a pun in this case indicating daughters (Mehr n.d.: 370-1). A uniquely tasteful erotic verse, with the potentially powerful image of nakedness transmuted to the remoteness of stars, so that the *fact* of nudity seems somehow innocent and playful, with no danger of obscenity: daughters (particularly daughters in mourning) are chaste, so that we can contemplate their abstract nakedness, safely and without guilt, across the stellar gulf.

6.28. A reference to the Qur'anic story of Jacob's weeping until his eyes became blind in grief, for what he thought was the death of his son Joseph, who in fact had been cast into prison (see 4.12, and Naim [1965]: 192). The play on eyes and windows is complex, centering around the visual correspondence between hollow, staring (or white) eyes, and the round, eternally open light-holes in a dark prison or dungeon; also there is the conception of protection by the power of sight, and of affection expressed in terms of eyes—*nūr-e-cashm* (light of the eyes) is a favorite phrase for a father speaking of his son. An unusual introduction into the ghazal of fatherly love, with the son as beloved (Joseph—see the next verse—is an ideal beloved). Comparison between eye and window, and possibly weeping and erosion of the walls of the prison (Mehr n.d.: 371-2); light (of

Jacob's white eyes) and dark (of Joseph's cell); and, implicitly, ignorance (in Jacob's intellect) and knowledge (in his fatherly intuition).

6.29. A reference to the story of Zuleikha, Potiphar's wife, in the Qur'an. Zuleikha was in love with Joseph, and was ridiculed by the women of Egypt for loving her slave. She took revenge by inviting them all to a feast, then calling Joseph, whose beauty so entranced them that they cut themselves with their knives as they were slicing lemons (Naim [1965]: 193). Joseph is invoked in epithet as the Moon of Canaan (moon-like in his beauty); not only was he incomparably handsome, but his fragrance (*bū-e-Yūsuf*) was also legendary. Contrast between unhappiness and happiness, with the reversal of the normal expectation that the lover is male, and that he (she in this case) is happy with the rivals.

6.30. An evocation of the traditional night of separation from the beloved (which is, of course, every night—see 4.18-19), with a typical exaggeration of crying to tears of blood (see 6.6), but here with the comparison of the lover's bloodshot, streaming eyes to a burning, melting candle, with the implicit opposition of water (or blood) and fire. See also 6.4.

6.31. A reference to the Islamic belief that the righteous will be attended in the Garden of Paradise by indescribably beautiful celestial maidens. Contrast between this earthly life and Paradise; and comparison of the fairy-faced ones of this world (unearthly in their beauty) and the *Houris.* This is a subtle, elegant expression of self-confidence, in the poet's knowing that *he* will be in Paradise. The revenge spoken of is for the extreme cruelty of the beloveds in their earthly existence, a cruelty so great that only God's power could enable them to reach, through a sort of divine pardon, the realms of Paradise.

6.32. An extraordinarily fine verse, and another example of *sahl-e-mumtana'* (effortless ease—see 1.2). Three simple statements of bliss—sleep, brain/pride/satisfaction/knowledge/intoxication, and nights (of union)—in the first line are fused into a totality by the intimacy and kinaesthesia of the second, in which the beloved's scattered tresses (perfumed with ambergris—see 5.54, black like the nights, and presumably dishevelled after dalliance and love-making) lie across the fortunate rival's arm. The inclusiveness of the experience is intensified by the multi-gendered sequence of the genitive: *kī, kā, kī* (plural), and *ke*. See 6.12 and 3.106 for other verses with the predictable linking of *zulf* (tress) and *pareshāṅ*; also 3.70.

6.33. The poet as a teacher of other poets (here as nightingale); a witty and accomplished piece of self-praise.

6.34. A typically Ghalibian verse of the deliciously rankling piercing of the beloved's eyelashes in the lover's heart (see 6.2 and 6.13 for *mizhgāṅ* as *qāfiya*; also 2.14, 3.67, 4.8-10, and 4.61). The unexpected here is in the shyness of the beloved.

6.35. The poet engaging in two other activities expected of the lover: sighing, and tearing his collar in frustration and grief (see 3.57 and 4.100; also 6.3 for *cāk-e-garībāṅ* as a *qāfiya*). The charm here, though rather contrived and typical of the *sabk-e-Hindī*, is in seeing the sighs as rising and being suppressed in the lover's breast, with the up-and-down motion of a needle mending the torn collar.

6.36. The beloved as typically cruel and abusive, protecting herself with an obstructive doorkeeper (see 4.29; also 6.15 for *darbāṅ* as *qāfiya*). Contrast between the beloved's abuse and the lover's supplicatory blessings and prayers, and between the undesirability of the doorman and the extreme beauty of the beloved. The *kyā javāb* (what answer?) also complements the curses.

6.37. A brilliant visual and kinaesthetic comparison between wine and blood, with the power of wine seen as causing each tiny line in the hand to swell and pulse like the jugular vein. See also 6.1.

6.38. A typically anti-sectarian Sufi statement, with a subtle echo in *miṭnā* ('to obliterate'—one of three occurrences in the ghazal of a retroflex sound—see also the *miṭnā* and *paṛnā* of 6.39) of the dust evoked in the first couplet.

6.39. The second use of *miṭnā*; a paradoxical statement of the circularity of perception, with the reversal of extreme difficulty passing all limits of tolerance to become easily tolerable. This verse has become proverbial in Urdu.

6.40. Another example of Ghalib's kinetic elemental imagery and hyperbole (see 4.108, 5.35-40, 5.47-8, and 6.17), with the lover's tears becoming floods, and entire cities throughout the world (instead of just the lover's house) being devastated by the power of his love and grief.

Ranges of Poetic Expression

A thorough survey of the individual couplets in this ghazal reveals a broad range of subjects, tones, and effects. Generally speaking, the ghazal is predominantly erotic in tone, with one verse (6.37) unambiguously anacreontic in its praise of wine, and two others tending toward the gnomic / mystical (6.38) and the more purely gnomic, or rational (6.39, with its epigrammatic observation on the difficulties of human existence). Sub-categories of tonal variety would included profound nostalgia (6.25-6); exquisitely veiled licentiousness (6.27); parental affection (6.28); allusion employed in a witty reversal of expectations (6.29); grief, and an almost religious devotion to that grief and its symptoms (6.30); envy overwhelmed by voluptuousness (6.31-2); subtle praise of one's own dedication to love (again, 6.31) and skills as a 'singer of ghazals' (6.33); ingenious invention, enriched by visual and kinaesthetic imagery, of the conventional duties of the poet lover—e.g., savoring of pain in 6.34, sighing and rending, then mending the collar in 6.35, and haunting the door of the beloved in supplicatory posture in 6.35; dedication to intoxication (6.37) and rejection of sectarianism (6.38); resignation to life's difficulties (6.39); and renewed dedication to dynamic love in a forceful statement that transcends petty boasting (6.40).

There are further breadths of variety to be found in this ghazal: a number of different time-senses, ranging from the extremely specific (*this* night of separation in 6.30) to the vast, stellar timelessness (in 6.27), and from the origins of humanity (6.25), through Qur'anic events (6.28-29) and one's own youth and age (6.26), to the afterlife (6.31), and the destruction of the human world (6.40). A number of different locations in space and geography, from the deserts (6.25) to oceans of tears (6.30); from the beloved's door (6.36) and festive gatherings in her presence (6.26) to the lover's lonely house (6.30 and 6.35) with its niche of oblivion (6.26); from prison (6.28) to school (6.33); from the garden of roses and tulips (6.25) and nightingales (6.33), and the lands of sects, with implications of mosque, temple, and church (6.38), to the world of the tavern (6.37); from Canaan to Egypt (6.28 and 6.29); and from the cities of the world (6.40) to Paradise (6.31) and the heavenly realms of the constellations (6.27). A range of states of being: memory (6.26 and 6.36), oblivion (6.26), sleep (6.32), union (6.32), separation (6.30), rapture (6.29), and death (6.25, 6.27, and 6.40). A full sequence of characters: beloveds, rivals, lover, doorkeeper, daughters, son, Jacob, Joseph, Zuleikha, the women of Egypt, religious communities, peoples of the world, humanity itself (*insān*—6.39), fairy-faced beauties, *Hourīs*, Fate, and God as Truth (6.31) and Lord (6.34). A catalogue of parts of the body—faces, eyes and eyelashes, brain (6.32), tresses, breast, heart, vein, arm, and hand—and of objects: flowers, decorations, adornments niche, bier, stars, veil, moon, window, wall, candle, stitches, collar, and goblet. References to modes of communication (news, glances, curses, blessings, answers) and of social concourse (*bazm*, funeral, feasting, school, and ritual). A spectrum of sensory evocations: visual (including black, white, red, and in 6.26, polychrome colors), auditory (songs and sighs), tactile (in the imagery of leached eyes and cut or pierced flesh), and kinaesthetic. Finally, there is scattered throughout the ghazal a network of typically Ghalibian references to substances in the four elemental categories: earth (dust), air (sighs), fire (candle, and again, sighs—see 6.4), and water (tears—in river, blood, and flood—and wine), with the latter three categories usually manifest in some aspect of their kineticism, and their capacity to change themselves and to alter other substances and forms.

Yet a recitation of this catalogue is not in itself sufficient for an understanding of the full effect of this ghazal, without some scrutiny of the unifying forces in the structure of the poetry—for without such unification, these diverse elements could not be truly reconciled, but would simply be 'heterogeneous ideas yoked by violence together', with the result that 'the poem simply explodes into incoherence' (Brooks 1973: 139). What is further required is an awareness of the structural techniques which provide the reconciliation and the unification necessary for the poem to be complete and coherent, yet successful as poetry because of its 'new insights, i.e. [its] new ways of putting into a pattern what we had usually taken to be unrelated and perhaps even irreconcilable elements' (Brooks 1973: 138).

Unifying Forces in the Ghazal

The most obvious feature unifying the verses in the above ghazal is, once again, the externally consistent structure of meter and rhyme. The meter is *ramal*, a structure of fifteen feet divided 1-s-1-1 / 1-s-1-1 / 1-s-1-1 / 1s-l (1 = long, s = short); the *qāfiya* syllable is *-āṅ*, and the *radīf* is *ho ga'īṅ*. The couplets, whatever the content, are thus similar in outer form through the adherence of each to this metric and rhyme scheme.

As is true with many ghazals, there will be a certain superficial unity imposed on the poem by the *radīf*: in this case, the phrase *ho ga'īṅ*, meaning 'became [feminine plural]', provides an engaging superstructure through the fact that the subjects of the verb are all grammatically or literally feminine, thus underscoring the essentially erotic character of the poem. Of the rhyming words (all ending in *-āṅ*), seven are adjectives, eight are nouns, and one is an adverb. Since the subjects of the verbal phrase *ho ga'īṅ* must all be feminine plural, there is a doubling of the effect of this emphasis on number and gender, from the flower-faced (feminine) ones manifest in the first line of 6.25, and the faces (feminine in both grammatical gender and implication, following the first line) hidden in the second line, to the habitations desolated in the last couplet.

There is a further unity of sound created indirectly in this ghazal through a recurrence of words ending in nazalized vowels: an astonishing total of 91 such vowels (9, 4, 7, 5, 4, 8, 6, 4, 6, 6, 6, 7, 3, 6, 5, and 5) in the entire ghazal, with the *āṅ* of the *qāfiya* repeated elsewhere as well in verses 6.25, 6.27, 6.33, 6.39, and 6.40, and the *ga'īṅ* of the *radīf* occurring once again in 6.38. In a similar fashion, a heavy emphasis on the Persian *eẓāfa* construction (as in the first ghazal in this chapter) provides the effect of an internal stitching of the ghazal, with a total of 19 occurrences throughout the poem; the Persian *va* (and) enhances this effect further (in 6.25 and 6.26), as does the Persian *bā* (with) in 6.35. These elements, like meter and rhyme, give the ghazal a conspicuous effect of external formal similarity in the individual couplets, though their contents are quite diverse.

In terms of the poet's engagements of the audience, there are several other techniques employed in this ghazal. Questions are asked in a total of six lines (*where* and *what* in 6.25, *what* in 6.27, *what* in 6.33, *why* in 6.34, and *what* in 6.36), though in 6.25 and 6.33 the interrogative particles serve the purpose of rhetorical negation of the question. There are direct addresses to the beloved (*terī*—your) in 6.32 (in many respects the central *she'r* of the ghazal), God (*yā rabb*—O Lord) in 6.34, and the people of the world in 6.40, as well as the imperatives 'let rivers flow' in 6.30, and 'see!' in 6.40.

Yet as efficient as these devices may be in imposing a formal unity of effect throughout the poem, it is in the presentation of a broad spectrum (as shown above) of familiar elements from the ghazal tradition in a consistent pattern of unexpected combination or reversals that Ghalib has achieved his most successful unity; each verse engages us in the play of familiarity and novelty, with the sense of newness and surprise inevitably prevailing in the effect of the couplet: 6.25) the faces which have *not* been reborn in flowers are invoked in place of those which have; 6.26) the niche in which we put our keepsakes as mementos of our youth turns out to be the niche of forgetfulness; 6.27) the daylight is portrayed as a veil for the naked stars; 6.28) eyes are suggested in several senses to resemble windows; 6.29) there is one lover who is *happy* with *her* rivals; 6.30) eyes and candles are compared in terms of shape, color, and kinetic flow; 6.31) though we will not have our way with our beloveds here, we will in Paradise, through God's intercession for those cruel ones; 6.32) an extraordinary compression, with apparent effortlessness, of several sensuous aspects of union with the beloved; 6.33) the presentation of the garden as a school, and the nightingale as a teacher; 6.34) eyelashes are seen as indications of shyness, not boldness—yet they still have the capacity to wound; 6.35) the up-and-down motion of stifled sighs is compared to the motion of the needle stitching the torn collar of the lover's shirt; 6.36) in spite of all our designs, the beloved's doorkeeper exhausts our resources of entreaty; 6.37) wine is compared, with vigorous kineticism and kinaesthesia, to pulsing blood in the hand's veins; 6.38) the paradoxical statement that the obliterated sects will become the constituent elements of the true faith; 6.39) another paradox, of difficulty increasing until it becomes ease—so that there *is* a hope for our survival; and 6.40) an exaggeration of the lover's *k͟hāna-k͟harābī* (house-destructiveness) to encompass all the cities of the world.

In these verses, in short, Ghalib uses the traditional topoi of the ghazal in his own distinctive style, fusing sensory and logical elements with striking success; whereas other Urdu poets such as

Mir (the poet with whom Ghalib is most commonly linked in greatness) rely heavily on feeling—empathy and pathos—Ghalib yokes together mind and eye, and brain and muscular sensor. He is interested in energy, logical as well as physical, potential as well as actual: something about to happen, or something already occurring; even when recalling some past energy, he still exploits the tension between that energy and its cessation.

It would be tempting to continue in an effort to characterize 'Ghalib's greatness'—*Ghālib kī 'aẕmat*—as so many essays (with precisely that title) and books have done in recent years (e.g. Suroor 1969, Farooqi 1969, Barelvi 1969). But it is probably wiser to say no more than I have already said with the evidence at hand.

In spite of the assertions made in the previous pages, of the ghazal's enormous potential for poetic expression, I do not mean to say that the ghazal is the most fertile genre of poetry in the world, nor that it can fulfill all the functions of all varieties of poetry. As Rashid Ahmed Siddiqi has observed, the g̱hazal is but one of the genres of Urdu poetry (1969: 12-13); it is not expected to be the vehicle for all of Urdu poetic expression, when there are all the various other forms—the *qaṣīda* (ode), *maṡnavī* (narrative), *marṡiya* (elegy), *hajv* (satire), *rubā'ī* (quatrain), *na't* (encomium—especially of the Prophet Muhammad), and *naẕm* ('free' poem) are only the most prominent of the many Urdu poetic genres (Pybus 1924: 59-68, Barker 1979: xxiii-xxx).

Given the highly prescriptive formal elements of the ghazal, moreover, there can be no doubt that it is easy to write bad ghazals, and that much ghazal poetry is of little worth. But there are bad poets and hack versifiers in every language, and the ghazal is not to be blamed for the failures of mediocre poets, any more than chess is to be condemned as a worthless pastime on the basis of badly played games. It is, rather, the challenge of the ghazal that is its greatest virtue—the challenge to make, in the limited scope of the couplet, a concise, highly evocative poetic statement that carries the maximum possible meaning. For an enormous span of time, the ghazal has survived extinction on the basis of this challenge, and through its adaptability to new languages and to the variety of poetic tastes in the different areas and eras of the Islamic cultural realm. At some points the ghazal's survival was only that—as witnessed by the frail and exhausted creations of conventional verse by the vast majority of ghazal poets. But the potential vitality and spirit of the genre have been accessible as well to the greatest ghazal poets—Ghalib among them—who with their passion and visionary originality have created some of the world's most eloquent lyric poetry.

Yet given its capacity to explore relationships and conflicts, the ghazal may be approached not only as poetry, but as a kind of broader noble play, both in Huizinga's sense, and in the sense that it is the primary aesthetic pursuit of the majority of cultivated Urdu speakers. The idea of some genre of thought and action which allows for a full expression of an identity both cultural and personal recurs in literature from Plato to such modern authors as Hesse (1949) and Borges (1962). The ghazal, it would seem to me, has come close to achieving the status of such a genre. The multitude of voices, personalities, relationships, arenas of action, and events that we have seen suggested—if not overtly stated—by the ghazal in so brief a compass as two lines, comprises indeed a rich expression of several identities: personal (in the vision of only one poet—Mirza Ghalib), cultural (in the idiom of the Urdu language, glimpsed here—like the beloved—only fleetingly, and then mostly in the imperfect medium of translation), and universally human (love, defeat, brief joy, and death are not peculiar to any single country or clime).

In short, it is the role of the ghazal to explore with us the relationships of our lives. The type of relationship may be old, familiar to us, so that we find pleasure in reflecting on some experience we have known. Or the relationship may be new, so that we find the delight of an unexpected discovery among familiar things. Perhaps most of the ghazal's critics are accustomed to thinking of poetry not so much in terms of relationships as of constituent elements; if this is the case, then it is easy to be deceived by the notion of the ghazal's 'monotony'. But as this book has attempted to demonstrate, it is the dynamics of the ghazal which need to be examined, albeit in the context of a tradition of somewhat restricted topoi, in order to understand fully the significance that these topoi acquire, from generations of poets, through the process of connotative accretion. Granted that the ghazal is in many ways spare and ambiguous; it is this spareness and ambiguity which demand so much from an audience. Yet these very qualities enable the ghazal, more than any other genre of Urdu poetry (and perhaps as much as the major poetic forms of other languages) to attain a high degree of visionary universality, and to provide a poetic mirror-palace in which every man may find portions of his own life reflected.

> When they read this poem of mine, they are translators.
> Every existence speaks a language of its own.
>
> ADRIENNE RICH (1969: 68)

Bibliography

This bibliography consists primarily of materials cited in this volume; in addition, certain works have been listed which were of particular assistance or interest in the preparation of the present work. For more detailed bibliographies on Ghālib, see Rahman (1969), Ziaee (1969), Silver (1970), and Pritchett (1979: 61-74).

Agha, Vazir (1969), 'Ghālib—ek jadīd shā'ir' (Ghalib—a modern poet), Lahore, *Saḥīfa* 46: 410-15.

Ahmed, Aijaz (ed.), (1971), *Ghazals of Ghalib,* New York: Columbia University Press.

Ahmed, Ilyas (comp.) (1957), *Gulhā'e pareshāṅ* [Scattered blossoms], Allahabad.

Ahmed, Sayyid Baha'uddin (comp.), (1970), *Gulistān-e-hazār raṅg* (The garden of a thousand colors), Amroha: Book Corner.

Alavi, Sayyid Zahiruddin Ahmed (ed.), (1941), *Ashk-o-rashk-e-Ghālib* (The tears and envy of Ghalib), Aligarh: Muslim Educational Press.

Ali, Ahmed (1966), *Twilight in Delhi,* Bombay: Oxford University Press.

——— (1969), 'Ghalib: selected poems', in *Ghalib,* pp. 1-70 (Serie Orientale Roma 39: Orientalia Romana 3), Rome: Instituto Italiano per il Medio ed Estremo Oriente.

——— (1973) (ed. and trans.), *The golden tradition: An anthology of Urdu poetry,* New York: Columbia University Press.

Ansari, Asloob Ahmed (1969-70), 'Some recurrent images in Ghalib's poetry,' in *International Ghalib Seminar, English volume,* ed. Yusuf Husain Khan, pp. 84-96, New Delhi: All India Ghalib Centenary Committee.

——— (1970), *Naqsh-e-Ghālib* (A picture of Ghalib), New Delhi: Ghalib Academy.

Arkoun, M. (1973), 'Ishk', in *Encyclopaedia of Islam,* New Edn., vol. 4, pp. 118-19, Leiden: Brill.

Arshi, Imtiyaz Ali (ed.), (1947), *Farhaṅg-e-Ghālib* (A dictionary of Ghalib), Rampur: Nazim Book House.

Askari, Mirza Muhammad (1937), *Ā'īna-e-balāghat* (The mirror of rhetoric), Lucknow: United India Press.

Baqar, Agha Muhammad (n.d.), *Bayān-e-Ghālib: Sharḥ-e-Dīvān-e-Ghālib* (A narative of Ghalib: Commentary on the *Dīvān* of Ghalib), Amritsar: Azad Book Depot.

Barelvi, Ibadat (1968), *Ghālib kā fann* (Ghalib's art), Lahore: Globe Publishers.

——— (1969), 'Ghālib kī 'aẓmat' (Ghalib's greatness), in *Tanqīd-e-Ghālib: Sau sāl* (Ghalib criticism: A hundred years), ed. Sayyid Fayyaz Mahmud, pp. 409-23, Lahore: Punjab University.

Barker, Muhammad Abd-al-Rahman (1977), *Classical Urdu poetry*, 3 volumes, Ithaca: Spoken Language Services.

Bausani, Alessandro (1956), 'Altaf Husain Hali's ideas on ghazal', in *Charisteria Orientalia*, ed. Felix Tauer, Vera Kubickova, and Ivan Hrbek, pp. 38-55, Prague: Ceskoslovenske Adademie Ved.

——— (1958), 'A way to a better understanding of the structure of western poetry', *East and West* (Rome) New Series 9: 145-53.

——— (1959), 'The position of Ghālib (1796 [*sic*]-1869) in the history of Urdu and Indo-Persian poetry', *Der Islam* 34: 99-127.

Bijnauri, Abdul Rahman (1969), 'Mahāsīn-e-kalām-e-Ghālib' (The beauties of the works of Ghalib), in *Tanqīd-e-Ghālib: Sau sāl* (Ghalib criticism: A hundred years), ed. Sayyid Fayyaz Mahmud, pp. 123-53, Lahore: Punjab University.

Bly, Robert (ed. and trans.), (1966), *The sea and the honeycomb: A book of tiny poems*, [Madison, Minnesota]: The Sixties Press.

Borges, Jose Luis (1962), *Labyrinths*, ed. Donald A. Yates and James E. Irby, New York: New Directions.

Briffault, Robert (1965), *The troubadours*, Bloomington: Indiana University Press.

Broadbent, J. B. (1964), *Poetic love*, London: Chatto and Windus.

Brooks, Cleanth (1973), 'I. A. Richards and the concept of tension', in *I. A. Richards: Essays in his honor*, ed. Reuben Brower, Helen Vendler, and John Hollander, pp. 135-54, New York: Oxford University Press.

Browne, Edward G. (1964), *A literary history of Persia*, 4 volumes, Cambridge: Cambridge University Press.

Chishti, Yusuf Salim (1959), *Sharḥ-e-Dīvān-e-Ghālib* (a commentary on the *Dīvān* of Ghalib), Lahore: Ishrat Publishing House.

Delhi University, Department of Urdu (1970), *Ishāriya-e-Ghālib: Kalām-e-Ghālib meṅ fārsī tarkībeṅ* (Persian compounds in the works of Ghalib), Delhi: Delhi University.

Faiz, Faiz Ahmed (1964), *Dast-e-tah-e-saṅg* (The hand under the stone), Lahore: Caravan Books.

Farooqi, Khwaja Ahmed (1969), 'Ghālib kī 'aẓmat' (Ghalib's greatness), in *Tanqīd-e-Ghālib: Sau sāl* (Ghalib criticism: A hundred years), ed.

Sayyid Fayyaz Mahmud, pp. 375-83, Lahore: Punjab University.

Faruqi, Shamsur Rahman (1969-72), Tafhīm-e-Ghālib (Understanding Ghalib), *Shabkhūn* (Allahabad) 33: 70; 34: 64; 35: 56; 36: 29; etc.

——— (1971), 'Ghālib kī ek ghāzal kā tajziya' (An analysis of one of Ghalib's ghazals), in *Armaghān-e-Mālik* (Presentation to Malik [Ram]), vol. 2, pp. 717-32, New Delhi: Majlis-e-Armaghan-e-Malik.

Ehrman, Jacques (ed.), (1968), *Game, play, literature,* Boston: Beacon Press.

Forster, E. M. (1952), *A passage to India,* New York Harcourt, Brace and World.

Ghalib, Mirza Asadullah Khan (1938), *Dīvān-e-Ghālib* (The Urdu poetry of Ghalib), Lahore: Taj Company.

——— (1958), *Dīvān-e-Ghālib,* ed. Imtiyaz Ali Arshi, Aligarh: Anjuman-e-Taraqqi-e-Urdu.

——— (1958), *Dīvān-e-Ghālib,* ed. Sardar Jafri, Bombay: Hindustani Book Trust. [A small supplementary volume consists of an Urdu-Hindi glossary.]

——— (1968a), *Khutūt-e-Ghālib* (letters of Ghalib), ed. Ghulam Rasul Mehr, Lahore: Shaikh Ghulam Ali and Sons.

——— (1968b), *Kulliyāt-e-Ghālib* (Persian poetry of Ghalib), ed. Amir Hassan Nurani, Lucknow: Ram Kumar Book Depot.

——— (1969a), *Dīvān-e-Ghālib,* ed. Malik Ram, Delhi: Ghalib Centenary Committee.

——— (1969b), *Mansūkh Dīvāṇ* (Ghalib's discarded Urdu verse), ed. Muslim Ziaee, Karachi: Idara-e-Yadgar-e-Ghalib.

——— (n.d.), *Dīvān-e-Ghālib,* ed. Malik Ram, Delhi: Azad Kitab Ghar.

Ghalib Academy (1969), *Whispers of the angel,* Delhi: Ghalib Academy.

Ghani, Abdul (1960), *Life and works of Abdul Qadir Bedil,* Lahore: Publishers United.

Gibb, E. J. W. (1958), *A history of Ottoman poetry,* vol. 1, London: Luzac.

Giffen, Lois Anita (1971), *Theory of profane love among the Arabs: The development of the genre,* New York: New York University Press.

Gilani, Arifshah C. Sayyid (1956), *Ghalib: His life and Persian poetry,* Karachi: Azam Book Corporation.

Goldin, Frederick (ed. and trans.), (1973), *Lyrics of the troubadours and trouveres: An anthology and a history,* New York: Anchor Books.

Hali, Altaf Husain (1963), *Yādgār-e-Ghālib* (A memoir on Ghalib), Lahore: Majlis-e-Taraqqi-e-Adab.

——— (n.d.), *Muqaddama-e-she'r-o-sha'irī* (an introduction to poems and poetry), Delhi: Ilmi Kitab Ghar.

Harrison, Jim (1972), *Outlyer and ghazals,* New York: Simon and Schuster.

Hesse, Hermann (1965), *Magister ludi* (*The bead game*), New York: Ungar Publishing Company.

Hillman, Michael Craig (1974), 'Unity in the ghazals of Hafez', unpublished Ph. D. dissertation, University of Chicago.

Huizinga, Johan (1955), *Homo Ludens: A study of the play element in culture,* Boston: Beacon Press.

Hunter, J. Paul (ed.) (1973), *The Norton introduction to literaure,* New York: Norton.

Hyder, Quratulain and Sardar Jafri (1970), *Ghalib and his poetry,* Bombay: Popular Prakashan.

Ikram, Shaikh Muhammad (1939), *Ghālib-nama* (A treatise on Ghalib), [no publication data given].

Islam, Khurshidul (1960), *Ghālib,* Aligarh: Anjuman-e-Taraqqi-e-Urdu (Hind).

Jafri, Sardar, (1958), Preface to *Dīvān-e-Ghālib,* ed. Sardar Jafri, pp. 5-49, Bombay: Hindustani Book Trust.

Kakorvi, Zaki (ed.), (1968), *Ghazal encyclopaedia,* Lucknow: Markaz-e-Adab-e-Urdu.

Kaul, J. L. (1957), *Interpretations of Ghalib,* Delhi: Atma Ram and Sons.

Keene, Donald (1955), *Japanese literature,* New York: Grove Press.

Khan, Kazim Ali (ed.), (n.d.), *Gul-pāre* (Flower fragments), Allahabad: Idar-e-Anis Urdu.

Khan, Yusuf Husain (1971), *Ghālib aur āhang-e-Ghālib* (Ghalib and the harmony of Ghalib), 2nd edn., Delhi: Ghalib Academy.

——— (trans.), (1977), *Urdu ghazals of Ghalib,* New Delhi: Ghalib Institute.

——— (ed.), (n.d.), *Urdu ghazal,* Aligarh: Anjuman-e-Taraqqi-e-Urdu (Hind).

Lane, Edward William (1863-93), *An Arabic-English lexicon,* 7 vols.: vol. 2 (1865); vol. 4 (1872); vol. 5 (1874), London: Williams and Northgate.

Lévi-Strauss, Claude (1967), *Structural anthropology,* New York: Anchor Books.

Latif, Sayyid Abdul (1924), *The influence of English literature on Urdu literaure,* London: Forster Groom and Company.

——— (1929), *Ghalib: A critical appreciation of his life and poetry,* Hyderabad (Deccan): Chandrakanth Press.

Mahmud, Sayyid Fayyaz (ed.), (1969), *Tanqīd-e-Ghālib: Sau sāl* (Ghalib criticism: A hundred years) (Publication of the Majlis-e-Yadgar-e-Ghalib 14), Lahore: Punjab University.

——— (1969), *Ghalib: A critical introduction* (Publication of the Majlis-e-Yadgar-e-Ghalib 16), Lahore: University of the Punjab.

Malik, Ram (1968), *Mirza Ghalib,* (National Biography Series), New Delhi: National Book Trust.

Matthews, D. J. and C. Shackle (1972), *An anthology of classical Urdu love lyrics: Text and translations,* London: Oxford University Press.

Mehr, Ghulam Rasul (n.d.), *Navā-e-surosh: Mukammal Dīvān-e-Ghālib ma'e sharḥ* (The song of the angel: A complete *Dīvān* of Ghalib, including a commentary), Lahore: Shaikh Ghulam Ali and Sons.

Mir, Mir Taqi (1968), *Kulliyāt-e-Mīr* (The poetical works of Mir), ed. Zil Abbas Abbasi, Delhi: Ilmi Majlis.

Mujeeb, M. (1967), *The Indian Muslims,* Montreal: McGill University Press.

——— (1969), *Ghalib* (Makers of Indian Literature Series), New Delhi: Sahitya Akademi.

Najmul Ghani, [Muhammad] [1957], *Baḥr-ul-faṣāḥat* (The ocean of eloquence), Lucknow: Raja Ram Kumar Book Depot.

Naim, C. M. (1965), *Readings in Urdu poetry and prose,* Honolulu: East-West Center Press.

——— (1967), 'Traditional symbolism in the modern Urdu ghazal', in *Languages and areas: Studies presented to George V. Bobrinskoy,* pp. 105-11, Ghicago: Division of the Humanities, University of Chicago.

——— (1970), *Twenty-five verses: Ghalib,* Calcutta: Writers Workshop.

——— (1972), *Ghalib's lighter verses,* Calcutta: Writers Workshop.

——— (1974), '*Ghazal* and *taghazzul:* The lyric, personal and social', in *The literatures of India: An introduction,* pp. 181-97, Chicago: University of Chicago Press.

Narang, Gopi Chand (1966), 'The tradition and conventions of classical Urdu poetry', *New Orient* 5: 50-3.

Niyazi, Mahmud (1972), *Talmīhāt-e-Ghālib* (The allusions of Ghālib), New Delhi: Ghālib Academy.

Nykl, A. R. (trans.) (1931), *A book containing the risala known as the Dove's Neck Ring, about love and lovers,* Paris: Librairie Orientaliste Paul Geuthner.

Oxford English Dictionary, (1971), Compact edition, 2 vols, New York: Oxford University Press.

Platts, John T. (1930), *A dictionary of Urdu, classical Hindī, and English,* London: Oxford University Press.

Pritchett, Frances W. (1979), *Urdu literature: A bibliography of English language sources,* New Delhi: Manohar.

Pybus, G. D. (1924), *A text-book of Urdu prosody and rhetoric,* Lahore: Rama Krishna and Sons.

Qureshi, Regula (1969), 'Tarannum: The chanting of Urdu Poetry', *Ethnomusicology* 13: 425-68.

Rahman, Sayyid Mu'inur (1969), *Ishāriya-e-Ghālib* (A bibliography of Ghalib), (Publication of the Majlis-e-Yadgar-e-Ghalib 15), Lahore: Punjab University.

Ramanujan, A. K. (trans.) (1967), *The interior landscape: Love poems from a classical Tamil anthology,* Bloomington: Indiana University Press.

Rich, Adrienne (1969), *Leaflets: Poems 1965-68,* New York: Norton.

——— (1971), *The will to change: Poems 1968-70,* New York: Norton.

Richards, I. A. (1929), *Practical criticism,* New York: Harcourt, Brace and World.

——— (1936), *The philosophy of rhetoric,* New York: Oxford University Press.

Russell, Ralph (1969), 'In pursuit of the Urdu ghazal', *Journal of Asian Studies* 29: 107-24.

——— (1970a), 'The Urdu ghazal in Muslim society', *South Asian Review* 3: 141-49.

——— (1970b), 'The development of the modern novel in Urdu', in *The novel in India: Its birth and development,* ed. T. W. Clark, pp. 102-41, Berkeley: University of California Press.

——— (ed.), (1972), *Ghālib: The poet and his age,* London: George Allen and Unwin.

Russell, Ralph and Khurshidul Islam (1968), *Three Mughal poets: Mir, Sauda, Mir Hasan,* Cambridge: Harvard University Press.

——— (1969), *Ghalib: Life and letters,* Cambridge: Harvard University Press.

Ruswa, Mirza Muhammad Hadi (1961), *Umrā'o Jān Adā,* trans. Khushwant Singh and M. A. Husaini, Bombay: Orient Longmans.

——— (1963), *Umrā'o Jān Adā,* Allahabad: Ram Narain Lal Beni Madho.

Saraswat, H. C. (trans.) (n.d.), *Selections from Ghalib,* New Delhi: The author.

Sadiq, Muhammad (1964), *A history of Urdu literature,* London: Oxford University Press.

Saksena, Ram Babu (1940), *A history of Urdu literature,* Allahabad: Ram Narain Lal.

Sauda, Mirza Muhammad Rafi (1973), *Kulliyāt-e-Saudā* (The poetical works of Sauda), ed. Muhammad Shamsuddin Siddiqi, Lahore: Majlis-eTaraqqi-e-Adab.

Schimmel, Annemarie (1975a), *Classical Urdu literature from the beginning to Iqbal* (A history of Indian literature, ed. Jan Gonda, vol. 8, fasc. 3), Wiesbaden: Otto Harrassowitz.

——— (1975b), *Mystical dimensions of Islam,* Chapel Hill: University of North Carolina Press.

——— (1979), *A dance of sparks,* New Delhi: Ghalib Academy, in association with East-West Publications, London and the Hague.

Shad, Naresh Kumar (1967), *Muḥāvarāt-e-Ghālib* (Ghalib's colloquialisms), Delhi: Kutubkhana-e-Anjuman-e-Taraqqi-e-Urdu (Hind).

Siddiqi, Rashid Ahmed (1969), *Jadīd ghazal* (The modern ghazal), Aligarh: Sir Sayyid Book Depot.

Silver, Brian (1970), 'A bibliography of English sources on Ghalib', *Mahfil* 5: 4: 115-26.

——— (1972), 'The Urdu *mushā'ira*', paper presented at the Association for Asian Studies, New York.

——— (1978), 'The Urdu ghazal as a musical genre', paper presented at international conference on 'The Urdu ghazal and prose fiction', Madison, Wisconsin.

——— (n.d.), 'English analogues to the Urdu ghazal', unpublished manuscript.

Singer, Milton (1972), *When a great tradition modernizes: An anthropological approach to Indian civilization,* New York: Praeger.

Steingass, F. (1892), *A comprehensive Persian-English dictionary,* London: Routledge and Kegan Paul.

Sud, K. N. (1969), *Eternal flame: Aspects of Ghalib's life and works,* Delhi: Sterling Publishers.

Suroor, Ali Ahmed (1969), 'Ghālib kī 'azmat' (Ghālib's greatness), in *Tanqīd-e-Ghālib: Sau sāl* (Ghalib criticism: A hundred years), ed. Sayyid Fayyaz Mahmud, pp. 277-89, Lahore: Punjab University.

Tabatabai, Nazm (1954), *Sharḥ-e-Dīvān-e-Urdu-e-Ghālib* (A commentary on Ghalib's Urdu *Dīvān*), Lucknow: Anvar Book Depot.

Tate, Allen (1965), 'Tension in poetry', in *Poets on poetry,* ed. Charles Norman, pp. 349-62, New York: The Free Press.

Webster's New World Dictionary of the American Language (1957), New York: World.

Wellek, René and Austin Warren (1956), *Theory of Literature,* 3rd edn., New York: Harcourt, Brace and World.

Wheelwright, Philip (1968), *Metaphor and reality,* Bloomington: Indiana University Press.

Wickens, G. M. (1952), 'An analysis of primary and secondary significations in the third ghazal of Hafiz', *Bulletin of the School of Oriental and African Studies* 14: 239-43.

Yagana Changezi, Mirza Yas (1969), 'A letter of Yagana', in *Taṣvīr kā dusrā rūkh* (The other side of the coin [literally, face]), ed. Tajassus Ejazi, pp. 9-25, Lucknow: Qaumi Avaz.

Ziaee, Muslim (1969), 'Ghalib: Some factual data' [bibliography], *Pakistan Quarterly* 27: 1: 111-18.

Preface to the Index

This index was created to expand upon, in a more extended and cross-referenced format, the basic premise stated in the introduction to this book: *For Ghalib, the traditional images of the ghazal are important, not in isolation, but rather, in the new ways in which he can configure their complex relationships to each other. For it is the primary function of the living ghazal, particularly in Ghalib's voice, to examine, analyze, and suggest in freshly created perspectives different tensions and dynamic connections among the individual topoi (images and words) of the traditional ghazal, so as to make them still relevant to the current era.*

This index, then, is designed to be, rather than a mere routine reference tool, a more useful interactive companion to the book itself, to be consulted as needed in order to aid the reader in following and connecting particular thematic strains in understanding Ghalib's poetry in a non-linear—we might say—nuclear way. This approach allows the reader to rise above the book itself to explore—separately from the prose flow of the text itself—the occurrences of, and most importantly, the relationships and linkages among the particular topoi discussed in the book. Hence, to avoid undue repetition in the index itself, I am listing below in this preface many of the frequent cross-references which, taken together, occur frequently in imagistic or conceptual clusters as part of Ghalib's distinctive voice, vision, and uniquely dynamic approach to the ghazal.

On the one hand, to avoid rendering the index too cumbersome, specific English words basic to a study of the subjects of the ghazal (beauty, beloved, emotion, friend, friendship, imagery, life, love, lover, mistress, sweetheart, etc.,) as well as the words associated with the genre itself (ghazal, couplet, hemistich, poetry, etc.—except for the rhyming aspects, for which see *qāfiya* and *radīf* below), as well as such general terms as India/Indian, conventional, etc., are not included in the index because of the extreme frequency of their occurrence.

On the other hand, returning to the purpose of the index stated just above, each single reference to specific Urdu words for love discussed at length in Chapter 3—*'ishq, muḥabbat, shauq,* and *ulfat,* (since Ghalib uses each of them in somewhat different perspectives)—as well as such English words as affection, dedication, devotion, erotic, friendship, longing, passion, etc., are cited in the index to enable us to explore Ghalib's own approach to some of these more nuanced words related to love—again, the central subject of the ghazal.

Furthermore, selected other topoi, even though they occur infrequently in Ghalib's *Dīvān,* are nonetheless cited in the index for one of two reasons. In the first case, certain words are noted for their comparative rarity in regard to the ghazal tradition—e.g., coral, crocodile, froth, henna, etc.—and for the striking and distinctive way Ghalib uses them. In an example of the second case of infrequent use: there is but one reference in the entire *Dīvān* to the moth—one of the traditional ghazal's most frequent and imporant images in the central triad of moth/candle/dawn (see p. 78)—images sometimes reviled as "clichés" by some critics, as stated in the introduction to this book. Yet this allegedly clichéd image is specifically included in the index to enable us to ponder why Ghalib used the common "moth" only once: perhaps because of its limited dynamism in merely fluttering fecklessly here and there around its beloved, the candle, before its easily predicted (and again, clichéd) annihilation in the flame, or perhaps also because of its dusky lack of visual vibrance, so important to Ghalib—again, see coral, crocodile, froth, and henna.

Yet, in contrast to the single appearance of the moth, there are countless references in this book to another basic element in the triad—the candle—as well as other fire/light-related topoi, which are central to Ghalib's dynamism and kineticism, in his exploration of active relationships, particularly those referencing the basic elements of fire, wind, and water (all constantly changing and in motion), as well as his extensive use of sensory images.

In short, many words, and some names, are cited in their occurrences in the *Dīvān,* as an indication of how Ghalib makes the traditional topoi of the ghazal distinctively his own in the two thousand or so couplets that we have, limited in number but incredibly rich in their reflection in a universal, and still contemporary, perspective of existence itself, and of existence's myriad complex relationships.

* * * * * * *

To assist the reader, here are some summary compilations of linked topoi in the *Dīvān*, most of which are itemized in the index:

The aspects of the nuclear (vs. linear) structure of the ghazal are discussed at length, particularly in Chapter 1. For specific instances (in both singular and plural forms) in the index, see: accretion, allusion, ambiguity, association, atom, cluster, comparison, compression, concordance, connection, connotation, dynamic (vs. static), electric, elision, ellipsis, energy, epigrammatic, epithet, exaggeration, extension, fusion, gnomic, hyperbole, interrogative, intonation, inversion, irony, kinaesthetic, linkage, network, opposition, oxymoron, paradox, personification, play, pun, punctuation, relationship, reversal, riddle, sarcasm, symmetry, synaesthestic, synecdoche, tension, triad. More conventionally, for specific poetic and rhetorical techniques and poetic devices used, see the summary in Chapter 1, especially pp. 21-2, and for a broad range of grammatic or semantic structures used by Ghalib in three selected ghazals, p. 201.

Similarly, for images of motion, see fireworks, flight, gait, kinetic, kineticism, launch, lightning, pulse, restlessness, running, rushing, scattering, shedding, spark, storm, surging, thrashing, turbulence, wandering, wind.

For the range of references to nature and the physical elements, many of which have their own dynamism, see:

Wind: air, breath, sigh, storm, wind (especially pp. 29-31).

Earth: desert, dust, mote, sand.

Fire: (especially pp. 22, 33, 102-3, 112-13); blazing, candle, flame, flare, heat, lamp, smoke, spark (with stone); see also lightning, crop, farmer, harvest, nest.

Water: dew, flood, froth, ocean, rain, river, sea, tears (also = blood), water, wave.

Astronomical imagery: celestial, creation (= universe), earth, firmament, heaven, moon, planet, sky, star, starry, stellar, sun, universe, world.

Garden imagery: cypress, flower (and flower-picker), gardener, narcissus, nightingale (as the lover of the rose), rose, tulip, weeping willow—and of course the convention of titling a poetry collection as a garden, scattered blossoms, flower-fragments (see p. 24).

And for typically Ghalibian evocation of scale and scope, see desert, desolation, dimension, distance, expanse, ruin, space, vast, wilderness.

For sensory references, see:

Auditory: cry, music, nightingale, sensory, shriek, sigh, singer, song, sound, speech, voice.

Olfactory: fragrance, musk, scent, smell, smoke.

Visual: balcony, blazing, bright, brilliant, color, decoration, eye (and related imagery: eyebrow = bow, eyelash/lash = arrow, launched with the attendant pricking/prickling resulting in the lover's heart, etc.), glance, glimpse, grain (of polished metal), illumine, luster, mirror, picture, radiance, sight, veil.

For the various treatments of love see the above reference to Chapter 3. More specifically, for the lover's emotional and mental states, see amazement, anguish, astonishment, awe, battle, boasting, competition, complaint, debilitation, delight, delirium, dementia, derangement, despair, desperation, disgrace, dishevelment, disorientation, distraction, embarrassment, envy, exhaustion, grief, jealousy, joy, longing, lust, madness, pain, pleasure (including the pleasure of pain), powerlessness, pride, punishment, restlessness, ridicule, sarcasm, separation, shame, sighing, sleep, strife, struggle, suffering, torment, torture, trial, tyranny, union, wandering, weeping (including tears, often of blood), wounded.

The range of the central characters in Ghalib's ghazals—*ma'shūq* (beloved), *āshiq* (poet-lover), and *raqīb* (rival), are discussed at length in Chapter 4. Within this triangular and conflict-ridden framework, see especially p. 118 for the phenomena and actions associated with love. See pp. 133-50 for a detailed discussion of the beloved, and his/her related attributes and typical behavior (usually exceptional cruelty to and torment of the lover). For some of the epithets used for the beloved in place of *ma'shūq*, see pp. 133-4. See particularly p. 150 for some of the lover's complex and wide variety of states of mind—in Ghalib's case, ranging from mostly suffering (as 'Asad') to a dominant exhilaration (as 'Ghalib') or at times, simultaneously.

For a summary listing of secondary players in the personae of the ghazal, including references to legendary names, see p. 78 for figures in some of the genre's traditional triads, as well as p. 119 and especially pp. 132-3 for the full cast of characters and roles evoked in the *Dīvān*.

For a general summary listing of places, locations, and settings cited by Ghalib, including specific geographical entities, see pp. 195-8.

In more general terms:

For death and dying (vs. life), see bier, bury, grave, mourn(ing), shroud.

For drinking, see anacreontic, bacchic, cup, cup-bearer, drunk, goblet, flask, intoxication, *sāqī* (vs. *shaikh*), tavern (vs. mosque), and of course, wine.

For the ghazal and its place in Urdu culture, see reader, and for its role in the *maḥfil* (both the public poetic gathering and the beloved's "court"), see assembly, audience, *bazm*, candle, competition, contest, gathering, listener, *mushā'ira*, recitation, riddle.

For religious references, see Ali, Brahmin, Christ, Christian, church, divine, God, Hindu, Houri, idol, infidel, Lord, Mary, mosque, Muslim, mystical, Paradise, Qur'an, Shi'a, temple, Zoroastrian.

Finally, see pp. 219-20 for the exceptionally wide range of anatomical features, objects, poetic expressions and tones, states of being, and time-sense that Ghalib can evoke, with his typical visionary powers of compression, in only three selected ghazals from among his master creations.

Note: When words are bundled, in the index as in "earthly/earth" to save space, the sequence generally appears in order of frequency of occurrence, not alphabetically—i.e., earthly occurs more frequently than earth. Also, when two words are closely related but significantly distinct in meaning and use, they are listed sequentially, as in "enemy and enmity".

Index

Tamām Shud